Changes in Statehood

# Changes in Statehood

## The Transformation of International Relations

Georg Sørensen
*Professor of Political Science*
*University of Aarhus*
*Denmark*

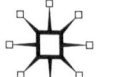

First published 2001 by
PALGRAVE
Houndmills, Basingstoke, Hampshire RG21 6XS and
175 Fifth Avenue, New York, N. Y. 10010
Companies and representatives throughout the world

PALGRAVE is the new global academic imprint of
St. Martin's Press LLC Scholarly and Reference Division and
Palgrave Publishers Ltd (formerly Macmillan Press Ltd).

ISBN 0–333–96300–8 hardback
ISBN 0–333–96301–6 paperback

This book is printed on paper suitable for recycling and
made from fully managed and sustained forest sources.

A catalogue record for this book is available
from the British Library.

Library of Congress Cataloging-in-Publication Data
Sørensen, Georg, 1948–
    Changes in statehood : the transformation of international
    relations / Georg Sørensen.
        p. cm.
    Includes bibliographical references and index.
    ISBN 0–333–96300–8 — ISBN 0–333–96301–6 (pbk.)
    1. National state. 2. International relations. I. Title.

    JZ1316 .S67 2001
    327.1′01—dc21
                                                    2001036480

10  9   8   7   6   5   4   3   2   1
10  09  08  07  06  05  04  03  02  01

Printed and bound in Great Britain by
Antony Rowe Ltd, Chippenham, Wiltshire

*For colleagues who are also dear friends and make it all worthwhile:*
*Lothar Brock, Robert Jackson, Atul Kohli, George Lopez, Michael Stohl,*
*and Michael Zürn*

# Contents

# List of Figures and Tables

# List of Abbreviations

| | |
|---|---|
| CIA | Central Intelligence Agency |
| ECOMOG | Economic Community of West African States Monitoring Group |
| EU | European Union |
| FDI | foreign direct investment |
| G7 | Group of Seven (the world's seven biggest economies: USA, Japan, Germany, Great Britain, France, Italy, and Canada) |
| G8 | Group of Eight (the Group of Seven plus Russia) |
| GATT | General Agreement on Tariffs and Trade |
| GDP | gross domestic product |
| GNP | gross national product |
| IGO | intergovernmental organization |
| IMF | International Monetary Fund |
| INF | intermediate-range nuclear forces |
| IR | international relations |
| LDC | less developed country |
| MITI | Ministry of International Trade and Industry (Japan) |
| NATO | North Atlantic Treaty Organization |
| NEP | New Economic Policy (the Soviet Union 1921–28) |
| NGO | non-governmental organization |
| OAU | Organization of African Unity |
| OECD | Organization for Economic Cooperation and Development |
| SAP | structural adjustment programme |
| SDI | Strategic Defence Initiative |
| TNC | transnational corporation |
| UN | United Nations |
| UNCTAD | United Nations Conference on Trade and Development |
| UNDP | United Nations Development Programme |
| US | United States (of America) |
| USSR | Union of Socialist Soviet Republics |
| WTO | World Trade Organization |

# Preface

The research leading to this book began some eight years ago. The basic idea concerning different types of state emerged from a project on world order after the end of the Cold War (Holm and Sørensen (eds) 1995). The contributions to that project by Robert Keohane and Michael Zürn were especially helpful, as were the discussions with my co-editor, Hans-Henrik Holm. The work got under way during 1994–95 when I was a visiting scholar at the Graduate School of International Relations and Pacific Studies, University of California, San Diego. I am grateful to Peter Gourevitch for making that stay possible. In early 1995, I was invited by Robert Jackson to give a seminar on my ideas at the University of British Columbia, Vancouver. Discussions there, and many later conversations with Robert Jackson, have had a strong influence on my work. Robert is a mentor and a close friend. We do not agree on everything, but at every turn he prompted me to clarify and strengthen my own argument.

Back in Denmark, Peter Nannestad gracefully took the position as head of department, leaving me with the much less demanding job of deputy and thus free to pursue what was slowly turning into a more focused project. An autumn sabbatical at the Freie Universität during 1999 gave me a chance to complete the first full draft of the manuscript. I am grateful to Helga Haftendorn for inviting me, and to friends at the Transatlantische Artbeitsstelle, in particular Anja Jetschke and Ingo Peters, for making it such a delightful experience. The BG-Bank Foundation kindly let me have the disposal of a wonderful Schöneberg flat in Berlin.

I am pleased to acknowledge economic support from Aarhus University's Research Foundation and from the Danish Social Science Research Council. Between 1998 and 2001, the Council supported a large project on 'Globalization, Statehood and World Order' of which I was the project leader. That fruitful context was decisive in providing the opportunity to tie together several scattered pieces of research and finally develop them into a coherent argument. Discussions with members of the globalization research group have greatly stimulated my own work. They were: Sven Bislev, Hans Krause Hansen, Hans-Henrik Holm, Robert Jackson, Knud Erik Jørgensen, Tonny Brems Knudsen, Jens Ladefoged Mortensen, Mehdi Mozaffari, Morten Ougaard, Jørgen Dige Pedersen, and Dorte Salskov-Iversen.

Robert Jackson, Peter Viggo Jakobsen, and Robert Keohane read an entire earlier draft and offered numerous suggestions that significantly improved the final version. Comments on parts of the manuscript from Knud Erik Jørgensen, Bernhard Zangl, and Michael Zürn have also been very helpful. I am extremely grateful for this assistance. Of course, responsibility for interpretations and arguments rests with me. Alison Howson and Steven Kennedy at Palgrave were very enthusiastic about the book from early on and they were always ready with advice and support. Jonna Kjær in Aarhus again did a great job in getting the manuscript ready for the publisher; thanks. Deborah Bennett was a very efficient copy-editor.

It has been a marathon, in some ways more strenuous than the one I ran in Hamburg a couple of years ago. Thanks to Lisbet, Sebastian, and Mathilde for keeping me alive during the project.

GEORG SØRENSEN

# Acknowledgements

The overall argument has not appeared in print before, but some of the themes contained in this book have been set forth in articles in scholarly journals and in book chapters published earlier. A number of ideas have also been presented at conferences and seminars. My thanks go to editors, reviewers, and participants; they have greatly inspired and enriched my understanding of the subject. The relevant earlier publications are the following: 'States are Not "Like Units"': Types of State and Forms of Anarchy in the Present International System', *The Journal of Political Philosophy*, 6:1, (1998:79–98) (Chapters 1, 4, and 6 through 9; 'An analysis of contemporary statehood: consequences for conflict and cooperation', *Review of International Studies*, 23, (1997:253–69) (Chapters 6 through 9); 'Development as a Hobbesian Dilemma', *Third World Quarterly*, 17:5, (1996:903–16) (Chapters 7 and 8); 'IR theory after the Cold War', *Review of International Studies*, 24, (1998:83–100) (Chapters 1 and 6); 'The Role of Western Politics and Research in Third World Democratization', Paper for Third Pan-European International Relations Conference, Vienna, September 1998 (Chapter 8); 'Development in Fragile/Failed States', Failed States Conference, Purdue University, (1999) (Chapter 8); 'Individual Security and National Security', *Security Dialogue*, 27:4, (1996:371–87) (Chapters 8 and 9); 'Strategies and Structures of Development. The New "Consensus" and the Limits of Its Promises', *The European Journal of Development Research*, 3:2, (1991:121–46) (Chapter 5); and 'Sovereignty: Continuity and Change in a Fundamental Institution', *Political Studies*, 47:3, (1999:590–604) (Chapter 10).

# Introduction: the Argument

The study of international relations is very often cut off from the study of domestic affairs. This is true for the dominant classical approach to the subject, realism. It is also true for recent influential approaches, such as for example constructivism. The insulation of 'international' from 'domestic' is wrong. International relations cannot be interrogated in separation from domestic matters and vice-versa: no analysis of domestic affairs is adequate if the connections to international relations are left out.

This book investigates the international–domestic connection from both sides: 'outside-in' and 'inside-out'. 'International' forces profoundly influence the core structures of sovereign statehood, including their political–military, economic, and normative substance. International forces have helped create three main types of state in the post-Second World War international system: they are termed the modern, the postmodern and the postcolonial state respectively.

Turning to the 'inside-out' analysis, different types of states display different security dilemmas. That is to say, the security dilemma in international relations is not based merely on the existence of an 'international' anarchy; it is also based on specific 'domestic' statehood structures. The security dilemma pertaining to postcolonial states is qualitatively different from that applying to modern states and the postmodern security dilemma is different again. Collapsing these security dilemmas into a single one, relevant for all sovereign states in the international system, is profoundly misleading.

Revisions are needed if the prevailing major theories on international relations shall face up to the challenge of adequately incorporating the international–domestic and domestic–international relationship. It will have to be accepted that the core values pursued by states, that is, security, freedom, order, justice, wealth, and welfare, each contain 'international' as well as 'domestic' aspects. None of those values can be reduced to a purely 'international' or a purely 'domestic' issue. Therefore, purely systemic or purely domestic analysis must be avoided; instead the international–domestic interplay should be at the centre of inquiry. The future of world order, that is, the configuration of forces that set the context for world affairs, cannot be adequately understood if the international–domestic relationships are left out.

The first chapter situates the argument in the debate about the connections between 'international' and 'domestic'. The major contributions made so far are briefly reviewed. An analytical framework is outlined which addresses the shortcomings of previous research efforts. In response to these problems, the framework contains both an 'outside-in' and an 'inside-out' analysis and emphasis is on the historical development of international-domestic dynamics, stressing the post-Second World War period.

Chapter 2 pursues the 'outside-in' examination. Two main theoretical views on the effects of international forces on domestic structures are identified; they are termed the logic of homogeneity and the logic of heterogeneity respectively. According to the first view, international forces pressure sovereign states in the direction of becoming more and more alike; they develop into 'like units'. The second view argues that dynamics of uneven development lead to the creation of qualitatively different kinds of state. Both theoretical positions have a point: homogeneity as well as heterogeneity can be the result of international forces. That takes me to an historical examination of how the political–military power (Chapter 3), international norms (Chapter 4), and economic power (Chapter 5) have conditioned the domestic development of sovereign states since 1945.

Neorealists claim that the Soviet Union represents a paradigmatic case of international forces leading to domestic homogeneity. The country wanted to be very different from its Western, capitalist competitors, yet it was pressured to emulate its more successful rivals. The dissolution of the Soviet Union and recent developments in Russia are seen to confirm that view. Chapter 3 rejects the idea of the Soviet Union/Russia developing into a 'like unit'. Innovation and the possession of nuclear weapons offered escapes from the external pressure to emulate. When states are not 'like units', the existence of different types of state will have to enter our analysis of international relations.

Chapter 4 focuses on the effect of international norms on domestic state structures. Liberals and neorealists argue that such norms lead toward homogeneity, that is, states becoming more and more alike. This has happened, but not nearly to the extent that these theorists maintain. Different domestic conditions lead to heterogeneity, that is, to states that are 'unlike'. International norms have helped create three main types of state in the post-Second World War international system, modern, postmodern, and postcolonial states.

Chapter 5 is about the consequences of international economic forces on domestic statehood structures. The chapter focuses on economic globalization and its consequences for statehood structures. It is argued that economic forces have furthered the development of three main types of state in the international system. Chapter 6 summarizes the combined effects of forces of homogeneity and forces of heterogeneity on sovereign statehood. Drawing on Weberian ideal types, the state types are presented in detail: the modern state, the postmodern state, and the weak postcolonial state. Each of these types displays distinct features on the core aspects of state: government, economy, and nationhood. The three ideal types of state are used as the starting point for the 'inside-out' investigation. That part of the analysis is focused on the different security dilemmas belonging to each type of state.

Focus is on the security dilemma, first because this is an appropriate way of tying together 'domestic' and 'international'; as Chapter 7 will demonstrate, different security dilemmas are based on different configurations of international and domestic conditions. Second, the security dilemma has been the classical way of articulating the security predicament of the modern state. The classical security dilemma as identified by John Herz is based expressly on the modern state. The present analysis demonstrates that other main types of state are characterized by qualitatively different security dilemmas. The security dilemma pertaining to the modern state and its historical forerunners is set forth in Chapter 7.

Weak postcolonial states are the subject of Chapter 8. These states are protected by strong international norms, backed by the great powers. Given the lack of external and internal constraint, state elites often pursued their own narrow interests; that has led to the creation of state structures which provided insecurity rather than security for most of the subject populations. Instead of the 'hard shell' of the state, protecting against external threat, there is an insecurity container exposing people to severe domestic threat.

Postmodern states, by contrast, make up a coordinated security community, an argument developed in Chapter 9. While the threat of war has been largely removed, new challenges to effective governance have emerged instead, in economic, political and societal domains. Postmodern statehood requires a redefinition of the concept of a 'strong state'; it also requires new reflections on security in context of a realm that is not easily defined in precise territorial terms. The pursuit of 'national security' is not as straightforward in the postmodern context as it was under conditions of modern statehood.

The consequences for sovereignty of the existence of different main types of state are taken up in Chapter 10. The focus on sovereignty is a way of further substantiating the claim that each type of state displays a particular pattern of international relations, based on a specific combination of substantial statehood characteristics and distinctive rules of sovereignty. Furthermore, a focus on sovereignty is warranted in order to clarify the confused debate about what happens to sovereignty as a result of changes in statehood. There is a distinct sovereignty game connected with each type of state. Because the relationship between 'domestic' and 'international' changes with the transformation of statehood, each sovereignty game contains a separate modality of the relationship between 'domestic' and 'international'. The modern sovereignty game is based on a clear distinction between what is 'domestic' and what is 'international'. Postmodern states are different. They are much more integrated with each other on the level of substantial statehood. That is true both for the economic level and for politics, which is characterized by 'multilevel' governance. The chapter explains how this substantial integration is reflected in the rules of the postmodern sovereignty game.

Weak postcolonial states display serious deficiencies in substantial statehood. They are in basic ways unable to take care of themselves; their statehood structures are significantly dependent on, and associated with, the international system. The rules of their sovereignty game have been modified accordingly. This is another peculiar modality of 'domestic' and 'international', different from that of both modern and postmodern states.

It is of course highly pertinent to examine the consequences of my analysis for existing main theories of international relations. This task is undertaken in Chapter 11; the chapter discusses how well existing theories of international relations can account for the emergence of different types of state, and how the assumptions, core contentions, and strategic recommendations of these theories are challenged by an international system containing different types of state. Five clusters of theory are addressed: realism, liberalism, the English school, neomarxist international political economy, and constructivism. With some modifications, several of the existing theories should be able to open up to forms of analysis which take on the domestic–international interplay in context of the development and change of sovereign statehood. But for sustained progress in this field, there will have to be more conscious efforts at reconnecting 'international' and 'domestic' political theory.

In the final chapter, the more general perspectives flowing from the present analysis are addressed. They concern the implications for the evaluation of the future world order, and the implications for the development of international relations (IR) theory. Reflections on world order, it is argued, must include both the 'international' issue of survival and the 'domestic' issue of the 'good life'; both are discussed in Chapter 12. The concluding reflections on IR-theory are less concerned with current debates on epistemology and ontology, because pluralism is considered healthy here: one position cannot, and should not, trump all others. Focus, therefore, is rather on the substantive issues, that is, what to study and why.

# 1
# An Analytical Framework

Scholars readily consent that in order to understand world politics, it is necessary to study both international relations and domestic affairs, and to analyse the interaction of the two.[1] The solid unanimity behind the need for treating international and domestic forces as a whole is not difficult to understand. 'International' and 'domestic' *are* parts of a totality, a whole; focus on only one element will always lead to questions about the role and influence of the other.

While most scholars agree on the need for a comprehensive analysis of the interaction between domestic and international, there also appears to be a consensus that this is a very difficult task. Kenneth Waltz, for example, finds that 'neither I nor anyone else has figured out how to construct a theory that comprehends both the international and the national level' (1994:6).[2] To set the context properly for the present study of the 'international–domestic–international' interplay, it is necessary briefly to review the major contributions made so far; their most important problems will be identified and it will be indicated how this study attempts to overcome them. I introduce the general debate about the issue first and proceed to comment on some more specific analyses of the role of domestic factors in international affairs.

In the early phases of the debate,[3] scholars could not agree on the relative importance of the international dimension as compared to the domestic dimension. With the idea of 'Primat der Aussenpolitik', Leopold von Ranke in the nineteenth century promoted a realist focus on the power struggle between states. Writing in that tradition, Otto Hintze (1906) analysed how domestic structures (in his case the constitution and the military forces) were shaped decisively by the external rivalries in which states were involved. Eckart Kehr (1970) and his followers, by contrast, stressed the 'Primat der Innenpolitik', arguing that German foreign policy before the First World War was due to the influence of particular domestic political coalitions. The emphasis on politics was called into question by Marxist theories of imperialism (Lenin 1917; Hilferding 1910); they explained foreign economic expansion with reference to economic structure instead. As with Kehr, however, their analytical model began with 'domestic' and moved from there to 'international'.

One-sided emphasis on either 'international' or 'domestic' also characterizes several contemporary approaches. Accent on the international system is characteristic of neorealism. The aim of Kenneth Waltz's neorealist theory of international politics (Waltz 1979) is to construct a systemic theory of IR. A systemic theory is focused on the way in which the structure of the international system explains international outcomes. A reductionist theory, according to Waltz, explains such outcomes through elements and forces at the level of the units, the states that make up the constituent parts of the system. By focusing on the systemic features of anarchy and the relative distribution of power, Waltz's theory is able to make a few, but powerful statements about the way in which the structure of the international system shapes the structure and behaviour of the units. 'Socialization' and 'competition' are the two major ways in which the anarchic structure affects states,[4] adaptation according to the requirements of the balance of power is the major way in which the anarchic structure affects state behaviour. Neorealism thus does not treat international and domestic politics as a whole. It rather tends to replace such a view with a notion of state units as merely adapting to the pushing and shoving of structure. Waltz is well aware of the problem even though he downplays it somewhat. What neorealist theory is waiting for in order to properly address the unit-level, says Waltz, is a theory of the state (1994:6).

The broader realist corpus of theory does contain reflections on the influence of domestic politics on relations between states. Drawing on a tradition going to back Rousseau, some realists identify variations in domestic societies as a source of more or less stable international systems. But they firmly remain part of realist theory in that the international structure of anarchy comes first. World politics is 'a state of war' and the role of domestic politics is of lesser, secondary importance. It can provide for more or less stable balances of power.[5]

Some scholars in the neorealist tradition have also attempted to theorize domestic politics. These scholars find that the systemic level explains too little state behaviour; consequently they focus on domestic politics. They are sometimes labelled 'defensive realists' (cf. Zakaria 1995). One of the most ambitious attempts in this group is Jack Snyder's *Myths of Empire* (1991). He studied the unsuccessful 'overexpansion' of great powers and set forth a model of domestic factors to explain such 'overexpansion'. In contrast to Waltz, Snyder argues that systemic factors cannot explain the kind of state behaviour he is studying; therefore, the major explanatory work has to be done by domestic factors. It may appear as if this approach treats international and domestic politics as a whole, but that is not the case. It separates the two and then one-sidedly stresses the importance of domestic politics. The neorealist who sympathizes with the Waltzian emphasis on the systemic level claims that defensive realists are driven to this erroneous stress on domestic politics because they 'miscon-strue the manner in which the system affects states' (Zakaria 1995:482). That is, the assumption made by defensive realists about the minimal systemic effects on state behaviour is not sound. When one explores the systemic factors identified by Waltz, namely 'socialization' and 'competition and selection', the importance of the systemic level comes fully into view. True or not, this is another argument for the importance of systemic factors; it is not an approach treating international and domestic factors as a whole. An approach meeting that requirement has yet to emerge from the neorealist debate. The result so far has been a more intense discussion of international and domestic sources of state policy.[6]

The liberal tradition in IR has presented the perhaps most well-known theory stressing domestic factors and claiming also to explain the relationship between those domestic factors and systemic forces. It is the republican liberal theory of democratic peace which is premised on the empirical observation that democracies do not fight each other. Why are democracies at peace with one another? The answer to that question has been most systematically addressed by Michael Doyle (1983; 1986) who based his argument on the classical liberal study by Immanuel Kant (1992 [1795]). There are three ele-ments behind the claim that democracy leads to peace with other democracies. The first is the mere existence of liberal democracies whose domestic political cultures are based on peaceful resolution of conflict. Democracy encourages peaceful international relations because democratic governments are con-trolled by their citizens who will not advocate or support wars with other democracies.[7] The second element is that democracies hold common moral values which lead to the formation of what Kant called a pacific union. Peaceful ways of solving domestic conflict are seen as morally superior to violent beha-viour and this attitude is transferred to international relations between democ-racies. Finally, peace between democracies is strengthened through economic cooperation and interdependence. In the pacific union it is possible to encour-age what Kant called 'the spirit of commerce': mutual and reciprocal gain for those involved in international economic cooperation and exchange. From the present project's point of view, the republican liberal argument has a weak point. Instead of a dynamic notion of an interplay between 'international' and 'domestic', the liberal analysis tends to build on the onesided view of 'domestic' democracy leading to 'international' peace.

Another strand of liberalism, institutionalist liberalism, has developed an argument about cooperation which focuses on the international level. It says that international institutions promote cooperation among states (Keohane 1989). Institutionalist liberals agree with neorealists about the major systemic constraint on state cooperation set by anarchy and the security dilemma, but they maintain that international institutions can mitigate the negative consequences of anarchy. Yet institutionalist liberals do not treat international and domestic politics as a whole. On most occasions they treat state preferences as given and do not attempt to theorize domestic politics.[8]

English school theorists (Bull 1995; Wight 1991; Jackson 1995a) draw a firm line between domestic politics and international relations; in that sense they are like most realists. They are not primarily investigating the domestic aspects of foreign policy. Yet there are at least two ways in which the English school approach touches upon the relationship between domestic and international. One is via the Kantian notion of cosmopolitanism; this leads towards the liberal idea that liberal institutions at home can form the basis for liberal institutions in the international realm and thus pave the way for 'more society' in international society. The other element concerns the role of state leaders. A major focus of the English school approach is the study of the moral choices confronting state leaders in foreign policy. Such statecraft may be considered a 'domestic' (state elite) influence on the international realm. It is clear, however, that the two factors mentioned here do not amount to any systematic investigation of the interaction between domestic and international. The domestic sphere – and by implication the domestic–international relationship – remains undertheorized in the English school approach.

Marxist theory contains two different strands of thought on the problem of state behaviour. They are in principal agreement about treating domestic and international politics as a whole, but their theories onesidedly stresses either one or the other aspect. As indicated above, theories of imperialism in the Hobson–Lenin tradition stress domestic factors; because of the contradictions of capital accumulation national capitalists are compelled to international expansion and the competition with other expanding capitalist states will eventually produce war (Lenin 1939 [1917]; Kemp, 1967). Such reasoning has been labeled reductionist in the sense that international outcomes are explained solely by reference to the domestic features of states (Waltz 1979). The treatment of international and domestic as a whole is accomplished by reducing the former to the latter.

Another main strand of Marxist theory stresses systemic forces. The theory of the capitalist world-system by Immanuel Wallerstein goes so far in that direction that it even hesitates to talk about 'societies'. Social science, says Wallerstein, would 'make a great leap forward if it dispensed entirely with the term' (1984:2; see also Ougaard 1989:85). Behind this view is the notion that there is only one world economic system with a single division of labour and that it is theoretically and empirically unsound to divide that economic level into units of national economies. There are different polities and cultures according to Wallerstein, but their development dynamics are fundamentally or even entirely shaped by the systemic forces of the world economy (Wallerstein 1979:53). In other words, the treatment of international and domestic as a whole is accomplished by reducing the latter to the former. The position creates at least two major problems. First, it is impossible to employ a notion of sovereign state which includes an economic level to some degree separate from the world economic system; second, it impedes a meaningful analytical conception of domestic forces.

Constructivist analysis stresses that anarchy need not lead to self-help. Whether that happens depends on an intervening variable: the intersubjectively constituted identities of state-actors. Their processes of interaction may instead lead to a cooperative anarchy as has happened in Western Europe. Interests and identities are constructed in interaction and not exogenously given; anarchy is what states make of it (Wendt 1992, 1999). Yet it must be stressed that constructivist theory, at least in the Wendtian version, is a systemic theory. It is recognized that domestic politics can play an important role in creating more of less cooperative anarchy, but that role is not systematically addressed because focus is on systemic interaction. It appears that the treating of international and domestic politics as a whole is no easy task. There is no real disagreement as to the necessity of the undertaking, but it has not been accomplished in a fully satisfactory manner in the various main theories of IR. It remains in this brief overview to introduce a number of more specific analyses that attempt to combine 'domestic' and 'international'. These analyses have been highly successful in demonstrating the importance of domestic forces for explaining variations in the response by different states to similar external stimuli.[9] Yet it will also be claimed that they have not fully achieved the goal of treating 'domestic' and 'international' as a whole.

In a pioneering study, Peter Katzenstein (1976) analysed the different responses by France and the United States to the energy crisis of the 1970s. He argued that the different historical development of state–society relations in the two countries had led to a situation where political power in France was concentrated in the state ('strong state', 'weak society') whereas in the United States it was concentrated in society ('weak state', 'strong society'). These differences of domestic structure explained why the response to the oil crisis varied, conforming to realist expectations in France and liberal expectations in the United States. Stephen Krasner (1978) used this distinction between 'strong' and 'weak' states as the central variable in the explanation of foreign policy.

Matthew Evangelista examined weapons innovation in the United States and the Soviet Union. Again, differences in domestic structure helped explain why a 'bottom up' bureaucratic-politics model applied to the United States whereas a 'top-down' realist state-as-unitary-actor-model applied to the Soviet Union (Evangelista 1988; 1997). Peter Gourevitch (1986) argued that the 'strong versus weak' dichotomy was insufficient to explain the influence on domestic forces on foreign policy, because the autonomy of the state in relation to society must also depend on the structure of the linkages between the two. Processes of domestic coalition building are of special importance in this context.[10] Finally, Thomas Risse has employed an expanded model of domestic structure[11] to explain the differences in behaviour of liberal democracies in their security policies.

These are sophisticated investigations of comparative foreign policy with elaborate conceptions of domestic structure. But they do not treat 'international' and 'domestic' as a whole. Domestic structure is employed to explain variation in policy response to given external challenges. Two areas, highly important for the domestic–international relationship, are not sufficiently addressed. The first concerns the effects of international forces on domestic structures; this is downplayed when focus is on policy responses.[12] The second is the link between domestic structures and the international political system. This is only addressed in the limited sense that different foreign policy responses emerge as inputs into the international system.

Recent attempts to theorize the relationship between domestic and international have focused on the twin pressures – domestic and international – on state decisionmakers (Putnam 1988; Evans *et al.*, 1993). This leads in the direction of identifying checklists of those domestic and international factors that influence state decisionmakers in their negotiation of specific issues. Such an approach is informative in revealing the different pressures on state leaders and indicating their respective rooms of manoeuvre. But it does not yield any systematic information about international and domestic structures and the relationship between them.[13] In that sense the relationship between international and domestic remains undertheorized in the approach. Furthermore, international and domestic structures are theoretically prior to the notion of two-level games since they concern the structure of the settings in which decisionmakers conduct their bargaining.

In sum, previous attempts to analyse the interplay between 'international' and 'domestic' suffer from various shortcomings. First, they are most often rather narrowly conceived, focusing on either 'outside-in' ('international' effects on 'domestic') or 'inside out' ('domestic' influences on 'international'); aspirations to include both aspects fully in the analysis have been very rare. Second, there is most often a focus on isolated aspects of the 'international' or the 'domestic'. The power struggle between states, or the international economic system, are the aspects most frequently in focus of the 'outside-in' analysis. Liberal democracy has been a favourite of 'inside-out' studies. It is highly uncommon to find a more comprehensive view of 'international' or of 'domestic' which includes several major elements of both in the investigation. Third, the 'international' –'domestic' interplay is frequently cast in terms of external and internal pressures on political elites whose foreign policy decisionmaking then becomes the central site where 'international' and 'domestic' influences meet and are weighed off against each other. A focus on such decisionmaking overly downplays the broader effects of 'international' forces on 'domestic' structures and vice versa. Finally, existing contributions tend to conceive of 'international' and 'domestic' as a static, unchanging relationship, where the dividing line that is the sovereign border determines once and for all which is what. Because sovereignty is an institution subject to historical development and change, it follows that the concrete content of what is 'international' and what is 'domestic' must also change in context of that historical development. In that sense, the relationship between the two is certainly not static and unchanging, but dynamic and changeable.

The present study makes an attempt to address these problems. First, both the 'outside-in' and the 'inside-out' perspective are given priority. Focusing on 'outside-in', the most comprehensive theory comes from neorealism. It argues that systemic forces tend to create 'like units'. Against this logic of homogeneity, Chapter 2 will argue that there is also a theoretical argument to be made in favour of a logic of heterogeneity, of states developing into qualitatively different kinds of units due to the effects of systemic forces. Yet the two positions are not as incompatible as they may seem; I shall argue that both logics have been in play in the post-Second World War period. In theoretical terms, the message is that systemic forces *condition* domestic structures of states; such conditioning can contain elements of homogeneity as well as of heterogeneity. International forces have helped create different main types of state in the international system.

In pursuing the 'outside-in' analysis, this study will take a comprehensive view of the 'international'; it comprises both political–military power, economic power, and international norms. These three elements of the 'international' are more precisely defined below. 'Domestic' will also be further defined below, in comprehensive terms, as salient aspects of sovereign statehood, comprising the political–military institutions of the state; the economic basis of the state; and the 'idea' of the state.

Focusing on 'inside-out', the most comprehensive theory, on the democratic peace, comes from republican liberalism. I attempt to show that the puzzle created by republican liberalism, about when democracy leads to peace and when it does not, can be solved by identifying changes in statehood on a broader scale than suggested by liberals. Different types of state (that is, different 'domestic' structures) *condition* 'international' structures in different ways. Three types of state will be identified; they are labelled the modern state, the postcolonial state and the postmodern state, respectively. These states exist in different forms of anarchy in context of different patterns of cooperation and conflict, typical of each main type of state. Specifically, these state types confront different security dilemmas and they play different sovereignty games.

The present study will focus on international and domestic structures rather than on actors and their decisionmaking. The focus on structure is not an attempt to separate structure and actors or an argument against the useful insight that the two are mutually constituted (Giddens 1984). But it is an emphasis of the fact that the present study is less about domestic and international sources of and pressures on foreign policy decisionmaking than it is an attempt to find out how international forces affect domestic structure and how different main of types domestic structure in turn affect the international system.

Finally, in making the argument I will also show that the very definition of what is 'domestic' and what is 'international' changes in the context of the transformation of statehood. Therefore, the 'international'–'domestic' interplay comes in different modalities; it is not a fixed relationship, as all previous theories have im-or explicitly argued.

## Definitions: what is 'international'?

The standard way of distinguishing between 'domestic' and 'international' in IR (and in Comparative Politics) is by following the sovereign border. The argument goes something like this. The fundamental unit in the international system is the sovereign state. States are entities with a delimited territory, a stable population, and a government. Sovereignty means constitutional independence, that is, independent, centralized authority over a specific territory and population (James 1986). Jurisdiction thus creates a 'domestic' and an 'international' space. In substantial terms, 'domestic' is what goes on inside that jurisdiction; 'international' is what goes on outside of it.

Three points may be noted about the domestic/international separation via sovereign borders. First, it requires an historical approach to the domestic/international puzzle. Borders between sovereign states are of relatively recent origin; only during the twentieth century has the institution of sovereignty spread to encompass the globe. For example, the relationship between 'domestic' and 'international' was fundamentally changed for a large number of countries a few decades ago, when they became independent in the context of decolonization. Should developments in British colonies before decolonization be considered part of the domestic affairs of Britain? How should the 'domestic/international' dynamic in those colonial areas be conceptualized? Another aspect of this point is that once established, sovereign borders may change their meaning and function. As will be demonstrated in a later chapter, such developments have taken place within the European Union.

Second, the use of sovereign borders to distinguish between domestic and international implies that the units involved in this distinction are of a special kind. They are members of a distinct society, the society of sovereignty states. It has been customary in the neorealist tradition to talk of an international system, invoking the image of states as billiard balls. The above definition of sovereignty immediately reveals why this image is misleading. Relations between sovereign states involve acts of recognition and of mutual obligations between states. The act of recognition confers a special status on states. The society of states only admits new members on specific and demanding conditions, and once entry is accepted members have to play by certain rules. In sum, the institution of sovereignty appears to require that the international realm cannot merely be conceptualized through the structure of anarchy as do neo-realists. International rules and norms – as emphasized by English school theorists – must enter the picture. This point will be developed further below. As for terminology, I am going to use the terms 'system' and 'society' interchangeably and give further specification where necessary.

Third, the sovereign border is a legal, juridical construct. It has never prevented a wide range of substantial connections between different societies, in the political, economic, social, cultural, technological, and other areas. The consequence of that is clear: what we at a given time consider 'domestic' is the result of a previous interplay between domestic and international – and vice versa. Even a snapshot picture of the domestic realm will reveal elements that could be considered non-domestic, such as foreign direct investment undertakings, minority groups that are not citizens of the country (for example, Russians in the Baltic republics); or the International Monetary Fund (IMF) officials who help formulate economic policies in many weak African states. Fernando Cardoso and Enzo Faletto put it in the following way: 'There are no metaphysical relations of development between one nation and another, between one state and another. The relations are made possible through a network of interests and coercion that bind some social groups to others, some classes to others' (1979:73). As noted by others (for example, Almond, 1989), in order to avoid circularity in the argument about domestic structure, it is necessary to 'explore the extent to which the structure itself derives from the exigencies of the international system', and vice versa. To overcome this problem calls for a sequencing strategy in the analysis of domestic and international and that will be attempted here: first it must be examined how the international system affects domestic structures. This will be followed by an analysis of the effects of domestic structure on the international system. More on this below. (Even that is only a second-best solution of course; an attempt to make analytical sense of 'domestic' and 'international' in a situation where the two are frequently more or less completely woven into each other.) This study, then, will focus on the 'international–domestic–international' or the 'domestic–international–domestic' connections, and the phrases 'domestic–international' or 'international–domestic' are merely shorthand expressions for that focus.

On closer view, therefore, the sovereign border is not in every respect an ideal demarcation line between inside and outside. Some sociologists argue that it is relevant to start with a truly global analysis right away, that is, to 'understand the global flux of social relations within which the international system floats, and to explore the manifold dimensions of these relations' (Shaw 1994:113). This point of view is similar to Wallerstein's position mentioned earlier; it makes the issue of the domestic–international connection uninteresting, even meaningless, because there is only one social totality comprising both. Whether one wants to proceed along such lines really depends on one's view of the importance of the sovereign state. If the increase in all sorts of transborder relations is interpreted to mean that 'we have to give up the notion and the concept of the state as well as the terminology that is traditionally connected to it' (Czempiel 1989:132) there is no need to study the relationship between domestic and international.

The position taken here points in the opposite direction. The debate about the possible decay or not of the state makes it more, not less, urgent to study the connections between domestic and international. A brief look at the main contending views in the debate will reveal why. The 'declinists' argue, for example, that the state is losing power to the market: 'domestic social and political relations are increasingly shaped by global capital circuits' (McMichael and Myhre 1991:84). Along similar lines, Susan Strange claims that the state is becoming 'just one source of authority among several, with limited power and resources' (Strange 1996:73). But against this it can be argued that states remain, not only the prevailing units of political organization, but also 'the principal units of economic organization and management' (Pooley 1991:28). Both of these views clearly have a point; in order to make sense of this debate it is necessary to study how sovereign states change in the context of political, economic, and social development. Different changes can either weaken or strengthen the state, of course. Every major aspect of modern statehood has been subject to substantial development and change, whether it be the institution of sovereignty, the economic basis of statehood, the political institutions of the state, the notion of nationhood and national identity, or the relationship between the state as government/institutional apparatus and civil society. A crucial dimension of that process of change concerns the dynamics of the interplay between domestic and international. In sum, the changes in statehood over time do not render the domestic–international relationship uninteresting, rather the contrary: they demand further analysis of how it has developed. It is relevant to note that several critical political economists have moved towards a similar view, that is, even if capitalism is a global system, analysis of its interplay with the sovereign state remains crucial (for example, Lipietz 1987:18–19).

To sum up so far: the distinction between 'domestic' and 'international' follows the sovereign border. Changes in sovereign statehood which may make the state weaker in some and stronger in other respects require a closer examination of the domestic–international connection. Such analysis must be historically specific because the sovereign border is an historical construct. The analysis also requires that international rules and norms are taken seriously, because the institution of sovereign statehood, that is, who gets to participate in the international game and what are the conditions of playing, is in part decided by those rules and norms. Finally, what we call 'domestic' at any given point in time is always the result of previous international–domestic interplay. That requires a sequencing strategy of analysis in order to reveal the extent to which 'domestic' is a creation of international forces.

The above reflections have defined the line of demarcation between domestic and international, but they have not defined the concrete content of either entity. What is the actual content of what is called 'international' or 'international system' or 'systemic' forces? In a rigorous analysis of that question Kenneth Waltz (1979:73–101) first defines 'structure' as 'a set of constraining conditions' (p. 73). Waltz is at pains to avoid a reductionist theory, where 'the whole is understood by knowing the attributes and the interactions of its parts' (1979:18). He therefore wants a definition of international structure which ignores how (state) units interact and concentrates on 'how they stand in relation to each other' (1979:80). That leads to a definition of structure with three elements. The first concerns the ordering principle of the system; domestic systems are hierarchic, international systems are anarchic. The second element concerns the functions of differentiated units. In anarchic systems this level drops out, 'since the system is composed of like units' (1979:101). The third element is the distribution of capabilities across units. Anarchy leads to self-help; a given balance of power leads to balancing or bandwagoning (Waltz 1979:126), because states want to survive and to maintain their positions in the system.

The sharp division Waltz makes between international structure on the one hand and state units and their interaction on the other hand may have theoretical advantages but it goes squarely against the point made above, about the need for an historically sensitive approach to the domestic/international division. First, Waltz assumes that an ahistorical division between state unit and system can be made but – as critics have pointed out – the attempt to do so while keeping the content of international structure as spare as possible has produced some odd results. Why, for example, are 'demographic trends, transnational flows, and military technology that affect all (or many) states assigned to the unit level? . . . by assigning everything except the distribution of capabilities to the unit level, that category becomes a dumping ground hindering theory building at anything but the structural level' (Nye 1988:243). Second, Waltz's ahistorical approach leads to reification, the move whereby historically produced structures are presented as unchangeable constraints given by nature. Anarchy becomes such a constraint, always leading to self-help, as emphasized by neorealist John Mearsheimer: 'Anarchy has two principal consequences. First, there is little room for trust among states...Second, each state must guarantee its own survival since no other actor will provide its security' (Mearsheimer 1991:148). A consequence of this view is that very few changes have taken place in the international system in the last several hundred years. Anarchy prevails; as for the relative distribution of power, multipolarity prevailed until the end of the Second World War; after the end of the Cold War the system in an early phase of change from bipolarity to multipolarity (Waltz 1993).

In order to avoid the reification of anarchy it is necessary to bring the concrete interaction between states back in; it is also necessary to expand on the neorealist view, according to which state behaviour is only (or at minimum largely) 'shaped by the *material structure* of the international system' (Mearsheimer 1995:91). There are two ways to do this. The first is to emphasize that 'material structures' in the international system are of different kinds; not all of them are related to the balance of power and the military confrontation of states. There are also institutions concerned with the creation of peaceful intercourse between states, such as the UN system and the institutions of international law and of various international regimes. The second way is to emphasize that the structure of the international system is not purely material; it is also norms, rules, and ideas. The emphasis on international norms and rules emerges from the Grotian (rationalist) tradition in the study of IR. Rationalism taken to the extreme, says Robert Jackson, is 'a perfect world of mutual respect, concord and the rule of law between states' (Jackson 1995a:114). According to English school theorists, any complete comprehension of international relations requires inclusion of a 'realist' dimension of the distribution of (primarily) material power and a 'Grotian' or rationalist dimension of (primarily non-material) rules and norms. Recent constructivist analysis also emphasizes that international norms defined as 'collective expectations about proper behavior for a given identity' shape 'the national security interests or (directly) the security policies of states' (Jepperson *et al.* 1996:54). In sum, material power matters, but so do norms.

The content of the 'international' or of 'systemic forces' now begins to come into view. I have identified two elements so far; the first is political–military power, that is, power embodied in control over political institutions and over the means of violence. We may call this the 'realist' element in the international structure. That political–military power affects domestic structures has often been demonstrated, perhaps especially in the aftermath of wars. As noted by Bruce Cronin, the winners of war take measures changing the domestic structures of the losers: 'after every major war since 1815, the victorious powers consciously reorganized the societies of the losing states. They did this...to make them into certain kinds of states' (Cronin 1994:17).

The second element is international norms, rules and ideas; in the present context it is considered sufficient to summarize this under the label 'international norms'. We may call this the 'English school' or 'liberal–constructivist' element in the international structure. That such norms influence the domestic conditions in states is immediately clear from a brief example. It concerns the formal recognition of new states, that is, their entry into the exclusive club of sovereign states. These rules of admission have changed in several ways over time. For a long period, sovereignty was exclusively for Europeans; other would-be sovereign states were held out because the Europeans found they did not satisfy the basic criteria for statehood. Sovereignty became a universal institution only in the twentieth century. In other words, rules of recognition decide what kind of entities that can get into the club; that is a very fundamental way of affecting domestic conditions. When the right to self-determination of colonial peoples became an international norm after the Second World War, a whole new group of previous colonies became sovereign states.

Realists will object that norms can be subsumed under material power; the powerful make up the rules in any case and change them as they see fit. Material power and norms do indeed interact, as will be explored below. But to subsume the latter under the former would be misleading. States, including powerful states, most often respect international norms; they consider themselves bound by treaties, that is, they keep promises even when it is no longer in their interest to do so. International norms constrain the way states pursue military power, for example by shaping arms races; they also affect economic competition between states by setting up the rules by which such competition is played out. Finally, states with insignificant material power can play an important role in international affairs by helping shape international norms. In that sense, international norms is linked to the notion of 'soft power' (Nye 1990).

The third and final element in international structure is economic power, that is, the capability to design, construct, produce, finance, and distribute economic goods. Economic power is possessed by those able to produce wealth in a world dominated by capitalism. We may call it the 'international political economy' or IPE-element in international structure. Many realists (Gilpin 1987 is a notable exception) will want to subsume economic power under other forms of material power. The two are linked of course, but they are also analytically and institutionally separate. The separation between an economic sphere of the market and a political sphere of the state is a feature of modern, capitalist society. The separation between state and market turns the economy into a relatively autonomous sphere of society; there is a logic of the market which is different from the political–military logic of the state. In an earlier project, we characterized this market logic for the contemporary period as one of 'uneven globalization' (Holm and Sørensen 1995). The major actors in the market (managers, firms, investors, and so on) must also be distinguished from the major actors in the political–military structure. It is immediately clear that the dynamics of economic power significantly affect the domestic structures of states as demonstrated most recently, for example, by the economic crisis in Asia. A state's position in the economic structure, as a core or a peripheral player, deeply affects and shapes what kind of entity it can aspire to be. I shall argue later, that the dynamics of uneven globalization have helped change sovereign statehood in significant ways in different parts of the world.

The content of 'the international' has now been spelled out; three elements of international structure have been identified, as indicated in Figure 1.1. The distinction between these three elements is analytical. Politics and economics are two sides of the same coin (Keohane 1984:18–31); it will often be extremely difficult to draw a clear distinction between economic power and political power. International norms affect and shape the exercise of political and economic power and are themselves affected by economic and political power. The three elements are considered equally important, that is, their relative influence can be identified only in the context of concrete, historical analysis. This view is of course different from many existing contributions which tend to either subject economics and norms to the logic of political–military power (for example, realism) or to subject norms and political–military power to the logic of economic power (for example, Marxist IPE), or indeed to attach extraordinary importance to international norms (for example, rationalism).

The three elements can be considered an historical structure in the sense defined by Robert Cox, that is, 'a picture of a particular configuration of forces. This configuration does not determine actions in any direct mechanical way but imposes pressures and constraints' (Cox 1996:97–8).[14] The aim here is to identify the ways in which international structure affects the domestic structures of states and, in turn, to trace the effects of these domestic structures on the international system. The next step is to identify the content of domestic structure.

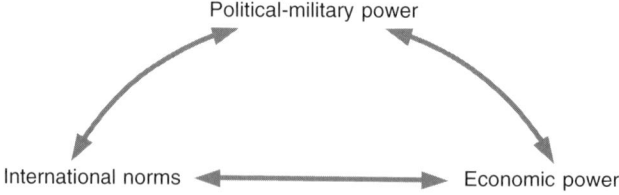

*Figure 1.1*   Elements of International Structure

## And what is 'domestic'?

It was argued above that 'domestic' is what goes on inside the territory of sovereign states, but that is obviously not a clear definition of 'domestic'. Much IR-theory is of little help in analysing the state and thus spelling out what is behind 'domestic'. It is an irony of the IR-discipline that it has combined a focus on states as the most important actors in the system with an astonishing absence of analysis of the state itself.[15] On this view, states are 'billiard balls', territorial entities with a government enjoying sovereignty over a people within a demarcated territory. It is implied that state elites enjoy 'a high level ... of autonomy in domestic and foreign affairs' (Zacher 1992:61). Based on this concept, IR-theorists have focused their analyses on relations between states (that is, governments), often largely ignoring what goes on inside states. Such a conceptual point of departure is correct in pointing to states as sovereign, territorial entities, but it is of course inadequate for the present study which wants the focus directly on the relationship between international and domestic.

The 'IR-view' of the state focuses on a sovereign territorial unit which is part of a larger system of states. The concepts of state from political science and sociology, by contrast, focus on the state as an institutional apparatus of government and on the relation between that apparatus and society. Theda Skocpol offers a Weberian definition with a focus on the state apparatus. The state is 'a set of administrative, policing and military organizations headed, and more or less well-coordinated, by an executive authority' (1979:29). The Marxist perspective pursued by Robert Cox is more interested in the underlying (class) structure of society and its relation to the state. That in turn leads to an analysis of the development of 'a plurality of forms of state, expressing different configurations of state/society complexes' (Cox 1996:86).[16]

It is not necessary here to engage deeply these various theoretical approaches to the state. My concept of 'domestic' and thus of the state is shaped by the purposes of the present study. I want to accomplish two things: first, to get an idea about how sovereign statehood develops and changes over time, in particular how international forces shape domestic structures in different ways. Second, I want to discuss the specific security dilemmas connected with three different types of state, the modern, the postmodern, and the postcolonial state.

For these purposes, the adequate starting point is the 'IR-view' of the state, as a sovereign, territorial entity with a population and a government. But in order to understand how state structures change over time and how security dilemmas vary in relation to that, some further specification of the salient aspects of statehood is needed.

In this regard, Robert Cox's notion of historical structures is a helpful starting point. Historical structures are a picture of a particular configuration of forces.

They consist of material capabilities, ideas, and institutions. It was noted above that the three elements of the 'international' could be considered an historical structure. Recall the premise set out in the opening paragraph of this chapter: 'international' and 'domestic' are parts of a totality, a whole. When 'international' and 'domestic' are considered part of a whole, we are looking for a structure that pertains to the whole, not merely to the 'international' or the 'domestic' parts of it. Put differently, not merely the 'international' but also the states are historical structures made up of material capabilities, ideas, and institutions.

Against this background it is possible to specify the principal elements of sovereign statehood that will be in focus here. In terms of institutions, focus is on the political–military institutions of the state, as emphasized by Skocpol. All sovereign states have those institutions; but there are huge differences between them in terms of efficiency, structure of power, and legitimacy. It cannot be taken for granted, for example, that all states enjoy a monopoly on the legitimate use of force. Such differences in 'domestic' structures, it will be argued, have consequences for the 'international' relations of states and for the ways in which they confront the problem of security.

In terms of material capabilities, focus is on the economy. The definition of the economy has been given earlier, that is, the capability to design, construct, produce, finance, and distribute economic goods. In context of the substantial analysis below it will be relevant to distinguish between various sectors of the economy at different levels of development in order to get a clear picture of the extent to which sovereign states do or do not have economic capabilities.[17] Some states have well-defined national economies, others do not; some states are highly dependent on the world market. Variation in 'domestic' economic structure significantly influences the 'international' relations of different types of state.

Finally, in terms of 'ideas', focus is on identity and community (that is, the nation). 'Nation' and 'state' are often conflated in the IR-literature, as indicated in such book titles as 'Games Nations Play' or 'Politics Among Nations' and even in organizational names such as the 'League of Nations' and the 'United Nations'. Nationhood concerns the kind of community and common identity that exists or does not exist among the members of the population. There are two aspects of this; one concerns the idea of a common community of the people in the nation; the other concerns the relationship between people and the state, the system of rights and duties, of obligations and privileges that are about citizenship. One major element in the development and change of sovereign statehood thus involves 'the idea of the state' (Buzan 1991:69–80), that is, the ways in which community and identity has developed in the population and the extent and concrete shape of citizenship. The actual character of community and citizenship, it will be demonstrated, have consequences for the distinct make-up of the security dilemma.

In sum, states are sovereign, territorial entities made up of material capabilities, ideas, and institutions. The salient aspects of sovereign statehood in focus here are: the political–military institutions of the state; the economic basis of the state, and the 'idea' of the state as expressed in the kind of community and citizenship that has developed (or has not developed) among the members of the population and in the relationship between people and state. In shorthand terms, the core elements of the state are: government; economy; and nationhood.

Which of the two came first in historical terms, 'domestic' or 'international'? Put differently, is the system derived from the states or are the states derived from the system? Antonio Gramsci made the argument that international relations come last: 'Do international relations precede or follow (logically) fundamental social relations? There can be no doubt they follow' (Gramsci 1971:240). This view dominates much Marxist thinking which is based on 'the primacy of the internal' (Ougaard 1989:102, my translation from Danish, GS). At the same time, it was noted above that what is at any given point 'domestic' is always the result of a previous interplay between domestic and international. As noted by Ronen Palan and Barry Gills, 'the "outside" becomes "inside" and inside becomes inseparable from the outside' (1994:61). On that view, then, 'domestic' and 'international' came simultaneously; in that sense there is a 'mutually constitutive relationship' (Buzan 1991:60) between the two. That is the view adopted here. It is not at odds with the sequencing strategy of analysis announced earlier. It merely emphasizes that the choice of where to begin the analysis – at the domestic or at the international level – is a matter of analytical convenience.

## A note on epistemology and ontology

Given the current debates in the discipline about ontology and epistemology, it is relevant briefly to situate the present argument in that context. This is the more so, because my argument is not particularly attached to any specific theory or cluster of theories; that is to say, it cannot be readily classified as, for example, a 'realist', 'liberal', or 'English school' argument. It should be clear already that the complex relationship between 'international' and 'domestic' is a concern for all the major theories of IR. The present study reflects that situation in that it draws on insights that originate in quite different theoretical traditions in IR.

Two major issues have provoked theoretical debates in recent years; one concerns ontology, the other epistemology (Sørensen 1998). The ontological debate is about the nature of the social world. There are two extreme positions in that debate, an 'objectivist' most frequently connected with neorealism and a 'subjectivist' often connected with various versions of 'post-positivism'

(Smith 1997). The 'objectivist' view is purely materialist or naturalist, that is, the social world of international relations is a world shaped by the material structure of the international system (for example, Mearsheimer 1995; 1994–95). The 'subjectivist' view is idealist, arguing that the social world is, more than anything else, constituted by our language, ideas, and concepts – the social world is 'what we make it' (Smith 1995:27). This is an important debate; but it is significant that the real extremes in it hardly exist in IR (or in social science) today. One would be hard pressed to find examples of theorists who would argue that the social world is purely materialist or purely idealist. The view taken here thus follows what is arguably the position among the majority of theorists; it is both.[18] The real debate is therefore not a matter of choosing between the two but of sorting out the proper relationship between them.[19] The aim of this study is not to seek further clarification of that intricate question, so it is not pursued in its own right in what follows.

The epistemological debate concerns the ways in which we are able to obtain knowledge about the world. At one extreme is the notion of scientifically explaining the world. According to this view, social science can be built upon a foundation of propositions that are empirically verifiable. At the other extreme is the notion of understanding the world. The task is to comprehend and interpret the topic under study. According to this view, the historical, legal, and moral problems of world politics cannot be translated into the terms of scientific explanation.

This is a long-standing debate, in the philosophy of science in general and also within IR. Hedley Bull famously defended what he called the 'classical approach', derived from 'philosophy, history, and law...characterized above all by explicit reliance upon judgment and by the assumption that if we confine ourselves to strict standards of verification and proof there is very little of significance that can be said about international relations...' (Bull 1969:20).

But again, the confrontation between 'explaining' and 'understanding' should not be overdrawn. It is possible to find a middle road, where inquiry into international relations contains elements of both. Indeed, Bull's rejection of what he calls 'the scientific approach' – defined as a theory 'whose propositions are based either upon logical or mathematical proof, or upon strict, empirical procedures of verification' (Bull 1969:21) – is not a rejection of any kind of causal reasoning (or explaining) whatsoever in IR. What Bull brings home is that the 'in *framing* hypotheses in answer to...empirical questions' and 'in testing them we are utter dependent upon judgment' (1969:27); but that does not mean that we cannot identify 'determinants' (1969:36)[20] or indeed consider rules and institutions to be 'part of the efficient causation of international order' (Bull 1995:71); in other words, the classical approach as defended by Bull is not an argument against any causal reasoning whatsoever.[21] It is an argument against taking such reasoning too far and never letting it escape the exercise of judgement. In that sense, Bull's position is similar to Weber's emphasis on 'interpretive understanding of social action' combined with 'causal explanation of its course and effects' (Weber 1964:88). Even if Bull emphasizes interpretive understanding of international relations and is sceptical about the extent to which causal explanation is possible, it is quite clear that both elements are present in his version of the classical approach.

In sum, there is an epistemological middle ground that avoids a stark choice between 'pure' explaining or 'pure' understanding. The present study is based on this middle ground – a space that it shares with many other scholars (see Sørensen 1998) – but there is no ambition in what follows to contribute to the epistemological debate or indeed to identify further different possible positions within this sizeable middle ground.[22]

## The argument summarized

I begin with the 'outside-in' analysis. Chapters 2 through 6 demonstrate how international forces (political–military power, international norms, and economic power) have helped create three different main types of state in the post-Second World War international system. They will be identified as ideal types and labelled the modern state, the postcolonial state, and the postmodern state, respectively. The next step is the 'inside-out' analysis in Chapters 7 through 10. It explains how the three types of state exist in different forms of anarchy and display different security dilemmas. It will be argued that the peculiar security dilemma of each state type is based on distinct 'domestic' statehood structures. Furthermore, the concept of 'sovereignty game' will be introduced as an adequate way of analysing the characteristic pattern of 'international' relations pertaining to modern, postcolonial, and postmodern states. Chapter 11 examines the consequences of the analysis for existing main theories of international relations. Finally, Chapter 12 reflects on the implications of the analysis for the evaluation of the future world order, and for the further development of IR-theory. Figure 1.2 sets out the argument in brief.

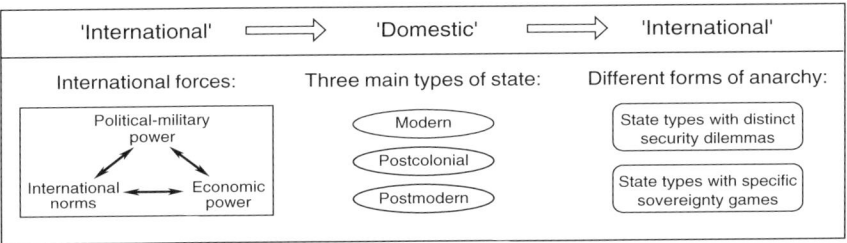

*Figure 1.2*   The argument in brief

# 2
# Theories on the Effect of 'International' on 'Domestic'

This chapter is the theoretical preface to the empirical 'outside-in' analysis that follows in the next three chapters. It sets forth the main theoretical views on the effects of international forces on domestic structures; they can be classified according to their main emphasis on either a logic of homogeneity or a logic of heterogeneity. The logic of homogeneity is one of competition for best place and thus most power and influence in the system; it is a logic of emulating more successful states, of imitating them to achieve similar success. The logic of heterogeneity, by contrast, is one of uneven development; of economic, political and other processes shaping types of state that are qualitatively different from each other.

I shall argue in favour of the view that there is both a logic of homogeneity and a logic of heterogeneity at work in the effects of systemic forces on domestic structures. The theoretical overemphasis of one at the expense of the other can easily lead to distorted analysis. Such relative emphasis can only be undertaken in concrete, empirical investigations.

Why is this issue of homogeneity versus heterogeneity so terribly important? First, because it offers insights into the consequences for countries of being members of a system or a society of states. The 'outside-in' perspective rests on the claim that international forces influence and shape domestic structures in basic ways. The whole trajectory of 'national' development is thus profoundly fashioned by the international context. When this is the case it is of utmost importance, of course, to be better informed about the precise ways in which international forces shape domestic structures. The major clusters of relevant theory are those on homogeneity and heterogeneity respectively.

Second, the domestic makeup of states has consequences for the international system or society of which they are a part. The 'inside-out' perspective rests on the claim that the domestic structure of states in basic ways influence and shape the international system. Therefore, it is supremely important to know about the extent to which states are homogenous or not; neorealism indeed builds its whole systemic analysis of the balance of power on the idea that domestic structures of states can be disregarded, because they can be considered basically homogenous, 'like units'. Several strands of Marxist analysis, by contrast, build their whole examination of the international system on the notion of groups of states that are highly heterogeneous. One cannot properly assess such views without due consideration of forces of homogeneity and forces of heterogeneity.

In sum, the relative importance of the logic of homogeneity and the logic of heterogeneity are profoundly important, both for an understanding of how domestic development is affected by international forces and for an appreciation of how domestic structures shape the international system.

## The logic of homogeneity

The dominant IR-theories emphasize the logic of homogeneity, of states becoming more alike as a result of international forces. That is the case for both neorealism, classical Marxism, and liberalism. The major arguments of each of these approaches will be addressed in turn.

Neorealism begins with the assumption of anarchy, that is, the absence of systemwide authority. Given that states at a minimum seek to survive they are driven, under conditions of anarchy, to emulate the more successful states in the system. 'The theory says simply that if some do relatively well, others will emulate them or fall by the wayside' (Waltz 1979:118). Socialization and competition are the two principal ways in which the anarchic structure affects states. Waltz draws an analogy between states in anarchy and firms in the marketplace. Both firms and states can succeed through coincidence, dumb luck, or whatever. Rationality, the conscious intention of wanting and trying to succeed, need not be involved. Provided they happen to do the right thing they will survive and prosper. 'Those who survive share certain characteristics. Those who go bankrupt lack them. Competition spurs the actors to accommodate their ways to the socially most acceptable and successful practice. Sozialization and competition are two aspects of a process by which the variety of behaviors and outcomes is reduced' (Waltz 1979:77).

Waltz's notion of Darwinian selection appears to be immediately applicable to the history of state formation in Europe. The number of states in Europe fell sharply between the sixteenth and the twentieth centuries. In many cases smaller and weaker units were swallowed by stronger ones which thereby consolidated their own sovereign statehood. In a similar way, the institution of sovereign statehood outcompeted rival forms of political organization: empires, city-states, and so on. The well-known formulation by Charles Tilly captures the important role of war in that process: 'states made war and war made states' (Tilly 1990:32). In addition to war and military technology there were other factors in play of course, economic change arguably the most important one (Spruyt 1994b:30).

Yet several indicators suggest that a pure Darwinian logic of selection cannot explain important elements in European state formation. There is great variation in the size of state units; no convergence on an optimum size has taken place. In particular, a number of small, weak states which ought to have been obliterated according to Darwinian evolutionary logic have continued to exist: San Marino, Andorra, Liechtenstein, and so on. Neorealists may counter that such weaker states are only allowed to exist because the greater powers have no interest in wiping them out; but this argument does not save the Darwinian logic because the fate of smaller units then depends on great power considerations instead of an automatic logic of selection. As noted by Buzan, Jones, and Little (1993), the balance of power can be constructed in such a way that it allows some weak states to persist. That means we would have to investigate the interests and preferences of great powers in any historical period to make inferences about the survival of states in the system. Such reasoning leads away from the neorealist view of an international system mechanically created by survival of the fittest and towards the notion of an international society of states (Jackson 1995a) containing states that are 'unlike units'.

Furthermore, if competition and socialization is non-mechanical and instead takes place through actors in social processes, it is necessary to make room for the possibility that some actors learn and adapt better than others (Spruyt 1994a). Moreover, it must also be expected that different domestic conditions, including different historical trajectories and varying political coalitions, affect the process. Additional considerations can be put forward which limit the homogenizing effects of competition and socialization. First, one way of competing is to innovate, to develop new institutional and other solutions that are superior to existing solutions (Alderson 1997). The special form of cooperation in the European Union, for example, can be seen as such an innovation which is neither a new regional state, nor a mere case of interstate collaboration. The argument can be made that this collaboration is pushed as a European answer to challenges from, among others, the United States and Japan; insofar that is the case, competition has led to heterogeneity rather than homogeneity. Second, the concept of socialization is not very clear. The scope and depth of socialization is not discussed by Waltz; who or what gets socialized to which extent (depth) and in which areas (scope)? Furthermore, socialization need not lead to homogeneity. States in the same system can be socialized to different roles (for example, 'trading states', or 'warrior states'). In short, competition and socialization may lead towards homogeneity, but may also involve significant heterogeneity. Neorealism is not clear in specifying the exact extent of similarity between states or how these processes have been affected by varying historical circumstances.

Neorealists respond to such views by emphasizing that their notion of homogeneity is a more limited one. That is, the logic of 'like units' pertains primarily to the great powers, not necessarily to smaller states; and no claim is made that the logic of homogeneity leads to identity. Rather, it leads to functional and structural similarity (Waltz 1979:96). In any case, the neorealist position is one of disregarding the domestic structures of states, because they are 'like units duplicating one another's activities' (Waltz 1979:97). This study will argue that neorealism takes the logic of homogeneity much too far and thereby creates a misleading analysis of international relations.

Another major argument in favour of homogeneity comes from Karl Marx. Marx's belief in a process of homogeneity is based on his analysis of capitalism and capitalist expansion. Capitalism is a force that eradicates previous modes of production; therefore, the expansion of capitalism results in the emergence of 'like units', not merely in functional form but in structural content. Material production is the core basis for any state and when material production is everywhere capitalist, states are homogenous in a profound structural sense. This argument is most forcefully made in the Communist Manifesto:

> The need of a constantly expanding market for its products chases the bourgeoisie over the whole surface of the globe. It must nestle everywhere, settle everywhere, establish connections everywhere. The bourgeoisie, by the immensely facilitated means of communication, draws all, even the most barbarian nations into civilization. The cheap prices of its commodities are the heavy artillery with which it batters down all Chinese walls, with which it forces the barbarians' intensely obstinate hatred of foreigners to capitulate. It compels all nations, on pain of extinction, to adopt the bourgeois mode of production; it compels them to introduce what it calls civilization in to their midst, i.e. to become bourgeois themselves. In one word, it creates a world after its own image.
>
> (Marx and Engels 1973:71)

There is a clear similarity between Marx and Waltz; both stress how a competitive logic leads towards sameness. As in Waltz's case, Marx's argument in the Manifesto contains an element of Darwinian selection: adapt or die; embrace the bourgeois mode of production 'on pain of extinction'. The difference is that Waltz's view is based on a focus on state leaders in a competitive game of power politics whereas Marx's view is based on the economic and social impact of capitalism in the broader society. Waltz's logic of homogeneity begins with the policies of state leaders and spreads from there to the rest of society. Marx's logic of homogeneity begins in the sphere of economic production and reproduction and spreads from there to the political and ideological levels of society.

The analysis of the capitalist mode of production in 'Das Kapital' can be seen as an identification of the basic structures and the laws of motion embodied in capitalism. This theoretical reconstruction of capitalism is not an ideal type in the Weberian sense, because Max Weber stressed that the pure ideal type had no empirical parallel (see Sørensen 1976:162–7). Marx, in contrast, stresses how the empirical reality moves closer and closer to his theoretical construct as capitalism develops; his ideal type is not pure theoretical construction, it is emerging empirical reality. When capitalism expands into noncapitalist environments, a process of homogenization is set into motion whereby new areas will gradually adopt the same basic socioeconomic structure as other capitalist countries. That is what Marx meant when he ventured that backward states saw a picture of their own future in the more developed capitalist states.

It was noted earlier that a pure Darwinian logic was not at work in the sphere of power politics; it was not at work in the socioeconomic sphere either. Capitalism did expand into new areas, but it did not create a world in its own image. On the one hand, concrete social conditions for capitalist expansion were radically different from North America to India, from East Asia to Africa; these varying conditions substantially shaped different varieties of capitalist expansion. On the other hand, the international context had also changed. Capitalist expansion in what became the Third World took place in context of a world market already dominated by the advanced capitalist states. Both of these elements helped create substantial deviation from the logic of homogeneity. Marx began to recognize this in his later work (cf. Shanin 1983; Halliday 1994:115–16), but it was left to later generations of Marxists, not least to Leon Trotsky, to draw the full implications as will be demonstrated below.

In summary, Marx bases the logic of homogeneity on the irresistible expansion of capitalism. Although his vision of homogeneity is not specified in detail, it is clear that it goes beyond functional similarity. Capitalist states and societies are alike in a basic, structural sense because they share a mode of production complete with specific laws of motion, defined social forces (bourgeoisie and proletariat), a capitalist state apparatus, and a dominant form of (capitalist) ideology. At the same time, there are barriers to capitalist expansion and Marx never worked out in detail to which extent these barriers would constrain the forces of homogeneity. In the absence of such addition, the classical Marxist analysis contains an erroneous overemphasis on the forces of homogeneity.

The final major argument in favour of homogeneity comes from the liberal tradition. Liberal thinking is closely connected with the emergence of the modern state. Liberal philosophers, beginning with John Locke in the seventeenth century, saw a great potential for human progress in the modern state and the modern economy. Modernity conjures a new and better life, free of authoritarian government and with a much higher level of material welfare. That is the basis for the liberal belief in progress: the modern liberal state invokes a political and economic system which will bring, in Jeremy Bentham's famous phrase, 'the greatest happiness of the greatest number'.

The notion of homogeneity is built into the liberal conception of progress. Social change is not merely natural, continuous, proceeding inexorably; it is also directional, moving towards modernity. Such were the ideas developed by the nineteenth-century evolutionary thinkers, Herbert Spencer, Auguste Comte, Emile Durkheim, and several others (Mitchell 1968; Nisbet 1969). This is the liberal version of the evolutionary optimism also found in Marx. A further development of these ideas came with liberal theories of modernization in the 1960s. Modernization theory is based on the notion of development as a spontaneous, irreversible process inherent in every society. The process implies structural differentiation and functional specialization; traditional social structures are eradicated by the more differentiated social structures of modernity. Domestic forces are the primary movers in the process of modernization, but the whole process is one of imitating the already modernized countries (Hettne 1990:60–1). External competition and military threat can spur the process, but it is a major point in most modernization thinking that less developed countries can take advantage of the technology and know-how of more developed countries and thus accelerate their own development (Gerschenkron 1962; Rostow 1960).

In sum, modernization is a unilinear process in which societies acquire the same social structures as those that are already modern and developed. In sociological terms, societies go from particularism, ascription, and diffuseness, towards universalism, achievement, and specificity. These are the pattern variables set forth by Talcott Parsons; the first three describe traditional society, the latter three describe modern society (cf. Hoselitz 1960). In economic terms, Walt Rostow portrayed the process of modernization as a movement through five stages which were seen to be undertaken by all societies: from traditional society, over the pre-take-off stage and take-off, to 'the road to maturity', ending up in modern mass consumption society (Rostow 1960).

According to modernization theory then, homogeneity is built into the process of modernization; as that process will eventually come to all countries they will also become more and more alike. However, more recent contributions to this literature distance themselves from the nineteenth-century sociologists of evolution. First, it is stressed that traditional social structures are not completely obliterated; they change in context of modernization but they continue to decisively influence the pattern of development in society and, by implication, the relations between societies (Gusfield 1971). Second, there is less optimism concerning the prospects for all countries to quickly reach a stage of modernity. Both of these qualifications point to a logic of homogeneity which is somewhat weaker than in early liberal formulations. In sum, the basic liberal view is one of increasing homogeneity, as expressed in the 'end of history' stage where all countries have reached liberal modernity. But there are bumps on that road which may lead to heterogeneity persisting for some time.[1]

To sum up this section: both neorealism, Marxism, and liberalism point to competition and socialization as important factors leading to a process of homogenization, of states becoming more and more alike. The neorealist argument is based on military–political competition in an anarchic realm. In its most radical formulations, the choice is between adaptation or liquidation, between emulating the successful states or falling by the wayside. The Marxist argument is based on the expansion of capitalism, but the choice is an equally stark one: adopt capitalism or be wiped out. Military–political and economic competition also play a role in liberal thinking, but the liberal view is in general a softer and less severe one; imitation is taking place in a context of modernization, but catch-up may be unsuccessful without fatal consequences. It is noteworthy that, with the partial exception of Marxism, none of the theoretical perspectives arguing for homogeneity appear to think beyond the sovereign state. Neorealism simply assumes that states want to survive as independent, autonomous units, and that their political, economic, military, and other arrangements are undertaken accordingly. Liberalism foresees mature modernity as the end stage of state development. Marx had some ideas of a socialist phase beyond that, but they were based on the false assumption that capitalism would inevitably create the conditions for its own destruction. In sum, there is a flavour of 'endism' in all of these perspectives, a teleological element of successful homogeneization leading to an end stage of mature, sovereign statehood.

It is clear that a pure Darwinian selection logic cannot be accepted as a general explanation of homogeneity. Weaker, non-capitalist, non-modern states have not, as a rule, died out. That leaves a more intricate issue of deciding in detail the types of pressures for homogeneity and their varying intensity in different historical periods. To which extent did states actually end up as 'like units'? That is the empirical issue to be addressed in later chapters. The theoretical issue is this: did states become 'like units' to such an extent that it is analytically defensible to substantially disregard the general patterns of variation in their domestic characteristics for the purpose of analysing international relations? As already indicated, my answer to that question will be a resounding 'no'. Before proceeding with these issues, however, it is relevant to set forth the main arguments for a logic of heterogeneity.

## The logic of heterogeneity

It is a branch of Marxist analysis which has set forth the strongest arguments in favour of a logic of heterogeneity, but an argument for this logic can also be based on international norms. I begin with the Marxist argument. Marx's position in the Manifesto was clear in claiming that the expansion of capitalism would lead to homogeneity. But there is another element in Marxist analysis which points in the opposite direction; that element is the notion of uneven development. Lenin, like Marx, expected capitalism to spread rapidly across the world. Yet he also emphasized that capitalist development is uneven:

> There can be no other conceivable basis under capitalism for the division of spheres of influence . . . than a calculation of the strength of the participants in the division, their general economic, financial, military strength, etc. And the strength of these participants in the division does not change to an equal degree, for under capitalism the development of different undertakings, trusts, branches of industry, or countries cannot be even.
>
> (Lenin 1939 [1917]:119)

The idea that capitalist development is uneven at every level, including firms, industries, sectors, and countries, need not in itself lead to heterogeneity; it might merely be a question of differential power within the same (that is, homogenous) structure of capitalism. That appeared to be Lenin's position: uneven development was mainly a question of uneven power within the same structure of capitalism. But it is clear that uneven development can easily lead to heterogeneity, to the creation of qualitatively economic and societal structures in different countries. That is the view adopted by neomarxist dependency theorists writing in the 1960s and 1970s. Andre Gunder Frank (1969) and Samir Amin (1976) argued that capitalism produced development in one part of the world (the core) and underdevelopment in another part of the world (the periphery) as elements of the same single process of global capitalism.

Samir Amin claimed that this process led to qualitatively different socio-economic forms in core and periphery respectively. The core is characterized by a basically self-sustaining capitalist model, with a foundation of capital goods combined with mass consumption industries. The social class structure is dominated by a domestic industrial bourgeoisie and a skilled working class. In essence, capitalist development in the core is accompanied by a tendency to approximate the pure model of capitalism characterized by Marx in 'Das Kapital' (Amin 1976:293). The peripheral formations, by contrast, exhibit a qualitatively different pattern of development sharing four main characteristics: '(1) the predominance of agrarian capitalism in the national sector; (2) the creation of a local, mainly merchant bourgeoisie in the wake of dominant foreign capital; (3) a tendency toward a peculiar bureaucratic development, specific to the contemporary periphery; and (4) the incomplete specific character of the phenomena of proletarianization' (Amin 1976:333). Samir Amin's analysis of global capitalism thus combines heterogeneity (qualitatively different structures in core and periphery) with homogeneity (shared characteristics within the group of core countries and within the group of peripheral countries).

The most radical version of the argument that unequal development of global capitalism leads to heterogeneity in the form of qualitatively different economic, social, and political structures in different countries can be found in the writings of Leon Trotsky. He rejected Marx's famous idea about capitalistic-ally advanced England showing other countries a picture of their own future; development in other countries would be different, often radically different, from the English experience: 'England in her day revealed the future of France, considerably less of Germany, but not in the least of Russia and not of India' (1980:378).

Trotsky's argument specifically stressed that uneven development was pushed by the different international contexts in which the rise of capitalism took place. On the one hand, there was a 'privilege of historic backwardness' (Trotsky 1980:5) which meant that latecomers could draw on technological and other advances made by the frontrunners. Germany effectively exploited that possibil-ity in its catch-up race against England and Trotsky found that Germany was already overtaking England economically by the late nineteenth century. On the other hand, late development such as it took place in Russia, spurred by state and foreign investment, led to distortion of the 'normal' capitalist class struc-ture. The indigenous bourgeoisie was weak or non-existent; capitalism was an urban affair that did not involve a transformation in the countryside although it did involve heavy taxation of the peasantry; this in turn led to a radicalization of political life, dominated by an autocratic state facing an extreme and violent opposition. Justin Rosenberg summarized Trotsky's analysis as follows:

> ... capital did indeed create one world, but not a homogenous world fash-ioned in the image of the capitalist societies at its centre. To understand why this is so, we have to grasp the peculiar international mechanism of capitalist expansion which, even as it incorporates other societies, fuses with them in unpredictable combinations. ... if we want to understand what the interna-tional system is today, we cannot begin with a logical model of homogenous states: the variety of political forms is simply too great; we would have to begin instead with a historical analysis which reconstructs the uneven and combined development of capitalism internationally which has produced such a variegated world of states.
>
> (Rosenberg 1996:8)

Several points may be noted about Trotsky's analysis. First, the argument is based on economics; uneven and combined capitalist development leads to variations in class structures which in turn imply different shapes of political institutions and political struggles. Second, the logic of heterogeneity is sharply emphasized while the logic of homogeneity is played down; the entire process is one of capitalist development on a global scale, but the forces of homogeneity which that process may contain are less important for Trotsky. Where Marx overemphasized homogeneity in capitalist development, Trotsky overemphasizes heterogeneity. While Marx did not spell out in detail the constraints on the logic of homogeneity, Trotsky did not address the relationship between the forces of heterogeneity contained in uneven development and the forces of homogeneity contained in global capitalist expansion. Third, the analysis by Trotsky in effect abolishes any sharp distinction between domestic and international; they are part of the same, whole process of uneven and combined capitalist development which one can choose to study either from an 'international' or a concrete 'domestic' starting point. This is a radical way of emphasizing the close interrelationship between domestic and international, but it is not a very clear position when the aim is to sort out the relationship between international and domestic.

I now turn to international norms which can support a different type of argument in favour of heterogeneity. Recall the neorealist argument set forth earlier: the international system is a self-help system; states are compelled to emulate the more successful members of that system or fall by the wayside. The logic of homogenization is driven by states competing for survival in an anarchic system. But this argument rests on the assumption that a struggle for survival is actually taking place; that conquest through war and a subsequent change of borders is a perfectly rational and legitimate way for state leaders to secure their power and position in the system. But what if self-help is seriously circumscribed by international norms, so that a struggle for survival is not on the agenda? If international norms delegitimize conquest by war and the change of borders without the consent of the parties involved, and if such norms were effective, then the argument about competitive struggle for survival leading to 'like units' would carry little weight. In effect, international norms may lead to heterogeneity because they have removed the competitive pressure for emulating the successful states.

This is exactly the claim made by several scholars. Hendrik Spruyt notes that 'because Darwinian selection occurs less frequently, there is increased space for variation in internal design' (1994a:33). Robert Jackson emphasizes that 'determinations of territorial jurisdiction by threat or use of force, or by any means other than consent, have no legitimate place in contemporary [that is, since 1945, GS] international relations' (Jackson 1995b:66). In short, the effect of international norms is to neutralize pressures for homogeneity and thus create room for variation. The argument contains little about the actual extent of such variation; it is a negative argument (that is, absence of push for homogeneity) rather than a positive argument about the precise extent of heterogeneity.

The above reasoning does not imply that international norms lead only towards heterogeneity. Sovereign states are expected to play by a certain set of rules as members of the society of states, in accordance with international law and the standards of diplomacy. They often set up international regimes which oblige them to meet certain standards or behave in certain ways. In short, international norms can also lead towards homogeneity. The extent to which that is the case would appear to depend on the extent to which there exists an elaborated set of international norms with which states are obliged to comply.

To sum up this section: several variants of Marxist analysis argue for a logic of heterogeneity based on the notion of uneven capitalist development. Samir Amin finds that capitalism leads to qualitatively different socioeconomic forms in core and periphery. Leon Trotsky goes one step further in arguing that uneven and combined development throws up different economic, political, and sociocultural domestic forms which must be analysed in their historically specific context. International norms can also lead to heterogeneity, because they can create an international environment where state survival is no longer directly threatened by other states; that decreases the need for emulation and increases the room for variation.

Both international norms and uneven capitalist development can also involve domestic changes towards homogeneity. It appears that there are elements of homogeneity hidden in the arguments for heterogeneity, and vice versa. That is what makes historical analysis necessary. Before moving in this direction, the theoretical positions reviewed in this chapter will be drawn together.

## Homogeneity and heterogeneity: a framework for analysis

International forces shape domestic structures in countless ways. This chapter has focused on what might be called the main macro-theoretical views on the effects of international forces. Those views have been presented under the main headings of the logic of homogeneity and the logic of heterogeneity. Serious arguments can be set forth in favour of each view; it is clearly impossible to maintain that there is only one single logic, pointing in only one direction. A more complex question is this: has one logic been relatively stronger than the other, seen over a longer period of time? This question opens up a larger issue which has not been directly addressed in the present chapter: the ascendance and rise to complete dominance of the institutional form that is sovereign statehood itself. The theoretical perspectives on homogeneity and heterogeneity tend to take the existence of sovereign statehood for granted. That is, they do not directly attempt to explain how the institution of sovereign statehood has outcompeted other forms of political institutions including political empires, the institutional form that has dominated most of human history.

One can deduce from Waltz that processes of competition and socialization have led to the victory of sovereign statehood, or from Marx that the most appropriate or functional political form for capitalism appears to be the sovereign state, but their considerations as summarized above are not very clear on this point.

The present analysis does not aim to take on this issue. Obviously a number of different and partially unrelated developments combined to produce the dominance of sovereign statehood.[2] The main issue here is this: does the fact that states have become 'externally isomorph', i.e. they all possess formal, juridical sovereignty, mean that the logic of homogeneity is at work in their domestic structures as well? That is the question addressed by the theoretical perspectives introduced in this chapter. The theories refer to the three aspects of 'international forces' introduced in the previous chapter: political–military power; economic power, and international norms. It is clear by now that each of these factors can lead in either direction, towards homogeneity or towards heterogeneity. In sum, the effect of international forces on domestic structure is indeterminate. While it is certainly true that international forces *condition* domestic structures, the precise content of such conditioning, that is, homogeneity or heterogeneity, cannot be determined in advance. There is therefore no way around an historically founded analysis to address the issue. That analysis is the subject of the next three chapters which make up the empirical part of the 'outside-in' analysis.

# 3
# Political–Military Power Shaping Domestic Structures: Homogeneity or Heterogeneity?

This chapter begins the empirical investigation of the effects of international forces on domestic structures. Focus is on the effects of political–military power; the chapter concentrates especially on the empirical study of the neo-realist idea that political–military competition leads to homogeneity. Even with this narrowing of the subject, an exhaustive empirical analysis is a daunting task. Fortunately, a complete empirical examination is not necessary for my purpose in this book. The aim in this and the next two chapters is to get a better grip on the way in which international forces condition domestic structures. It has already been indicated that both forces of homogeneity and forces of heterogeneity have been in play. To which extent have they led to the emergence of 'like units'? Without an answer to this question it will be impossible to properly understand the present international system.

## The Soviet Union: a case-study

Instead of a more superficial discussion of the overall effects of political–military power on domestic structures, this chapter conducts an in-depth case-study of the Soviet Union/Russia. The country appears to be a tremendously strong case for the neorealist thesis that international political–military power pressures states towards homogeneity.[1] The argument might run as follows: Here is a great power that very consciously set out to become an 'unlike' state in an international system dominated by Western capitalist countries. The vision was that of a communist country with a political, social, and cultural system dramatically different from its capitalist counterparts. This included staying out of traditional Western practices of diplomacy and the like. Trotsky, the first Commissar for Foreign Affairs, explained his task in simple terms: 'To issue a few revolutionary proclamations to the peoples of the world and then shut up shop' (Trotsky 1930:341). But it quickly turned out that the Soviet Union had to accommodate to established practices if it wanted to survive. The armistice at Brest-Litovsk was therefore not only a substantial defeat for the Bolsheviks who lost a third of their population, a third of their cultivable land, plus more than half of their industry; it was also a defeat for the alternative foreign role of rebel and outsider. Even revolutionaries had to play by the rules of the diplomatic game.

The concession to diplomatic practice was only the beginning. The attempt to build 'Socialism in one country' was a miserable failure; the Soviet system was comprehensively unable to compete with its main rival, the United States, on every important dimension: economy, military, politics, and ideology. In August 1991 the Soviet Union finally caved in and the successor states began doing exactly what the neorealist theory of homogeneity claims: to imitate their more successful rivals in the capitalist West. A stronger confirmation of the homogenizing effects of competitive and socializing international pressures appears hard to find.

But closer scrutiny of the Soviet Union/Russia warrants a different conclusion, because forces of homogeneity have not worked in the way and to the extent indicated by neorealists. First, the initial premise for the argument is wrong. Bolshevik leaders did not set out to create a communist country, that is, a highly 'unlike' unit. They were in no doubt that the Russian revolution would be doomed to failure without support from revolutions elsewhere. The Russian revolution was understood by these leaders, not as the main event, but as the spark which would set off revolution in Germany and elsewhere. Revolutionary success in Russia depended on a revolution in Germany. That is the context for understanding Trotsky's statement about revolutionary proclamations, quoted above. A group of Bolsheviks led by Nikolaj Bukharin were so convinced about the need for revolution in Germany as a precondition for a revolution in Russia that they found any peace with Imperial Germany unacceptable. Thinking along similar lines, Trotsky attempted to stall the peace talks, hoping that the German proletariat would rise against Kaiser Wilhelm. Lenin justified Russian socialism and Soviet power on the grounds that it would create a 'temporary headquarters of socialism' (Hobsbawm 1994:376). In short, the Bolshevik leaders entertained no long-term visions about communist development in the Soviet Union alone; they were engaged in a short-term struggle for survival, attempting to meet the needs of the front while also responding to the mobilization of the urban working class and the masses of peasants in the countryside.

Second, international pressures in these early years did not push the Soviet Union towards 'sameness'. The opposite is closer to the truth: Bolshevik initiatives to create a more 'like unit', that is, a domestic structure much closer to capitalism than the revolutionaries actually wanted, were rejected by the international capitalist system. To understand how this came about, a few words about Soviet developments since the early crisis strategy of 'War communism' are necessary. 'War communism' came to involve the nationalization of the 'commanding heights' of the economy, that is, the major industrial enterprises, the banks, and the mining activities. It also involved the takeover of landlord estates by the peasantry, who divided up the land. A centralized state organ took control over industry. The creation of a centralized, military-like, political and party structure began. But centralized economic and political command structures do not mature overnight; food shortages were extensive with famine in parts of the country; steel production was down from 4.2 million tons in 1913 to 200 000 tons in 1920 (Hobsbawm 1994:378). The Bolsheviks could claim victory in the civil war in 1920, but the economy was in a terrible shape and the population was exhausted and decimated (two million emigrated, among them many of the educated).

'War communism' left the newly established Soviet regime increasingly isolated, both internally and externally. No revolutions had taken place in other countries, although some Russian revolutionaries were still hopeful they would. Surrounded by hostile powers, the Bolsheviks had to realize the limitations of an economic course which requisitioned 'surplus' grain from the peasantry by force and used similar means in ordering them to grow crops for the government. The answer to this situation was the 'New Economic Policy' (NEP) between 1921 and 1928. NEP was a compromise with capitalism; it allowed the peasantry to produce for sale in a market and it sought integration in the capitalist world market via the expansion of foreign trade and the welcoming of foreign investment in the Soviet Union. 'There is much that can and must be learned from the capitalists', Lenin declared in 1921 (quoted from Carr 1963:276).

NEP can thus be viewed as a temporary defeat of the socialist and communist ambitions of the Bolsheviks; that is indeed what many of them argued at the time. NEP set the Soviet Union on a course closer to that of the capitalist systems with which it had to compete. The aim was of course to strengthen Soviet power by building a stronger economic basis. Foreign investment was seen as an important element in this strategy. In 1925, Trotsky declared:

> We are still very backward in a technical sense. We are interested in using every possible means to accelerate our technical progress. Concessions are one way to do this . . . we are now more inclined than a few years ago to pay foreign capitalists significant sums for . . . their participation in the development of our productive forces . . . We are becoming a part, a highly individual but nevertheless component part, of the world market.
>
> (quoted from Day 1973:132, 134)

In sum, the Bolsheviks started to take some basic elements of the capitalist system on board, to move in the direction of more homogeneity. But the attempt found very few takers in the international system; instead of drawing the Soviet Union into a network of interdependencies via economic and political integration, the leading capitalist countries wanted no business with the Bolsheviks. Where the Bolsheviks sought integration and cooperation with the capitalist system, the major representatives of that system refused to have anything to do with the Soviet Union. Where the Bolsheviks steered towards taking significant elements of a capitalist system on board, the capitalist countries refused to be part of such a strategy (Pisar 1970:14).

That rejection was not merely economical in the sense that capitalist countries wanted no economic intercourse with the Bolsheviks. It was also political in the sense that those same dominant members of the international society of states did not want to recognize the Soviet Union as a legitimate member. The United States did not extend official diplomatic recognition to the USSR until 1933. In the 1920s, therefore, the Soviet Union was developing closer relations with that other pariah state in the capitalist camp, Germany. The Treaty of Rapallo from 1922 gave the Soviet Union access to German technology and even to German military equipment (Kennedy-Pipe 1995:14).

This leads to a third point concerning the pressures for homogeneity. By 1927 it was clear that NEP would not be able to produce a sufficiently fast rate of economic development.[2] With the road to integration in the capitalist system cut off for the Soviet Union, other ways had to be found to confront the competitive burden of the international system. By 1928, Stalin was talking about the need to 'catch up and surpass' the capitalist countries; he termed it 'a life and death question' (quoted from Kemp 1983:57–8). Industrialization by force emerged as the solution to the NEP crisis. That was innovation, the creation of a new, untested strategy of development. International competitive pressure did not lead to emulation and 'sameness' as neorealists indicate; it led to a decisive push towards the creation of a modern economy that was dramatically different from the modern economies of the capitalist countries. If you can innovate, you don't have to emulate.

In some ways, forced industrialization produced impressive results, especially compared with the crisis-ridden capitalist economies of the 1930s with their high levels of unemployment. Forced industrialization produced consistently high growth rates, terminated unemployment, and eventually provided the majority of the population with a low level, basic standard of living which included low cost housing, education, and health care in addition to work, food, and other basic necessities (for example, the economy produced a little more than one pair of footwear per person in 1940). It was this system that was capable of defeating Germany, the militarily most powerful state in Europe (the war came as a shock to Stalin who believed that the Nazi–Soviet pact of August 1939 would not be betrayed).

The Soviet Union that emerged victorious from the Second World War was, if anything, an 'unlike' unit. It was an isolated entity, with few external economic and political relations. Politically, it was an autocracy with all power vested in the communist party. The government merely carried out the will of the party. Party decisionmaking was centralized and nondemocratic. Ultimately, supreme power belonged to one man, the General Secretary. He did not follow laws, the several constitutions that were adopted meant little. 'The Soviet Union was governed by men, not by laws. And no one could ever be sure exactly how the system would work in a particular case. The system was largely rule-less' (Barner-Barry and Hody 1995:50). The workings of government and party were kept secret; the Soviet people were not citizens, but subjects. Rule was based on coercion, repression, and terror; inordinate power was vested in the repressive apparatus. Repression worked from the lowest to the highest level: Stalin not only filled the *Gulags* with millions of 'ordinary' people; he also eliminated a generation of political leaders, substituting them with persons of complete loyalty.

Economically, it was a command system with a collectivized agriculture, geared towards developing heavy industry. On top was an enormous bureaucracy, powerful but under Stalin always also in mortal danger; in the bottom were the millions of slaves in the labour camps, often living below subsistence. Then the peasants, a little better off, at least after the famine of 1932–34, and the forced collectivization which altogether killed between 13 and 14 million people (Conquest 1986:300–5). And finally, between the peasants and the cadres, the workers in industry.

To the extent that the state enjoyed legitimacy in the population it was based on a bond of sacrifice, economic, political, and military, between the people and 'Uncle Josef'. The basis for legitimacy in the developed countries in the West, by contrast, consists of two elements; a material factor of welfare, security, and order provided by the state; this is the basis for citizenship and for the vertical legitimacy between citizens and state. And a nonmaterial factor which is the idea of national community provided by mythology, interpretations of history, and ideology; this is the horizontal legitimacy of political community (cf. Holsti 1996). Neither vertical nor horizontal legitimacy was much developed in the USSR (Barner-Barry and Hody 1995).

I have argued that the neorealist thesis about competitive pressures leading towards homogeneity cannot be confirmed in the case of pre-1945 Soviet developments. What about the postwar period? Stalin died in 1953; by then it was clear to all that the Soviet system suffered immense problems. Command economies are geared to meeting plan targets; they are very poor innovators. The Soviet Union and other planned economies never mastered the transition from extensive to intensive growth, where flexibility and innovation are crucial. The problems manifest themselves in decreasing productivity, inter-industrial bottlenecks and lack of economic efficiency. The economy tends to be in a state of permanent crisis due to its own internal structure (Andreff 1984). Nikita Krushchev, who emerged as Stalin's successor, wanted to confront the economic problems. He was well aware of the need for meeting the material and nonmaterial needs of people as a precondition for generating support for the Soviet system. But Krushchev was also a firm believer in central planning and top-down reforms. As was the case with later reformers, including Gorba-chev, Krushchev thought that a number of isolated measures would reinvigo-rate the system; but those measures merely added new contradictions to a system that could not be reformed because the problem was the system itself. For example, Krushchev to his credit emptied the Gulags and wanted to increase the living standards of workers and peasants. But he also wanted to continue a centralized system that was based on extremely low-cost labour and geared to heavy industry. In the crucial agricultural sector, one grand scheme after another was put forward, to no significant effect. The basic problems with the command economy remained in place (Barner-Bary and Hody 1995:169).

At this point a significant puzzle emerges for the idea that competition and socialization lead to homogeneity: why did Krushchev not throw in the towel during the 1950s or, at the latest, in the early 1960s? It was abundantly clear that the Soviet command economy was no match for the capitalist market economies that were growing at immense speed in the 1950s. This was the time of the West German *Wirtschaftswunder* and of rapid reconstruction in Japan. Welfare societies emerged in Western Europe, Japan, and North America. If anything, this was a time to imitate Western success, to become a more 'like unit'? One possible answer is that despite the problems, the 1950s was a time of respectable growth in the Soviet Union, which was involved in a process of rebuilding after the war. According to this view, serious economic stagnation commenced only around 1970 (Barner-Barry and Hody 1995:171). Further-more, the *Sputnik* success indicated that the country was capable of some technological innovation.

But why were Krushchev's successors then not compelled to throw in the towel? There was a Cold War going on which required efficiency and competi-tive capability of the Soviet system. Perhaps the elite knew that basic changes would lead not only to abolishing the system, but would also sweep away the reformers themselves? Very well, but were they not involved in an 'emulate or fall by the wayside' competition with the West which ought to inspire prudent risk-taking? The question remains: why did more than forty years of unrelent-ing military and economic pressure not lead a stagnating Soviet Union much more in the direction of emulating the substantially more successful competi-tors? Stalin had responded to the competitive challenge with innovation instead of emulation. His successors did much less in terms of innovation. Given the competitive pressure, how could they get away with it? Why did emulation not set in, as neorealists predict?

The simple answer to this puzzle appears to be the fact of nuclear weapons. The United States had the atomic bomb in 1945. Stalin refused to let that fact influence his thinking about military affairs, but he was also determined to catch up; the Soviet Union exploded a fission bomb in 1949 and a hydrogen bomb in 1953. Malenkov declared in 1954 that the Soviet nuclear capability had created a deterrent which meant that war was no longer inevitable. He further argued that behind this new shield the USSR could divert resources away from military and heavy industry and push for more rapid increase in living standards. In 1956 Krushchev launched the idea of peaceful coexistence. 'This redefinition of Soviet thinking about the outside world had been made possible by the Soviet acquisition of nuclear power' (Kennedy-Pipe 1995:185).

Nuclear weapons ensured that the competitive pressure on the Soviet Union was no longer a matter of life and death. A shelter had been set up behind which the USSR could continue to be autocratic, coercive, inefficient, stagnant, and corrupt compared with its developed Western counterparts. For that situation to emerge, emulation had been required in one area: the obtaining of nuclear weapons. That event neutralized the need for efficient competition in all other areas. Even in the field of nuclear capability itself, imitation did not have to be very effective. In 1962 McNamara claimed that a 17:1 advantage for the United States in nuclear weapons still effectively meant nuclear parity, because the mere possibility that a few nuclear weapons could reach American soil was sufficient to create deterrence (Soviet leaders did not believe in this and kept pushing for actual parity). The nuclear stalemate indefinitely postponed any urgent need for effective catch-up in other areas. A side-effect was that 'the Cold War went on much longer than it might have had nuclear weapons never been invented' (Gaddis 1997:292).

But did not Mikhail Gorbachev finally throw in the towel by yielding to competitive pressures through a process of emulation? No, he didn't; first, the competitive pressure was not that hard in the first place. It is true that under Ronald Reagan, the American defence budget rose from $171 billion in 1981 to $376 billion in 1986; it was abundantly clear that the Soviet economy was unable to shoulder the burden of such increases in defence spending. The defence share of the USSR GNP went up from 12–14 per cent in 1965 to 15–17 per cent (25 per cent according to some estimates) in 1985; the corresponding figure for the United States was 6–7 per cent and 2–5 per cent for Western Europe (Powaski 1998:252). In addition, Reagan launched a Strategic Defence Initiative (SDI) aiming at giving the United States a ballistic missile defence. The SDI initiative threatened to decisively tip the nuclear balance in US favour and Reagan rejected, on Iceland in 1986, to discontinue SDI as part of a comprehensive agreement on nuclear arms reduction. That further increased the pressure on Gorbachev.

But Gorbachev successfully initiated a series of initiatives to call off the Cold War and reduce Soviet military commitments abroad, especially in the Third World and Eastern Europe. And the SDI remained a loose scheme; several scientists severely doubted its distant prospects for success; furthermore, nuclear disarmament did take place with the conclusion of the INF (intermediate-range nuclear forces) Treaty in 1987. So there was no acute external danger; substantial portions of the USSR nuclear capability remained in place and the Cold War was ending.

Second, what Gorbachev initiated was not a process of emulation. He was certain that the Soviet system could be reinvigorated. In *'Perestroika'* (1987:44), he wrote: 'We are convinced of its [socialism's, GS] capacity for self-perfection, for still greater revelation of its possibilities and for dealing with the present major problems of social progress . . .' The initiatives to end the Cold War can be seen a a contemporary version of Brest-Litovsk (cf. Cronin 1996:223): a tactical retreat to provide breathing space for addressing the urgent domestic problems. Successful domestic reform was a precondition for the Soviet Union's great power role: 'Only an intensive, highly developed economy can safeguard a reinforcement of [the] country's position on the international stage and allow her to enter the millennium with dignity as a great and flourishing power' (Gorbachev, quoted in Åslund 1995:15). Gorbachev knew that basic reform was necessary, but he was also confident about the abilities of the socialist system to come up with innovations which could make it master the difficult transition from extensive to intensive growth and revitalize the political system.

We now know that such innovation was not forthcoming. The old economic system, that is, the existing productive relationships, had to be replaced by something more efficient; that was the core of *perestroika*. Without sufficient growth, the regime was unable to fulfil its part of the unofficial 'social contract' under whose terms the public renounced any say about public affairs in return for a slowly rising standard of living' (Mandelbaum 1991–92:171–2).

The old political system also had to be fundamentally reformed; that was the core of *glasnost*. Political reform aimed at the establishment of a democratic state, complete with civil liberties and the rule of law. The centre of government was transferred from party to state. Dismantling the old system was relatively easy because it did not enjoy active popular support and most of the old elite could envisage new roles for themselves under a reformed system. But building a new, reformed socialist economic and political system in a very short time proved impossible.

The reason for this was not so much resistance from the old *Nomenklatura*; their coup attempt in August 1991 was dismantled by a vigorous Boris Yeltsin accompanied by merely a few supporters. The main reason was that there was no positive vision, not to mention a detailed plan, of what was going to take its place. Gorbachev knew what he did not want: a coercive, internationally isolated, economically outdated system with very little active popular support. It was much less clear what should be put in the old system's place: 'Nobody had the slightest idea of how, in practice, the transition from a centralized state command economy to the new system was to be made and – equally to the point – how what would inevitably remain a dual state and non-state economy for the foreseeable future would actually work' (Hobsbawm 1994:482).

So emulation set in by default rather than due to competitive pressures. Nobody could come up with an alternative to the liberal market economy as a means to faster economic progress. Nobody could come up with an alternative to liberal democratic procedures as a means to basic political rights and liberties. At the same time, there were groups in the former Soviet Union, often tied into transnational networks, who wanted to move in the liberal direction, not for reasons of competitive pressure, but out of positive support for a liberal political and economic model.

## Russia today: a 'like unit'?

We do not know what will be the final outcome of the dramatic changes set in motion by Gorbachev but utterly uncompleted under Yeltsin. In some basic ways imitation has set in: Russia is now a more open, pluralist political system and in the economic sphere there are some elements of a market economy. Opening up to the West has increased external influence; Western actors are, however slowly, moving Russia in the direction of a more 'like unit'. But successful economic and political development can not be executed by outsiders. My evaluation of the situation as at spring 2000 did not provide much ground for optimism. Economic and to a large extent political power was in the hands of a small elite, the oligarchy that emerged in control of the profitable economic sectors: raw materials (mainly oil and gas); banking; and some services. Yeltsin dismantled the Soviet Union after the August 1991 putsch but did little to create a new political framework (cf. McFaul 1997). A new constitution was not promoted; neither was the creation of political parties and elections.

The division of power and responsibility between branches of government and between central and local authorities remained unclear. The creation of a new parliament and the adoption of a new constitution came late, in 1993. Civil society is weak and disorganized; the state has little capacity to enforce laws; there is only very slow progress in establishing a rule of law. Basic services that citizens expect from a functioning state, such as order, security, welfare, and education are not public goods in Russia today. The state lacks both the will and the capacity to act upon citizen preferences. In short, Russia is a weak state, 'dominated by big business and insulated from societal pressures' (McFaul 1997:48).

The economy is plagued by persistent crisis; negative growth rates (minus 10 to 15 per cent during 1992–95); huge budget deficits; inflationary pressures; and a highly unstable currency. The standard explanation for this is that corruption and crime combined with poor tax collection has halted the diffi-cult early transition to a market economy, but eventually these obstacles will be overcome. A recent analysis is much more sceptic; instead of making slow progress most of the Russian economy 'is actively moving in the other direc-tion' (Gaddy and Ickes 1998:53). A large part of the economy is made up of an unreformed industrial sector. These enterprises produce goods but they take away more value than they add; that is, they not merely lag in productivity, they are counterproductive. This fact is hidden by a variety of mechanisms: tax arrears; underpriced inputs; and overpriced outputs. The result is a virtual economy, as described in a recent Russian commission report: '[This creates] illusory, or "virtual" earnings, which in turn lead to unpaid, or "virtual" fiscal obligations, [with business conducted at] nonmarket, or "virtual" prices' (quoted from Gaddy and Ickes 1998:56). The virtual economy persists because its elimination would negatively affect large groups: jobs would be lost in industry, pensions would have to be cut and tax delinquency would be exposed in the value-adding sector of the economy (Gaddy and Ickes 1998:60). By providing jobs, the virtual economy functions as a social safety net, but the system cannot persist, because it is based on virtual, not real production. That is, the Russian economy is even smaller than the official figures ($466 billion in 1997, that is, six per cent of US GDP at market exchange rates) suggest. Without a continued borrowing from abroad, the system will eventually break down. In short, a very substantial part of the Russian economy has not made any progress towards market conditions; instead counterproductive enterprises persist in a virtual economy.

The dissolution of the Soviet Union has turned the Russian Federation into a more homogenous entity, but the extent to which there is a national commu-nity can be questioned. The Federation has 87 political subdivisions (21 repub-lics, 1 autonomous region and 10 autonomous districts, 49 administrative regions and 6 provinces) (Slater 1994:24). The material basis for citizenship has not developed because the basic state services upon which this rests are not supplied. Whether the non-material, horizontal legitimacy of political community will develop remains to be seen. Direct attempts at secession have been limited to Chechnya, but movements for autonomy are strong in a number of republics. Some sort of federal arrangement is likely to persist but the precise division of power between the centre and the subunits has not been worked out (Barner-Barry and Hody 1995:299).

In sum, Russia did not emerge as a 'like unit'. It is rather like a drifting supertanker; it is uncertain what kind of substantial statehood it will end up with. Political institutions are impotent, lacking capacity and legitimacy; the virtual economy is in constant crisis; nation-statehood is not in the cards; the development towards liberal democracy and a market economy is by no means assured. At the same time, this rather pessimistic view must be balanced against the fact that significant elements of liberal political and economic institutions have been firmly established in Russia.[3]

## Conclusion

We began with the simple idea, derived mainly from neorealism, that competitive pressures would push the Soviet Union in the direction of homogeneity, a process consummated with the dissolution of the Soviet Union in 1991. Reality turned out to be somewhat more complex. The first Soviet move in the direction of sameness, the NEP policy, was rejected by the international capitalist system; in the 1930s Stalin proposed to innovate rather than emulate: forced industrialization was the response to the competitive challenges posed by the international capitalist system. The quest to successfully compete need not lead to emulation; there is always the alternative of innovation. The result is that political–military pressures do not lead to a process of homogenization, the creation of 'like units'. Innovation sooner leads to heterogneity, the creation of 'unlike units'.

The postwar period revealed a second possibility of escape from emulation and homogeneity: nuclear weapons ensured that the Soviet Union could stay in the competitive game even without being able to compete effectively in all other areas. Nuclear weapons set aside the neorealist logic of 'emulate ... or fall by the wayside' (Waltz 1979:118). If you have nuclear weapons, you don't have to emulate; you don't even have to innovate. When some emulation finally set in, it was sooner by default rather than due to competitive pressures.

It is clear that the pressures toward homogeneity due to political–military competition are not nearly as strong as claimed by neorealists. In effect, it is not warranted to disregard the domestic structures of states and to consider them to be 'like units'. Competitive pressures need not lead towards basic homogeneity; depending on the specific combination of external and internal conditions such pressures may lead towards homogeneity or towards heterogeneity as evident in the case of the Soviet Union/Russia. The Soviet Union did develop some basic elements of modern statehood, but it also – even in the case of Russia today – remained qualitatively different from the Western, liberal version of the modern state. Systemic forces do condition domestic structures of states; but depending on the circumstances, such conditioning can contain homogeneity and heterogeneity in different combinations.

When states are not 'like units', the existence of different types of state will have to enter our analysis of international relations. This argument will be developed in detail in later chapters. Presently, we must continue the 'outside-in' analysis. This chapter focused on political–military power. The next chapter will focus on international norms.

# 4
# International Norms Shaping Domestic Structures: Homogeneity or Heterogeneity?

The task in this chapter is to examine the influence of international norms on the domestic structures of states. From a neorealist view, international norms are expected to lead towards homogeneity because of their content; that is to say, international norms express successful practices in a situation of competitive, systemic pressures. Therefore, the 'socialization of nonconformist states proceeds at a pace that is set by the extent of their involvement in the system' (Waltz 1979:128). Liberals expect processes of modernization, including closer contact with the modern world, to have similar effect of homogenization in context of a process of modernization. Yet it was also indicated earlier that international norms might lead to heterogeneity because they removed the pressure for emulating the successful states. In the beginning of the twentieth century, prevailing international norms were explicated in a so-called 'standard of civilization' which set forth the requirements for the acceptance of new members of the society of states. The content of that standard and its implications for domestic conditions in prospective new member states will be taken up first. I then turn to the situation after 1945. The development of what is now a set of rules of recognition is recorded and two types of cases are singled out for additional treatment. First, the treatment of the defeated powers, Germany and Japan, whose compliance with international norms was secured through internal restructuring. The second case concerns the peculiar new class of member states that emerged in international society through the relaxation of membership requirements made in context of decolonization. Both types of cases will demonstrate distinct combinations of the forces of homogeneity and the forces of heterogeneity.

The analysis of the effects of international norms will reinforce the conclusion from the previous chapter, that states cannot be considered across the board 'like units'. For reasons explored below, states are only to a limited extent socialized to 'sameness' due to their integration in international society. Furthermore, this chapter will suggest that there are distinctive patterns in the ways in which international norms have affected states in the postwar period. That is to say, the combinations of forces of homogeneity and heterogeneity emerge in typical modalities of sovereign statehood. International norms (in combination with political–military power analysed in the previous chapter and economic power analysed in the next chapter) have helped create three main types of state in the post-Second World War international system: modern, postmodern, and postcolonial states.

## International norms and the society of states

International norms are standards of behaviour connected to the possession of sovereignty. Sovereignty is itself an institution, that is, 'persistent and connected sets of rules, formal and informal, that prescribe behavioural roles, constrain activity, and shape expectations' (Keohane 1990:732). Sovereignty emerged in Europe between the fifteenth and the nineteenth centuries. It is common to connect the rise to European dominance of that institution with the peace of Westphalia in 1648.[1] For a long period, sovereignty and thus membership of the society of states was a privilege of European countries. Non-European areas were not considered qualified for membership; they lacked the necessary civilizational and religious (Christian) qualifications.

The extension of European influence on a global scale was not undertaken primarily through diplomatic negotiation, but via coercion and control. In North and South America Spaniards and Portuguese, and later Frenchmen and Englishmen, colonized the 'New World'. Indigenous civilizations were almost completely annihilated and a large number of slaves were imported from Africa. The natives of America never achieved sovereignty; that was bestowed on descendants of the European colonizers who took the lands into possession. To qualify for sovereignty the new rulers had to meet the standards set by Europe.

Some of the ancient civilizations in Asia were not subjected to colonization; instead, Europeans imposed unequal treaties in order to open up the areas for European economic and political interests. This is what happened in the case of China after the opium wars (1839–42). Europeans in Shanghai, for example, were not subject to Chinese authority. In its place, European jurisdiction was extended to include Europeans in China. Africa, by contrast, was colonized. The Europeans felt certain that they had a civilizational mission to undertake; according to Sir Frederick Lugard, 'The African holds the position of a late-born child in the family of nations, and must as yet be schooled in the discipline of the nursery'; this was simply, according to M. F. Lindley, a part of the obligation that 'the advanced peoples collectively owe to backward races in general' (both quoted from Jackson 1993a:71). In sum, it was clear to European international lawyers in the late nineteenth century that 'international law is a product of the special civilization of modern Europe, and . . . cannot be supposed to be understood or recognized by countries differently civilized, such states can only be presumed to be subject to it' (Hall, quoted by Wight 1977:115).

At the turn of the twentieth century international society consists of a small number of consolidated states in Europe and North America; a number of countries in Latin America and Asia are on the way to becoming full members of the society of sovereign states; and a large number of areas in Africa and Asia are part of the colonial empires of European powers. By this time, the European states had fleshed out what was called a 'standard of civilization'. It contained the criteria that non-members had to meet in order to become members of the society of states. The standard has been summarized as follows (Gong 1984:14–15):

1. a 'civilized' state guarantees basic rights, that is, life, dignity, and property; freedom of travel, commerce, and religion, especially that of foreign nationals;
2. a 'civilized' state exists as an organized political bureaucracy with some efficiency in running the state machinery, and with some capacity to organize for self-defence;
3. a 'civilized' state adheres to generally accepted international law, including the laws of war; it also maintains a domestic system of courts, codes and public laws which guarantee legal justice for all within its jurisdiction, foreigners and native citizens alike;
4. a 'civilized' state fulfils the obligations of the international system by maintaining adequate and permanent avenues for diplomatic interchange and communication . . .;
5. a 'civilized' state by and large conforms to the accepted norms and practices of the 'civilized' international society, for example suttee, polygamy, and slavery were considered 'uncivilized' and therefore unacceptable.

A certain level of substantial, effective statehood was thus required to be recognized as an equal member of international society. It appears that the international norm as expressed in the 'standard of civilization' would often require significant amounts of domestic change in order to meet that standard; in other words, international norms to a large extent pressed new members towards the level of homogeneity expressed in the standard. This is undoubtedly correct; international norms did encourage and lead to homogeneity in that specific sense. But the specific extent of homogeneity as a result of the standard varied substantially, for two reasons. First, the standard always had to be interpreted and applied; it is clear from the above formulations that the demands of the standard were sufficiently imprecise to lead to significantly different interpretations. Several Latin American countries that achieved independence in the early nineteenth century could not have met the standard requirements had they been applied to them (Jackson 1993a:62). But on the one hand, they were offspring from the European civilization and were thus considered to incorporate the fundamental characteristics of European states; on the other hand, in the case of Spanish and Portuguese possessions, the British were keenly pushing for their sovereignty. The Foreign Secretary, Lord Canning, noted in 1824: 'Spanish America is free; and if we do not mismanage our affairs sadly, she is English' (quoted from Gunder Frank 1969:285). In short, a number of countries that split off from European empires achieved independence without strictly meeting the norms that were later set forth in the standard of civilization.

Second, the level of homogeneity sought by prospective candidates much depended on domestic conditions in the country in question. Abyssinia, for example, had demonstrated its ability for self-defence by defeating a large Italian army in the famous Adowa battle in 1896. Ras Tafari (later Haile Selassie) sought to promote some Westernization and modernization in the country. He pushed for Abyssinia's recognition by international society through application for the country's membership in the League of Nations. League members were clear about the fact that Abyssinia was far from modernized. Yet it was also argued that membership would 'enable her to rise gradually to the level of other Members, and that as a matter of fact, the League recognized different degrees of civilization' (Joseph Cook of Australia, quoted in Gong 1984:125). A telegram from Ras Tafari to the League, assuring that his government had already 'prohibited, under penalty of death, the purchase of slaves throughout its territory' (quoted in Gong 1984:127) paved the way for Abyssinia's entry to the League in 1923. Abyssinia was now accepted in the good company of civilized nations. It had undoubtedly demonstrated a capacity to meet several of the demands in the standard of civilization. But a modernized country it was not; it was an empire where peasants were subjected to the sort of feudal domination that characterized European serfs in the middle ages. In 1935 a militarized Italy claimed that the backward people of Abyssinia were in need of Italian 'assistance' and the League of Nations again complied; the standard of civilization could obviously be 'bent according to the exigencies of the balance of power' (Gong 1984:128). Ethiopia's independence was restored in 1941 and Haile Selassie ruled until 1974; but he continued to pursue inadequate, token reform, designed to boost Ethiopia's external image but not contributing the least to long-term, substantial state-building (Harbeson 1988:52).

Japan is usually seen as the case where socialization to Western standards happened extremely fast and paved the way for a process of homogenization which was completed in an extraordinarily brief period of time. Merely four decades lie between the unequal treaties imposed by Perry in 1854 and the acceptance of Japanese membership of international society on equal terms in 1894. The Meiji restorers of 1868 formulated a firm commitment to economic and political modernization of the country. Where previous regimes had attempted to cope with the Western challenge by way of isolation, the state now put itself in charge of promoting economic development, in part by obtaining modern technologies from the West. Legal and administrative reforms were implemented, together with a fundamental reorganization of the army. A market economy was promoted, supported by a modern infrastructure in transport and communication; mass education was further encouraged.

But the Japanese developments had as much to do with domestic preconditions as they had to do with external socializing pressures. This can be seen from the fact that the unequal treaties imposed on Japan were not different from those imposed by the West on China from 1842. Yet the unequal China treaties did not spark off a catch-up race in China anywhere near to the one that took place in Japan. In other words, the strong Japanese reaction was due to special domestic conditions in Japan.[2] The extent of emulation cannot be inferred from the mere existence of external pressure; it heavily depends on internal preconditions.

In sum, international norms in the form of a 'standard of civilization' did lead to processes of homogenization before 1945, but on the one hand, the degree of external pressure contained in the standard varied substantially; for example, it was not strong at all in Latin America. On the other hand, where such pressure was applied, the resulting degree of homogenization depended very significantly on domestic conditions in the affected countries. By no means did international norms lead to across the board creation of 'like units'.

## International norms after 1945

The United States and the Soviet Union emerged as the dominant powers after the Second World War.[3] The bipolar relationship between the two superpowers and their respective block of allies henceforth made up the framework for international relations between 1945 and 1991.

It was a hostile confrontation in the sense that a contest between two heavily armed ideological rivals with different political and economic system was involved. Both had global ambitions and attempted to recruit other countries to their side. The war in Korea and the Cuban missile crisis reminded the world that real war between the contenders was a possibility. But even at those points elements of moderation were involved. The superpowers created an international order based on a subjective balance of power (cf. Bull 1995:97–122), that is, the balancing in which they engaged was not automatic or mechanical; balancing was a conscious effort, a common objective of achieving international order based on a set of commonly acknowledged rules which regulated their military competition as well as other key aspects of their international behaviour.

The two superpowers dominated economic and political developments within their respective blocs, especially during the first decades of the Cold War. But it is relevant to emphasize that they also agreed to some substantial limitation on the nature of that dominance. Intervention by the superpower in its domain, including intervention involving the use of force, was accepted; but the change of borders and the expansion of territorial control by conquest was not. Existing borders were considered legal and legitimate; attempts to change them by force was not. The change of given boundaries must involve the acceptance by the sovereign states affected by that change.[4]

Given those parameters of action, there were significant variations over time in the willingness of the superpowers to intervene; there were also big differences in the use of means: the Soviet Union was always more ready to use force, especially in Eastern Europe, beginning with military occupation. To the extent that the United States created an empire containing Western Europe and Japan, it came to be based on popular acceptance and support, as demonstrated through democratic elections. It involved the active support of most political elites in the affected countries; in the words of one historian, it was, in Western Europe, an 'empire by invitation' (Lundestad 1986).

It would appear that the Soviet combination of coercion and centralized control worked to support the rapid creation of 'like units', that is, clones of the Soviet Union. Communist parties took over, forced collectivization followed land reform, heavy industry was given priority, the state apparatus was bureaucratized and autocratic power vested in the Nomenklatura. But it was a creation without legitimacy, without popular support. The system was based on the threat of outside force, as spelled out in the Brezhnev doctrine, which dictated Soviet intervention in Eastern Europe against 'unacceptable' regime changes. Under Gorbachev, that doctrine was replaced by the so-called Sinatra doctrine: 'You do it your way'. Release of the iron grip immediately demonstrated how shallow homogenization had been; not only the populations, but also the major parts of the ruling elites immediately rejected the Soviet political and economic system. In short, the creation of 'like units' can not take place through external pressure alone; it needs domestic support.

That was a lesson which the United States and her allies also had to learn in the case of Japan and Germany, as we shall see below. In the Western camp, the process of homogenization worked more by incentive than by coercion. The underlying idea was that rapid economic recovery would be the best way to contain the spread of communist influence. The Marshall Plan and the Bretton Woods institutional framework were the basic instruments of implementation. Seen in retrospect, they worked very well; the economies quickly gained steam in a system of 'embedded liberalism' (Ruggie 1982), that is, a blend of economic liberalization and increased intercourse between countries combined with social cushioning provided by interventionist governments at home.[5]

The trajectories of Japan and Germany are of special interest in the present context, because they were the primary targets of American efforts at reconstructing statehood in the countries that were responsible for the destruction of the Second World War. On immediate impression, developments appear to be in line with notions of homogenization: the United States and her allies picked up the defeated autocratic, militarized systems and turned them into liberal, democratic market economies that quickly became devoted members of the Western alliance; in short, they were homogenized, turned into standard versions of the modern, liberal state.

On closer view, however, there are two huge paradoxes in the cases of Japan and Germany. The first is that the US and her allies did come to seek the creation of 'like units', that is, nation-states complete with solid economies and strong armed forces. After all, the initial allied top priority was demilitarization and basic reform, ensuring that Japan and Germany never again could emerge as belligerent threats to international peace. Why did allied priorities change toward the creation of 'rich and strong' states? The second paradox follows from the first: given that the winners of the war wanted this to happen, why did it not come to pass? Why was the end result a rather different one, the creation of militarily weak 'trading states'?

The answer to the first question is related to the confrontation between the United States and the Soviet Union in context of the Cold War. The Cold War profoundly changed American policies in Japan. Instead of economic and military 'deconstruction' of the country, the goal was now to make Japan 'internally stable', 'industrially revived' and more 'amenable to American leadership' (Records of Kennan's Policy Planning Staff, quoted from Schaller 1997:16).

The new priorities led to remarkable changes in American policies in Japan. No longer was industrial deconcentration a goal; that programme was terminated in 1949. It was indeed US policymakers that encouraged the Japanese to set up a Ministry of International Trade and Industry; the later all-powerful MITI was 'modelled on the wartime Munitions Ministry and staffed by many of that agency's veteran bureaucrats' (Schaller 1997:18). Purges had never been indiscriminate anyway; most of the bureaucracy and government continued in their positions, albeit under American supervision. Given the new communist threat from China, the Americans were now ready to help Japan revive the old 'Co-Prosperity Sphere' in Southeast Asia, the Japanese area of economic hegemony. It was arms production on a massive scale, supplying American efforts in Korea and elsewhere, that set the stage for the Japanese economic 'miracle' (Samuels 1994). The US policy guidelines set out in 1945 had stipulated that 'the existing economic basis of Japan's military strength must be destroyed and not permitted to revive' (quoted from Samuels 1994:131); the Cold War clearly had imposed new priorities.

The most controversial element in American policy, bitterly resented by Australia and other former victims of Japanese aggression, was to seek rearmament of the country. The US first sought the rebuilding of a small army of 100 000 men. After the outbreak of the war in Korea, the American aim was for a Japanese army of at least 300 000. This was considered sufficient for the defence of Japan and thereby enabling the freeing of US troops for assignments elsewhere. In the case of Germany, The Morgenthau-Plan, which was supported by President Roosevelt until the fall of 1944, went very far. It proposed the division of Germany into agrarian territories; following a complete dismantling of industry, the industrial areas in Saar and Silesia would go to France and Poland respectively. The remaining industrial areas in Ruhr und Rheinland were to be controlled by a United Nations authority (Merkl 1965:13). The actual instructions for the American occupation forces were softer, but contained nothing about reconstruction of the country (Smith 1990:238). And France continued to advocate dismemberment.

Again, it was the emerging confrontation with the Soviet Union that changed the Western outlook. When Germany surrendered in Potsdam in May, the four allies agreed to let the country continue as one economic entity. Soviet support for this quickly came to be seen as a way of extracting war reparations from the entire country. The United States and Britain discontinued payments in kind of German reparations to the Soviet Union in May 1946. US and British steps towards the construction of a West German state prompted the blockade of Berlin in early 1948, followed by a Western counterblockade of the Soviet zone. Both blockades were lifted in 1949; by then the Cold War was a reality. The German Federal Republic and the German Democratic Republic were born in 1949.

Given that the United States and her allies now wanted to create 'rich nations and strong armies' in Japan and Germany, why did they end up differently, as 'trading states', weak in military might? Because domestic political forces wanted it that way. In the case of Japan, the government firmly resisted US proposals for rearmament. The old system had been a thoroughly militarized society; the population resolutely opposed the reconstruction of a strong army. The government's strategy was to concede no more than was sufficient to ward off the American pressure. By 1951, Japan had created a 'National Police Reserve' of 110 000 men. It is thus fair to say that Japan successfully withstood American demands for remilitarization. In other words, the Japanese people and the vast majority of the political elite accepted only the 'rich nation' project, but rejected the 'strong army' proposition. Japan developed a 'trading state' national identity as a nation 'that concentrates on economic development while foregoing the pursuit of political–military power' (Berger 1996:338).

In the case of West Germany, domestic political forces responded to the new situation by seeking to integrate West Germany as much as possible into Western Europe and the Western alliance. The commitment to Europe was explicitly laid down in the provisional constitution for West Germany, the so-called Basic Law. The preamble read: 'The German people, animated by the resolve to preserve their national and political unity and to serve the peace of the world as an equal partner in a united Europe ... have enacted ... this Basic Law' (quoted from Gruner 1992:202). Konrad Adenauer's 'great concern was to integrate Germany completely into Western Europe. Indeed, he gave this end priority over reunification of unhappily divided Germany' (Dean Acheson 1949, quoted from Alter 1992:171). The Social Democrats in West Germany were in complete agreement; their leader, Kurt Schumacher had made it clear already in 1945 that the party 'wants to see Germany as part of a new European confederation from the start' (quoted in Alter 1992:172).

The devotion to Europe became embedded in the popular consciousness surprisingly quickly. A public opinion poll of 1948 showed strong support for policies of European integration. Public debate in the early 1950s frequently had proposals for a replacement of the national anthem by a European, 'supra-national' anthem. Political elites and people were in accord about seeking to develop national identity, not at the level of the nation-state, but at the supra-national level of Europe and the subnational level of the *Länder*. Germany was to 'regain her character of a "nation of nations"' (Wilhelm Röpke, 1945 quoted from Alter 1992:170), and similarly, on the supranational level, Europe was perceived, following Montesquieu, as a nation made up of several nations.

The development of the Cold War only further amplified West German efforts of integration with their Western neighbours. Stalin's 1952 proposal for reunified, neutral and demilitarized Germany was rejected. West Germany locked herself into the West. This was also true for the economy; West German reconstruction led to the creation of an economy closely integrated with the partners in Western Europe and with the United States. In that sense, the West German economy would become 'the most European of all econo-mies' (Cronin 1996:91).

In sum, the West Germany that was created after the World War was not a 'like unit' compared to the modern, liberal states that led the Western alliance. It was different politically, economically and in nationhood terms. The polity not merely had a Montesquieuan division of powers; its peculiar federalism in combination with European integration created a configuration of 'multilevel governance' different from the standard centralization of authority in sover-eign states.[6] The economy was from early on directed towards close integration with the West. National identity was fixated less on the national than on the subnational and supranational level. In short, it was not mere homogenization; the priorities of reconstruction under the conditions of the Cold War led to heterogeneity in basic respects.

West Germany entered NATO in 1955; the United States had pushed for a West German contribution to the defence of Europe since the outbreak of the Korean war. The rebuilding of an army followed a pattern similar to that of the rebuilding of the country; the West German military capability was firmly embedded in a Western alliance and, in contrast to earlier, the armed forces were integrated in civil society through conscription and through the concept of 'innere Führung' (internal leadership) emphasizing democratic ethos and civil rights in the army. It was a 'non-nuclear, non-aggressive' approach to defence (Berger 1996:338).

In conclusion, outside pressures combined with specific domestic reactions created a peculiar combination of homogenization and heterogeneity in the cases of Japan and West Germany. They became liberal, modern states with a twist: militarily weak and – in the case of West Germany – economically and politically integrated in Western Europe. West Germany came to create the prototype of what I shall term the postmodern state. And instead of being the exception, the peculiar political and economic structure set up in West Germany after the war, complete with multilevel governance, a closely integrated economy, and a mixture of 'national' identities at different levels is emerging, mutatis mutandis, as the typical anatomy of European statehood in an era of economic globalization combined with extremely high levels of cooperation across borders.

This is not what the United States and the other winners of the war had foreseen. That is one reason why historical analysis of the forces of homogeneity and heterogeneity is necessary. The next section will show how changes in international norms helped create another peculiar type of state in the postwar world: the postcolonial state.

## Decolonization

The normative framework concerning colonies changed dramatically in the post-Second World War period. Before the war, the possession of colonies was considered legitimate and even necessary, given the backward conditions of the colonized areas. After the war, colonialism came to be considered fundamentally wrong, even 'a crime' (UN General Assembly Resolution 3103, quoted from Jackson 1993a:107). That normative change led to decolonization which in turn helped produce a peculiar type of weak player in the international system, the postcolonial state.

As recorded earlier in this chapter, it was European ideas about cultural and civilizational superiority that justified colonial empire. Unsurprisingly, it was the colonial powers that held on to such notions the longest. According to the official British view in 1946, there were four obstacles to 'early and effective self-government': (1) the colonial populations were 'too unaware' of the operations of modern government to be capable of citizenship; (2) there was no national unity; (3) there was no economic basis which could support a modern state; (4) a number of colonies were simply too insubstantial to allow for 'anything more than a limited internal self-government' (Perham 1946, quoted in Jackson 1993a:90). What the British suggested as an alternative to independence was a diverse range of forms of semi-autonomy which were seen as appropriate for the different levels of development of the colonies. There was nothing new in this; the League of Nations had employed a distinction between 'A', 'B', and 'C' Mandates indicating different degrees of 'readiness for self-government' of the territories that were perceived incapable of sovereignty.

Against this background, how could the right of self-determination for colonies become the accepted international norm so quickly after the war; how could colonialism, in contrast, become 'an absolute wrong: an injury to the dignity and autonomy of those peoples and of course a vehicle for their economic exploitation and political oppression' (Jackson 1993a:48)? A number of different sources combined to produce that profound change. First, colonialism never sat well with liberalism in the first place; liberalism is profoundly anti-paternalistic and thus in essence anti-colonialist. The middle-class professionals who founded the Indian National Congress in 1885 were convinced liberals. In the name of liberalism, they quickly denounced British rule in India as 'unfortunately unBritish'! Second, ideas about equality and independence grew rapidly stronger during the World War, where the main imperial powers were under the boot of the Germans and the ties to the colonies much weaker than earlier. Several colonial dependencies provided troops to aid allied efforts against the Axis powers and expected something in return when the job was done. Third, those Asian and African states that had achieved independence by the early 1950s immediately started pushing for comprehensive decolonization. In 1955, 23 Asian and six African states convened in Bandung, Indonesia. Their declaration emphasized the principles of national sovereignty and equality among nations. These countries also applied pressure through the United Nations; the General Assembly Declaration (Resolution 1514) of 1960 proclaimed that 'all peoples have the right to self-determination'. The efforts of these countries combined with push from Third World intellectuals powerfully attacking colonialism in their writings; the best known book is probably 'The Wretched of the Earth' (*Les Damnées de la Terre*) by Frantz Fanon who fought in the Algerian liberation movement, FLN. In a review of one of the later editions, Time Magazine called the book 'a rock thrown against the window of the West' (quoted in Betts 1998:38).

Last but not least, there was a new distribution of power in the world after the war. In Europe and in Japan that new distribution was abundantly clear from

1945. Eleven years later, on the occasion of the French–British invasion of the Suez Canal, its presence in the Third World was demonstrated. Eisenhower and Dulles demanded the immediate withdrawal of British and French troops. The Soviet Union also repudiated the invasion. As a result of American and Soviet efforts, Nasser remained in power in Egypt. The main colonial motherlands no longer controlled the agenda in the Third World.

Even though the United States was generally pleased to watch over the dissolution of colonial empires, she was not from early on a staunch, across-the-board supporter of decolonization. The US picked up the imperial mantle after France in Indochina; both the United States and the Soviet Union gave high priority to securing stable alliance partners in the Third World, some of which were former empires themselves (Iran, Ethiopia). Overall, however, the new postwar power relations aided the process of decolonization. The old colonial powers now held second rank in the international system. And they saw what was coming: British Prime Minister Harold Macmillan recognized the 'wind of change' in a speech in Cape Town, South Africa, in 1960.

The UN declaration mentioned earlier talked about the right of 'all peoples' to self-determination. The formulation did not mean that individuals and groups were to decide about which communities they wanted to belong to. Declaration 1514 explicitly declared that 'any attempt aimed at the partial or total disruption of the national unity and the territorial integrity of a country is incompatible with the purposes and the principles of the Charter of the United Nations'. The 'nations' that were entitled to self-determination were not nations in any community sense. They were the people living behind given colonial borders. The right of 'peoples' effectively meant the right to independence of existing colonies. In a large number of cases such colonies contained a variety of ethnic groups; ex-colonies were not nations in any community sense.

Nor did many ex-colonies possess much in terms of political and economic substance. State-building had not been high on the agenda of the colonial powers; they were most often satisfied with control, despite the ideas about a civilizational mission in the colonies. We saw earlier that a certain level of substantial, effective statehood was required to be recognized as an equal member of international society, even if that norm was not always consistently interpreted. With the UN declaration on colonial independence, any requirement for state substance as a precondition for independence was explicitly abandoned: 'inadequacy of political, economic, social or educational preparedness should never serve as a pretext for delaying independence' (quoted in Jackson 1993a:77).

What emerged from decolonization then, was a new type of very weak player in the international system. Ex-colonies became independent, that is, they were granted juridical sovereignty in spite of the fact that they contained very little in terms of substantial statehood, politically, economically or as regards nationhood, that is, cultural and political community. This development goes squarely against the neorealist logic of intense competition between states, the logic of 'emulate or fall by the wayside'; the society of states took measures that created a group of weak players. A sharper contrast to the image of the strong states swallowing the weak appears hard to find. No single factor is solely responsible for this surprising new development as regards the composition of the state system. It was pushed by a complex set of factors, including political and intellectual liberation movements in the colonies; changes during the Second World War; the transformation of international power relations; and a sharp decrease in the colonial rulers' own convictions about the legitimacy of their rule. These developments were validated by the sea-change in international norms whereby colonial empire was completely rejected and the right of self-determination for colonies was firmly established.

Decolonization led to homogeneity in the broad sense that the institution of sovereignty achieved global dominance. The vast majority of the world's population are citizens of a sovereign state. All other forms of political organization, especially empire, became extinct. But in context of that globalization of sovereignty, highly significant variation in the concrete content, the substance of statehood, was introduced. Martin Wight characterized the new situation created by decolonization in the following way: '. . . heterogeneity has returned. The states represented at the United Nations are more various in origin, size and structure than were the states represented at the Congress of Westphalia' (Wight 1977:41).

## Conclusion

This chapter has discussed international norms and the ways in which such norms (in combination with political–military and economic power) have affected domestic structures. The starting point was the neorealist and the liberal views, according to which international norms lead to homogeneity. Focus was first on the 'standard of civilization' which became explicit at the turn of the century. That standard did lead towards homogeneity, but because it was applied in very different ways and because of the variation in domestic conditions, significant elements of heterogeneity remained. I then turned to the discussion of international norms in context of the Cold War. The 'clones' created in the Soviet camp looked like their hegemon, but homogeneity was not more than inch-deep. As soon as the Soviet Union gave the green light, the rejection of imposed homogeneity set in.

In the Western camp, homogenization worked primarily through incentive; an exception was the defeated countries, Japan and West Germany. The Western Allies reconstructed these states along liberal, capitalist lines, but because of domestic reactions, the end result of these efforts were countries that in significant ways were different from the 'standard' model of modern states, complete with a national economy, a national polity and a national defence. West Germany became the first of its kind: a postmodern state. Many others were soon to follow.

During the same period, decolonization gave birth to a new type of weak member of the society of states, the postcolonial state. Overall then, international norms, combined with political–military and economic power, do produce some measure of homogeneity, but not in a consistent way: great variation remains. Theorists emphasizing the forces of homogeneity are prone to see that process of convergence culminating in a system consisting of modern nation-states. This chapter has begun to demonstrate how the postwar period helped create two additional main types of state in international society: the postmodern and the postcolonial state. The next chapter will argue how economic forces have led in the same direction.

# 5
# Economic Power Shaping Domestic Structures: Homogeneity or Heterogeneity?

The present unfolding of economic forces on a world scale is labelled 'globalization' by most observers; that is a proper place to start this brief examination of the effects of economic power on domestic structures. Economic globalization[1] is the intensification of economic relations across borders. Two features pertaining both to globalization in the broad sense and to economic globalization must be emphasized. First, far from all processes of globalization are global in scope. Many take place on primarily regional or even less extended levels.[2] In other words, globalization is uneven in both geographical scope and intensity. Second, globalization is uneven in an additional, basic sense: it leads to integration as well as to fragmentation and marginalization. Successful participation in economic globalization requires preconditions that are possessed by some states (and individuals) much more than by others.

Therefore, whereas the spread of globalization conjures an image of homogeneity in that the countries of the world are increasingly parts of the same global market economy, the notion of uneven globalization indicates heterogeneity in that specific countries may take up very different positions in that process. In sum, economic globalization creates a more homogenous world in some ways, but this is combined with unevenness which leaves much room for heterogeneity, because economic globalization unfolds in qualitatively different ways.

The homogenizing and heterogeneity-enhancing effects of economic globalization are already hinted at in the main theoretical positions introduced in Chapter 2. Karl Marx emphasized how capitalist expansion 'creates a world after its own image'. Liberal economic modernization theory described a process of five stages of development which were seen to be undertaken by all societies: beginning with traditional society, over the pre-take-off stage and the take-off, to 'the road to maturity', and ending up in modern mass consumption society. Classical Marxism and liberal modernization theory thus both stress homogeneity as a result of globalization, with the emergence of the modern, capitalist state as the end result. Trotsky, in contrast, emphasized how capitalist development is uneven and combined; it may have created one world, but it is not a homogenous world modelled after the first capitalist societies. It is a world characterized by heterogeneity. A particular aspect of this heterogeneity has been analyzed by neomarxist dependency theorists such as Samir Amin and Andre Gunder Frank. They argue that capitalist expansion has led to qualitatively different socioeconomic forms in core and periphery respectively.

The following sections look at postwar developments in the light of these different theoretical positions. It will be argued that economic globalization has indeed led to homogenization through the global expansion of the market economy. At the same time it will be shown how, for several reasons, heterogeneity has persisted. Heterogeneity in particular pertains to two groups of countries. On the one hand, the weakest, least developed ones in the Third World; they are the marginalized, peripheral players in the global economy, the weak postcolonial states. And on the other hand, the advanced countries in Western Europe, North America and Japan, who have been most involved in economic globalization and who have therefore been most exposed to the changes invoked by the new aspects of economic globalization;[3] they are the postmodern states. In sum, my argument in this chapter is that economic globalization reinforces the emergence of the three different main types of state identified earlier: the modern, the postmodern, and the postcolonial state.

## Economic globalization and homogenization: the spread of the market economy

Economic globalization has led to the integration of an increasing number of countries in the global market economy. In context of that integration, a process of homogenization has taken place: countries tend to converge on a similar model of economic development, namely the modern, industrialized, open, capitalist market economy. The following remarks about the trajectories of the South on the one hand and the former planned economies in Eastern Europe and China on the other will briefly indicate the main elements in this development in the post-Second World War period.

Many of the less industrialized countries in the South emerged as independent states only after the Second World War. They first lived in relative isolation from the postwar international economic order; the Bretton Woods system was not for them, and they hesitated to seek full integration in the international market economy. Heeding the infant-industry argument that a degree of protectionism and import-substituting industrialization would make them better equipped to compete eventually in full with the industrialized countries, they pursued a policy of relative isolation from the world market. The GATT, as noted by one observer, was 'a rich man's club' (Spero and Hart 1997:216) with only sixteen developing country members by the end of the 1950s.

Some developing countries were rather successful in constructing a solid industrial basis, but in many cases protectionism led to ineffective and non-competitive industrial undertakings. By the 1960s many countries in the South sought export expansion and integration in the world market instead of import substitution. The rapid expansion of world exports is reflected in the fact that whereas the World Export index and the World Real GDP index both moved from 100 to around 200 between 1950 and 1960, the Real GDP index reached 600 by 1993, whereas the export index climbed to 1,300 in the same period. (Cornett 1996:8 based on GATT figures).

The strategy of export expansion was especially successful for a small group of East Asian countries led by Taiwan and South Korea. These countries were able to combine an emphasis on exports on the one hand with, on the other hand, taking in foreign investment from transnational corporations in order to help upgrade their own industries. Taiwan and South Korea had a head start in export expansion.[4] Other countries from the South who did not enjoy such special advantage faced bigger problems in their attempts at promoting exports. The industrialized countries erected barriers to trade, especially in those areas – such as textiles – where Southern exporters were particularly competitive. Nevertheless, the share of manufactured goods in developing country exports increased steadily, from some 20 per cent of the total in 1970 to more than 50 per cent by 1990. But so did the differences between groups of countries.

While the economic structures of several Southeast Asian and some Latin American countries are now rather similar to many Western industrialized countries, the poorest countries in the South, especially in Sub-Saharan Africa, are lagging increasingly behind. Sub-Saharan Africa had close to 10 per cent of the global population in 1998, but a mere 1.3 per cent of global GNP and 1 per cent of global trade. The 1980s was a particularly difficult decade for most countries in the South because real interest rates rose sharply and they had to confront a debt crisis in a situation where rapid increase of exports to Western industrialized countries was difficult because of a general slowdown in economic activity. In sum, a process of modernization and convergence on the same basic model of economic development took place, but some countries were substantially more successful in those efforts than others.

The other group of countries relevant in this context is the former planned economies in Eastern Europe and China. China followed its own unique path, first combining a centrally planned economy with a policy of rather extreme self-reliance. That was not entirely by choice: the Cold War confrontation with the West and the breakup of relations with the USSR more or less forced China to pursue autarky. Until Mao Zedong's death in 1976, the trajectory of Chinese socialism can be seen as the struggle between two different strategies: the 'economics in command' strategy associated with the name of Liu Shaoqui with emphasis on industrial accumulation, centralized planning, and economic principles; and the 'politics in command' strategy associated with Mao's name, emphasizing politics and class struggle and the development of socialist values. Since the late 1970s, economic reforms have been implemented on a scale hitherto unseen in planned economies. The economic reforms in China have been characterized by two features: a restriction of state power over economic affairs, that is, a more prominent role for market forces; and an opening up of the economy towards more world market integration. With staggering growth rates of more than 10 per cent annually, China now has 82 per cent of its output in industry and services, compared to only 18 per cent in agriculture. External trade was 13 per cent of GDP in 1980; by 1995 it was as high as 40 per cent (World Bank 1997, 1999).

The planned economies in Eastern Europe[5] have been locked in an evil circle of stagnation, lack of innovation, and low productivity. Earlier attempts at injecting change into the planned economies left the groundwork of the system basically unchanged. The current metamorphosis, in contrast, aims at transforming the basic structure of the system. Three fundamental economic changes must take place so that the economies are transformed (1) from being relatively closed off to being integrated in the world market; (2) from being centrally planned to be market guided; and (3) from being collectively and state owned to being based on private ownership. In other words, the former planned economies are homogenizing in the sense that they attempt to adopt the modern, capitalist market economy.

To sum up so far: in economic terms, the post-Second World War system was divided into three main groups: the modern, industrialized market economies of Western Europe, North America, Australia, New Zealand, and (increasingly) Japan; the planned economies of Eastern Europe (including the Soviet Union), China and a few other countries, such as North Korea, Vietnam, and Cuba; and the less developed countries of the South, many of which achieved independence only after the end of the war. After several decades of economic globalization, the system is tied together by a much higher degree of economic interdependence than earlier. This is connected to a general change of development strategy in both South and East. The former is no longer pursuing overly protectionist or even autarkic policies; the latter has rejected the planned economy and is actively seeking integration in the world economy. The result is a global market economy which encompasses almost all countries with very few exceptions, the most notable of these being North Korea. In that sense, a process of homogenization has taken place; we have a world of interdependent market economies that are pursuing a roughly similar strategy of development.

That strategy is different from the state-oriented, protectionist strategy of the 1950s and from the neo-liberal, 'pure market' strategy of the 1980s. We might call it 'social-liberal' in that it attempts to combine market forces with a significant role for the state; it also combines an openness towards world market integration with ideas of national autonomy (Sørensen 1991b).[6]

Homogenization has thus taken place in the sense that countries are increasingly part of a global market economy within which they pursue a roughly similar strategy of economic development. In that way, the dynamics of economic globalization have led to the homogenization of the world predicted by classical Marxism and by liberal modernization theory. Countries tend to converge on a common model of a modern, capitalist market economy.

Yet it is also clear that significant heterogeneity remains. In one group of postcolonial states, modernization has not been successful; in another group of advanced capitalist economies, economic globalization has led beyond modernity. This will be developed below.

## Globalization and heterogeneity: the modalities of economic development

That the diffusion of the market economy was and is an uneven process has already been indicated. It is easy to see why this must be so: the timing of industrial modernization was vastly different, beginning with Britain in the sixteenth and seventeenth centuries, then moving to continental Europe, to North America, and only much later to many other parts of the world. In each country, there were specific economic, social, political, and cultural preconditions that shaped economic development in distinct ways. And each country faced a particular international context shaped by the trajectories of development in other countries.

Could the large number of newly independent countries emerging from the process of decolonization plainly follow in the industrial footsteps of the advanced states? The latecomers that began industrializing in earnest only after the Second World War faced huge gaps in relation to the already industrialized countries. It was not immediately clear that they could undertake a rapid process of development.

Two principally different answers emerged from the 1960s and onwards, to the question about prospects for economic development in the decolonized states. Liberal modernization theory expected these countries to follow the path of the those before them and move relatively fast from traditional to modern through a process of industrialization. Marxist dependency theory saw development in the Third World as blocked or at least seriously hindered by the dependence of the less developed countries on the economically advanced states (see Chapter 2). Real developments gave some credit to both views; economic modernization was a success in some countries, but certainly not in others.

The East Asian countries were a confirmation of the proposition that successful economic modernization demanded specific external and internal conditions. Take the case of Taiwan. The historical preconditions for development on the island were shaped by Japanese colonization during the first half of the twentieth century. The Japanese did create a dependent society in Taiwan, with an agricultural economy geared to Japan's needs to import foodstuffs, and with decisionmaking concentrated in Japanese hands, as was competence and ownership in the non-agricultural areas of the economy. But it was not underdevelopment: good agricultural productivity together with a sound infrastructural basis including a comparatively high level of education and the existence of some industrial undertakings provided a healthy basis for further economic advancement. External conditions were extraordinarily favourable because of the Cold War and US involvement. The United States was instrumental in securing the immediate survival of the Guomindang regime; the US provided economic aid and favourable market access and pushed for agrarian reform as well as for the creation of a dynamic private sector. Domestic political conditions were also unusual: Zhiang Kai Shek and the Guomindang were compelled to push for economic development, both in order to create a basis of support on the island and in order to qualify for continued American support (Sørensen 1991a:122).

Taiwan's success can be compared to the failure of most Sub-Saharan African countries to get modernization effectively underway. Historical preconditions were more adverse; the colonial masters in Africa had most often been preoccupied with maintaining control and exploiting profitable raw materials and primary goods. After independence, Sub-Saharan Africa also got involved in the Cold War confrontation but in a very different way from Taiwan. In Taiwan, the US was eager to help create a showcase of successful capitalist development in face of the confrontation with China; in Sub-Saharan Africa, by contrast, it was more a question of finding local allies, not caring much whether or not they promoted development. Several decades of CIA support for one of the worst predators, Mobuto Sese Seko of Zaire (now the Democratic Republic of Congo), is a case in point (Kelly 1993). Domestically, the African state was relatively isolated from society. The state did not face a nation in the sense of a community; it faced various ethnic groups sharing a colonial border and the 'community' provided by a common struggle against the colonizers. That created a difficult starting point for the pursuit of economic development and in many cases state elites abandoned that project and focused on looking after themselves and a group of supporters, most often defined in ethnic terms.

Summing up, modernization did not happen to any significant extent in a number of states; most of the Sub-Saharan states in Africa are examples of that.

These countries are integrated in the global market economy, but they are peripheral players and their domestic economies look radically different from those of the economically advanced countries. They are highly dependent on the world market for critical inputs of production technology and a host of other items. There is a highly heterogeneous domestic economic space, consisting of sectors on very different levels of development (including a variety of precapitalist domains) with low levels of intersectoral exchange. Different historical preconditions, combined with different internal and external situations, have joined to create heterogeneity. The previous chapter indicated how norms of decolonization had helped create a new type of weak entity: the postcolonial state. The lack of economic success in these countries further emphasizes the need to single out the marginalized, nonmodern economies as 'unlike units'; the postcolonial state is qualitatively different from the modern state.

## Economic globalization and the advanced economies

The lack of successful participation in economic globalization has promoted the creation of a postcolonial state. Highly successful participation in economic globalization, by contrast, also promotes a change in statehood. Intense economic globalization has led to a change in the economic foundation of the advanced economies. The purpose in what follows is to identify that change and to indicate the major differences, in economic terms, between modern and postmodern states.

The major part of foreign direct investment (FDI) before the Second World War was in raw materials, including minerals and agriculture, but today such activities are much less important. Foreign investment in manufacturing began in earnest after the war, led by companies based in the United States. This reflected American economic superiority in that period. Traditionally, firms were strong players in their domestic markets before they set up activities abroad. Raymond Vernon's theory of the product cycle showed how the advanced, affluent domestic market in the US helped created an ideal environment for the development of sophisticated products. The resultant technological lead could then be exploited through FDI (Vernon 1966). Stephen Hymer emphasized that technological superiority was only one out of several 'monopolistic advantages' which could spark foreign investment; other possibilities were, for example, competent leadership; an efficient sales and distribution network; financial capability; and an efficient organizational structure (Hymer 1975:48).

The notion of a global economy signals several important changes in this traditional picture of postwar foreign investment. First, manufacturing no longer goes through a sequence from domestic maturing to international expansion. Production, design, and distribution are increasingly spread across a large number of countries from the beginning. A number of different developments have made this change possible: (a) advanced communication and transport technology makes production much less dependent on geographical distance; (b) advanced production technology makes it possible to split up complicated production processes in segments each of which can be placed where it is most favourable; (c) the availability of cheap, but also often skilled, labour in several Third World countries and now increasingly in Eastern Europe (Fröbel *et al.* 1977).

Second, the United States no longer dominates as the source of FDI. A host of other countries participate, mainly from Western Europe and Japan, but increasingly also from some Third World countries. In context of this change 'New Forms' of investment have emerged as an alternative to the traditional Majority Owned Foreign Affiliate. The new forms involve participation of local companies in the host country, that is, joint ventures, licensing and franchising, and subcontracting (Oman 1979). Third, manufacturing is of decreasing and services are of increasing importance. A large number of different services, including transport, communication, insurance, banking, publishing, and filmmaking, now contribute as much as one-third of the global production of wealth; another third is traditional manufacturing, and the remaining third is education and health care (Drucker 1989).

A recent study by the OECD (1993) has sketched out a five-stage path through which companies develop towards undertaking global operations. It emphasizes how firms at the latter stage sustain all core activities, including research and development, production, marketing, financial operations, and management on a global scale. In that sense, economic globalization can be seen as involving 'the growth of economic activity which functions beyond national economies and is organized with reference to the world as a whole' (Albrow 1996:130).

The importance of the 'global economy' is difficult to measure precisely. The number of transnational corporations (TNCs) has climbed from 7,000 in 1970 to 53 000 parents with 450 000 affiliates by 1998, but this does not include all new forms of investment. TNC sales reached $9.5 trillion. When local suppliers and subcontractors are included, it is estimated that TNCs control more than one-third of the world's productive assets (figures from UNCTAD 1997). But in terms of employment, the TNC share remains relatively small, about five per cent of the global workforce. A better indicator of the 'global economy' may be the magnitude of intra-firm trade, but it is only US statistics that precisely record these figures. In 1989, 33.5 per cent of US exports and 41.4 per cent of imports (as percentages of total trade) were intra-firm trade (UN 1997).

One significant aspect of the 'global economy' concerns finance. The liberalization of capital movements has created a global money and capital market which more than anything else symbolizes current economic globalization. For simple reasons: the financial actors can move their assets around on a global basis within seconds; together with a much increased relative importance of short-term, often speculative capital movements compared with long-term investment flows, individual countries can easily become 'financial hostages' of global money markets. As emphasized by Paul Kennedy, 'more than 90 per cent of... trading in the world's foreign exchanges [is] unrelated to trade or capital investment' (Kennedy 1993:51).

These developments must be seen in context of a further intensification of 'old' processes of economic globalization. They include high, historically unprecedented levels of trade and of foreign direct investment (Beisheim *et al.* 1999). The economic processes of globalization, in turn, are embedded in a larger context of globalization processes taking place in the realms of culture, communication, increasing mobility of individuals, and so on (Zürn 1998; Albrow 1996). Sovereign states are not mere objects of these processes, they are deeply involved in them as acting subjects. More than anything else, it is the liberal world economy created after the Second World War by the leading states, in particular by the US, which has paved the way for globalization. But states are also being changed by these processes. The states mostly involved are no longer based on purely 'national economies'; they are significantly integrated in a global economic framework. Uneven globalization therefore contributes to the creation of heterogeneity is two basic ways; one is marginalization and peripheralization as in the case of the least developed countries discussed earlier; another is through increasing interdependence and integration among the advanced economies.

In sum, the effect of economic power on domestic structures has been to further the development of three different main types of state in the present international system: modern, postmodern, and postcolonial states.

## Conclusion

The market economy is sometimes considered the 'great homogenizer' in that it leads towards an integrated world of similar production and consumption patterns (the 'coca-colaization' or 'McDonaldization' of the world), even of similar life styles in general. There is a core of truth in that claim: economic globalization has led to the expansion of the market economy on a world scale and today the vast majority of countries are part of that system. Homogeneity has developed in the sense that the structures of a modern, capitalist market economy now increasingly characterize the global system and single countries pursue uniform strategies of development that are compatible with membership of that system. But there are sharp limits to the actual degree of homogeneity, because a number of different factors lead toward heterogeneity: They have to do, for example, with the different timing of industrialization; with specific preconditions in individual countries; and with the exploitation of different types of comparative advantage. Finally, the process of economic globalization itself contains its own inbuilt dynamic of heterogeneity: the advanced economies which have been most intensely involved in economic globalization have had their economic bases qualitatively changed as a result, away from being primarily national economies, towards being integrated parts of a regional-cum-global economic framework. The least developed states in the South, by contrast, have become increasingly marginalized.

The overall result of these processes is that one group of weak, postcolonial countries remains highly heterogeneous compared with the modern world, because economic modernization has only taken place to a very limited degree. Another group of advanced, postmodern economies have developed in new economic directions as a result of globalization. Their heterogeneity compared with modern economies rests on the fact that globalization produces new forms of integrated economic structures which change the economic basis of statehood in important ways.

The next chapter discusses the overall consequences for statehood of the international forces (political–military power, international norms, and economic power) analysed so far. The 'outside-in' analysis in this and the two previous chapters have pointed to the existence of three types of states in the present international system. The next chapter systematically identifies the core features of modern, postmodern, and postcolonial states.

# 6
# Types of State in the Present International System

This chapter considers the empirical findings of the three previous chapters in context of the theoretical debate about homogeneity and heterogeneity. Both processes of homogenization and processes of heterogenization have been at work in the international system; they have been so in a combination which has led to the emergence of three main types of state in the present international system: modern, postmodern, and postcolonial states.

Theorists emphasizing homogeneity tend to overgeneralize when it comes to sovereign statehood, arguing, as do neorealists, that all states are 'like units'. I have demonstrated that there are empirical and theoretical problems with the neorealist statement about socialization and competition leading to 'like units'. Classical Marxism also argued in favour of homogenization based on competition and socialization, but the Marxist idea is based on the notion of capitalist expansion. The market economy has indeed expanded to encompass the globe, but the result has not been the creation of uniform structures of capitalist economies and societies, as emphasized in Chapter 5. Industrialization took place at different points in time with vastly dissimilar national preconditions; together with a number of other factors that created a solid barrier against homogeneity. This is also a critique of the liberal notion of modernization as a unilinear process leading to the same end result, modern society.

While it is easy to demonstrate the persistence of heterogeneity, that notion can also be taken too far. The realization that every sovereign state is unique does not allow a general conceptual handle on the development of sovereign statehood in any historical period. Giving in to historical specificity will not permit us to address core theoretical debates about the development of sovereign statehood, about the effects of uneven globalization, about current patterns of cooperation and conflict, and about a host of other acute issues in world politics. Furthermore, such a notion excessively downplays the effects of the forces of homogeneity. Convergence towards distinctive common forms of sovereign statehood has surely taken place, pushed by political–military power, by international norms, and by economic power. Such convergence means that there are general patterns in the development of sovereign statehood, even if they fall short of the one-dimensional idea of 'like units'.

The identification of three main types of state in the present international system solves this problem by allowing for significant variation in sovereign statehood without getting lost in less important historical detail. The classification of states is of course nothing new. Various types of classification are integral parts of theoretical constructs; realism distinguishes between states according to their relative possession of aggregate power resources and according to their aligned or non-aligned position in a given balance of power. Liberalism classifies according to different levels of political and economic modernity; neomarxism works with different main types of capitalist development (that is, core and periphery); and so on.

What is sought here is less a typology in the conventional sense of empirical classification than a way of distinguishing typical forms of statehood in the postwar world. The main types of state presented below are Weberian ideal types. Such types cannot be found empirically and they are by no means the expression of empirical averages. Ideal types are analytical constructs which seek to express 'pure' forms by accentuating selected aspects of historical reality. Ideal types make up a 'conceptual pattern which brings together certain relationships and events of historical life into a complex which is conceived of as an internally consistent system' (Weber 1949:90).

Sovereign states are human contrivances; they develop and change every day. A large number of those changes are uninteresting from a longer term macro perspective, but some of them accumulate to become more significant changes. Significant change is by definition structural change. Structures, in a most general sense, are the patterns of regularities which enable and constrain human behaviour. The ideal type is an attempt to capture core characteristics of a given type of state in its pure form. In so doing, the ideal type consciously disregards elements that are considered less important. This should not be mistaken for a failure to appreciate the concrete complexities of actual historical statehood.

Ideal types of state rest on a common foundation; all states have a (more or less precisely) defined territory, a population, and some form of government (at least at the point of independence). The states discussed here share one more characteristic: they possess constitutional independence which means that they are recognized under international law as legally valid members of the society of states. But beyond these four basic common characteristics sovereign states are very different; it is the most important of these differences that the three ideal types developed below aim to capture. In later chapters the argument will be developed further, with the claim that each of the identified ideal types behave in certain, typical ways in conducting their international relations and that each of them confronts the problem of security in a distinct way.

The three ideal types contain my answer to the question of how sovereign statehood has developed so far. Therefore, they are also an answer to the question of how the forces of homogeneity and heterogeneity have affected sovereign statehood. The discussion of the ideal types will be structured on the core aspects of substantial statehood developed in Chapter 1: government; economy; and nationhood. In the later discussion of state behaviour, typical features of the institution of sovereignty connected with each type of state will be drawn in. I begin with the modern state. It is the implicit basis for most theorizing in the field of IR, including realism and most liberal approaches. Theories emphasizing homogeneity have tended to consider states 'like units'. The structure of the modern state as identified below is the substance of those 'like units'. Therefore, according to the theories stressing homogeneity, the 'like units' making up the international system are sovereign states which share the characteristics of the modern state. Against this view I have argued that there are three main types of states in the present international system, the three types presented below. Therefore, the modern state never came to be the universal format of sovereign statehood; furthermore, the modern state, where it developed, was not fully in place until the early twentieth century. Only by then are we able to talk of strong states in the sense of states with law, order, legitimacy, and a well-developed resource base in the form of a national economy. Only by then does a description of a national realm with 'authority, administration, and law' (Waltz 1979:113) fully make sense.

In other words, neither contemporary nor historical theorizing about IR can base itself on the 'like unit' of the modern state. The implications of this will be developed later. The task in this chapter is to present the three types of state, the modern, the postcolonial, and the postmodern state.

## The modern state

The modern state emerged first in Europe; the system of states was European for a long period before it became global (see Chapter 4). Why did the modern state emerge in Europe? A large number of different circumstances were involved, among them the relative weakness of imperial structures in the Holy Roman Empire; the emergence of new forms of production and technology in what was to become capitalism; the competition between religious and secular elites for power and position; and the competition among kings for territory and resources.

It is clear that the issue of state formation can be approached in radically different ways.[1] No exhaustive account of state formation and the relative merit of different theories is necessary here. But it is relevant to situate briefly the core elements of modern, sovereign statehood in the proper historical context, partly in order to indicate their origins, partly in order to emphasize how those elements have changed and developed over time.[2]

### Government in the modern state

The ancient Roman state displayed some of those features that characterize the modern state. Roman rule involved representation; the governing Senate represented the ruling class of patricians and the Senate developed political institutions which allowed for mediation and compromise between patricians and plebeians, the ordinary people. Political rule came to be based on law; Roman law included civil law, regulating exchange and contract relationships between private citizens; public law defining the rights and duties of citizens towards the state; and criminal law, designed to keep the lower classes under control, 'a social safeguard for the whole ruling order' (Anderson 1974:74). The Roman state contained an ideology of ruling based on civic virtue. Holders of political office saw themselves as guardians of the public good, not as selfish caretakers of their personal fortunes. Their legitimacy in the eyes of citizens was based on the positions they held, not on their individual qualities.[3]

The appropriate framework for this form of government was the city-state of Rome; but as a city-state, the system was unable to sustain itself economically. The ruling class was a warrior class; the revenue it produced came from the appropriation of slaves and of land for agricultural production. That required a continuous expansion of empire, a process which fed on itself: the larger the army, the more land was needed to sustain it; the larger the territory, the more soldiers were needed to defend it (Davies 1996:159). The process of expansion created contradictions which, over several centuries, led to the decline of Rome. The rulers in Rome came in conflict with the large landowners over the distribution of agricultural revenue; in Rome itself, tensions grew between a 'senatorial plutocracy' (Anderson 1974:102) and the army. The empire was threatened from below by peasant and slave revolts; and finally from the outside, by the invasion of Germanic tribes. The last Western Roman emperor was deposed by a German chieftain in 476 A.D.

Government in the Germanic kingdoms was fragmented and personalized, without the formal political and administrative organization of the Roman Empire. Public power was privatized (Strayer 1965:15–20), held by individuals who had full power in both military, judicial, and economic matters. Larger kingdoms were subdivided into counties or fiefs, where the same structure of power was replicated on a smaller scale. The central institution was vassalage, 'a system in which a free man binds himself personally to a lord, offering him loyalty and military service in return for protection and the use of property (usually land)' (Russell 1968:193). The nobles pledged loyalty to their king; lesser knights to their dukes and counts, and so on; in the bottom, peasants cultivated a plot of land owned by the lord of the manor. They depended on him completely, for the land to yield their livelihood, for his interpretation of the law, and for military protection. In return, they paid rent in the form of labour, produce, or money.

Kings held advantages over the nobles, for example through their control over the distribution of fiefs, but they also depended on them in several ways, most importantly for military power. The king's army was made up of the groups of private forces provided by the vassals. Several developments between the eleventh and the seventeenth centuries, especially from 1550 to 1650, combined to produce an increase in the power of kings; in that way, the basic political framework for the modern state was created.

One such development has been called the military revolution; it concerns the scale, organization, and technology of warfare. Gunpowder came to Europe from China during the fourteenth century. The military balance was now in favour of the offence. The stone walls of medieval castles were no match for artillery. The defensive answer was the *trace italienne*, the low, star-shaped, earthen bastions. Large arsenals of artillery and infantry armed with muskets became necessary elements in a strong army. Armies grew much bigger and so did the costs of maintaining them. Successful kings found ways of doing that; nobles with private armies could not. These private armies were replaced, in due course, by a professional standing army under the king's command (Porter 1994:63–105).

Large armies require money and organization. Borrowing, selling land, or pawning jewels were not sustainable ways of raising money. Kings took to taxation of estates and of the bourgeoisie; this was early mercantilism in operation: the accumulation of wealth in order to create a strong state. Both estates and bourgeoisie resisted on many occasions but eventually came to accept the new system. On the one hand, kings now had superior means of coercion making them able to overcome threats against their increasing power, as in the 1648 Fronde in France, when provinces rising against royal tax collection were defeated by Louis XIII and Richelieu. On the other hand, kings and their finance ministers gradually created a new monetary and legal order with a dependable system of credit, a guarantee of the value of money, and a legal framework for commodity exchange. This greatly helped to pave the way for capitalist expansion and the bourgeoisie came to accept the cost involved in terms of taxation. The writing of legal codes had another important effect; it cultivated the development of national languages, such as French, English, Russian, Spanish, and Portuguese (Opello and Rosow 1999:55).

These developments spawned bureaucratic organization, in the military itself, and in financial and legal institutions. A state apparatus began to emerge and that in turn required more bureaucracy for the coordination of activities. This was the early form of the modern state: a centralized system of rule, headed by the monarch, based on a set of administrative, policing and military organizations, sanctioned by a legal order.[4]

Finally, this system came to claim control over the means of violence. Centralized rule involved the monopolization of the means of violence. Private armies were suppressed and kings tore down private fortifications; 'all fortresses not on the frontier must be razed' was the advice by Richelieu to Louis XIII (quoted from Porter 1994:78). The bearing of arms by citizens was sharply restricted. As a result, a territory was created, where the state was able to claim 'the monopoly of the legitimate use of physical force in the enforcement of its order' (Weber, quoted from Mann 1993:55). Only by then did a distinction between an 'inside' of state-based law and order, and an 'outside' of anarchy and possible violent conflict begin to make sense.

None of the above was fully in place, not even in Europe, before the eighteenth, in some cases the nineteenth century. By then the process of state formation was relatively complete in terms of external territorial demarcation and in terms of internal centralization of power and authority combined with domestic pacification; strong states in that sense did not emerge until then. It is easy to see, therefore, why this whole process of statemaking in Europe has little to do with a modern image of international relations of strong states that are domestic 'hierarchies' face each other in an international 'anarchy'. There was no domestic hierarchy until relatively late; and much of the violent conflict that this period generated was 'domestic' in the sense that it was related to the struggle between would-be rulers attempting to consolidate their power and internal rivals contesting them. Before the consolidation of state power, would-be rulers always had to think in terms of two-front battles, against 'domestic' as well as against 'international' opponents. If we make a distinction between statemaking, defined as 'attacking and checking competitors and challengers within the territory claimed by the state', and warmaking, defined as 'attacking rivals outside the territory already claimed by the state' (Tilly 1990:96), there can be no doubt that statemaking was the principal activity for several centuries, even though a clear empirical distinction between the two endeavours will often be difficult.

If the modern state represents the end result of a long historical process of homogenization, it is clear that heterogeneity persisted, even in Europe, well into the twentieth century. And by the early twentieth century, there was little evidence that modern statehood would emerge on a global scale, even if Japan and a handful of other countries had begun a process of modernization. Paradoxically, the modern states of Europe chose the building of colonial empire on a global scale as a dominant form of competition and that was to lead to the creation of a different type of non-modern state. I return to these developments below. It is necessary first to address the two other core aspects of modern statehood: the nation and the national economy.

## Nationhood in the modern state

The modern state is, in ideal–typical terms, a nation-state. The contemporary understanding of what a nation is assumes a basic identity between state (as government) and nation (as people within a territory). That identity signifies a specific understanding of the relationship between state and society; the state is an expression of the nation, representing it and catering for its basic social values: security, freedom, order, justice, and welfare. National security can thus refer to the state and the nation simultaneously: security for the state is security for the nation. A current definition of nation reflects this relationship: 'a uniquely sovereign people readily distinguishable from other uniquely defined sovereign peoples who are bound together by a sense of solidarity, common culture, language, religion, and geographical location' (Davies 1996:7–8).

Feudal bonds were personal, demanding that oaths of allegiance had to be repeatedly renewed. Modern bonds of loyalty are de-personalized; the nation is an imagined community and the loyalty of nation towards state is directed towards the institutions of the state, not towards the concrete individual currently in charge. That transformation took several centuries and it is intimately connected with the political changes described above and the economic changes addressed below. A core element in the idea of nation concerns group identity; it has to do with what goes on in the heart and minds of people when they think about who they are and to whom they owe their allegiance. But it is misleading to perceive of the nation as based only on ideas of community, common culture, or ethnic heritage. There is a material side which is of equal importance; it concerns the duties and obligations of individuals to the state and the rights and privileges that they receive in return, the complex of relations that is the development of citizenship. Following the distinction from Toennies (1955), we can conceive of this material aspect as the *Gesellschaft* component of nationhood and the cultural–ethnic idea of a community of people defined by the nation as the *Gemeinschaft* component.[5]

To the extent that a distinction between the material and the non-material does make historical sense, the material aspect most frequently came first. The move away from private armies and the centralization of power undertaken by medieval kings created the basis for a direct relationship between the king and his subjects. Domestic pacification of the territory and the development of the rule of law erected a barrier separating the population and the sovereign from the outside. A notion of common purpose could emerge; the good of the state and the good of the people depended on mutual support and shared obligation towards defending and supporting the state.

In close connection with this came the battle over hearts and minds. The Catholic church had claimed authority over its subjects everywhere, including the right to oversee disputes between kings and other national rulers. The Reformation meant a revolt against that religious hierarchy, claiming that religious practice was in essence a personal relationship between the individual believer and God. Protestantism revolted against the whole Catholic hierarchy of power, including priests, bishops, archbishops, and pope. The culmination of that struggle, the thirty years' war, amounted to a dramatic strengthening of secular power, because political freedom without church interference now became possible. Religious identification took second place compared to national identification.

Despite these developments, the idea that the state is based on the nation defined as the people within a certain territory emerged only with the American and French revolutions. The Declaration of Human and Civil Rights of 1789 put the nation at the centre of the nation-state construction: 'The nation constitutes the principal source of all sovereignty. No assembly or individual may exercize a power that does not derive expressly from the nation' (quoted from Schulze 1996:155). The Declaration for the first time recognized ordinary people as citizens with rights instead of subjects and granted them equality before the law. Yet for a considerable period of time that did not mean much to most people. The Declaration was more a piece of political theory than of actual practice. The main practical expression of citizenship was connected to war; the *levée en masse* from 1793, and the payment of taxes to finance war which made up the primary activity of the state until the mid-nineteenth century.

The *Gemeinschaft* component of the nation gathered strength during the nineteenth century; Johann Herder considered language and culture the real core of the nation. Nation-building in that respect concerned the elaboration of a common language and the construction of a common cultural and historical identity based on literatures, myths, symbols, music, and art. Only some 12 per cent of the French citizens spoke the language well by 1789; 3 per cent of Italians spoke Italian by 1860; to a significant extent, national identity was forged from above, by the state, primarily through mass education. Compulsory education laws and universal (male) suffrage, began to emerge by the mid-nineteenth century. A national identity anchored outside elite circles, in the general population, became firmly established in several states in Europe rather late, by the early twentieth century. Passports, making clear distinctions between national citizens and aliens, were introduced as late as the First World War (Soysal 1994:141).

A common definition of nationalism takes the concept to mean that 'the political and the national unit should be congruent' (Gellner 1983:1). That was the principle set forth by Woodrow Wilson after the First World War as the basis for redrawing the map of Europe, but it created a large number of demands from various ethno-national groups for recognition. To follow that course quickly proved both politically and practically infeasible. As a consequence, few contemporary states are nation-states in the strict sense of clearly defined ethno-cultural groups possessing their own state. But it is not necessary here to go into the issue of various degrees of multinational statehood. As the concept is used here, a state does not have to be based on a homogenous ethno-national group in order to qualify as a nation-state. It is sufficient that the population of the state makes up a community in two senses of the term, namely the *Gesellschaft* and the *Gemeinschaft* senses as they were defined above. Together they provide the basis for the legitimacy of the state, the belief in its right to rule (Holsti 1996).[6]

In sum, the modern state is characterized by a high level of cohesion; nation and state are bound together by a complex set of rights and obligations. Important non-material aspects of this relationship is community, legitimacy, and solidarity. Important material aspects are the resources and services exchanged between the state and its citizens.[7]

### The economic basis of modern states

The development of a capitalist economic system on the one hand and a modern state system on the other hand are closely connected. State rulers depended on a solid economic basis for the creation of strong states and economic actors benefited from the creation of a monetary system, organized credit, and a legal framework stipulating contractual rights and obligations. The modern state is based on a national economy which may well have much interaction with other economies, but remains separate from them. It has been noted earlier how the separation of 'internal' and 'external' is created only with the growth of modern, sovereign statehood. That separation pertained to the economic sphere as well. Sovereignty created a territorial space within which rulers could shape and regulate national economic systems. Competition with other rulers was not limited to the military sphere, of course, it took place in the economic field as well.

The close relationship between state strength and the strength of the national economy is clearly expressed in the theory of mercantilism. Mercantilism was the world-view of political elites that were at the forefront of building the modern state. They proposed that economic activity is and should be subordinated to the primary goal of building a strong state. In other words, economics is a tool of politics, a basis for political power. Mercantilists see the international economy as an arena of conflict between opposing national interests, rather than an area of cooperation and mutual gain. And states have to be worried about economic gain, because the material wealth accumulated by one state can serve as a basis for military–political power which can be used against other states.

The strongest theoretical proponents of mercantilism have come from states attempting to catch up with economically more advanced rivals. Alexander Hamilton argued that the United States needed trade protection and a that the government was required to support forcefully the development of domestic industry; Friedrich List made the point even more strongly on behalf of nine-teenth-century Germany: 'The prosperity of a nation is not...greater in pro-portion in which it has amassed more wealth... but in the proportion in which it has more developed its powers of production.' (List 1966:144).

The extent to which the emerging modern states did actually create nation-ally segregated economies has been subject to much debate. World systems theory, especially associated with the work of Immanuel Wallerstein (1974) maintains that capitalism was from the early beginning a global system, where the development of what was first a European core was closely connected with underdevelopment in what became the periphery of the Third World. Critics argue that capitalist development in Europe was predominantly a Euro-pean affair; to the extent that there was exchange and interdependence involved, it was primarily between the emerging national economies inside Europe (Senghaas 1985). Avoiding the extreme positions, both views appear to have a point: national economies were indeed created, yet it took place in a context which was from early on characterized by extensive economic relations across borders and regions, and some countries were much more successful in the economic area than others (for a similar view, see Giddens 1992:167). The national economy is not self-sustaining in the sense that it is autarkic; it is rather what some development theorists call auto-centric, meaning that the decisive intra-and inter-sectoral links in the economy are domestic (Senghaas 1985); there can be a high level of foreign trade, but the economic structure is introverted rather than extrovert.

Classic economic liberalism on first impression appears to be a stark rejection of mercantilism and the idea of national economies. After all, Adam Smith believed that markets tend to expand spontaneously for the satisfaction of human needs, provided that governments do not interfere. But liberals also strongly believed in viable national economies; they forcefully argued that a certain minimum size of nations was needed for economic viability and they also urged states to support economic development (Hobsbawm 1993:25–35). Classical liberalism can be seen as a mercantilism of the strong; free trade and non-state interference is preferred when the economy is capable of competing in its own right. Finally, even the early economic liberals were aware of the need for a politically constructed legal framework as a basis for the market. *Laissez-faire* does not mean the absence of any political regulation whatsoever; it means that the state shall only set up those minimal underpinnings that are necessary for the market to function properly.

Liberalism has remained strong in the twentieth century, but the liberal perspective has developed to embrace even higher levels of state control and regulation of the economy. Keynesian ideas paved the way for a significantly reformed liberal thinking which remains based on a market economy, but one with a considerable degree of state interference and direction. That recent form of modern state has been called the 'managerial state', it 'continuously monitors, organizes, controls, and regulates the social, economic, and political activities within it' (Opello and Rosow 1999:134).

In sum, modern states are characterized by national economies which are clearly demarcated from other national economies in that the major part of their economic activity takes place at home. How far can such a notion of national economy be projected backwards in history and to which extent is it a relevant concept today?

First, it must be noted that the national economy developed from a peculiar combination of long distance external trade on the one hand and highly localized economic spaces on the other hand. The role of external trade was addressed above; as regards the domestic space, it was only during the nineteenth and early twentieth centuries that localized economic networks gave way to larger integrated economic spaces. To a great extent, that had to do with physical infrastructure and with the scope of regulation. As for infrastructure, a trip between Paris and Lyon took about a week in 1800; it was down to 55 hours by 1848. Localized networks were penetrated only to the extent that national transport and communication infrastructures opened them up. A legal framework for capitalist development including the securing of private property and a commercial rule of law emerged in the nineteenth century as well (Zürn 1998:41–63; Zürn 1995).

Second, the notion of a national economy tends to overlook the fact that the consolidation of a 'national' economic space was frequently based on two types of expansion. One is the swallowing up of adjacent territories; the consolidation of Germany, the United States, or Italy, for example, meant the disappearance of a number of areas less viable, economically, politically and militarily. The other type of expansion is imperialism and the creation of dependent entities. The historical development then, is much more one of a process of establishing consolidated national economies instead of such completed entities facing each other.[8] Before further discussion of this, it is relevant to sum up the main features of the modern state and to identify its main modalities in the postwar period.

### Summary: the modern state

The major features of the modern state have been identified above. They can be summarized as follows:

| | |
|---|---|
| Government | A centralized system of rule, based on a set of administrative, policing and military organizations, sanctioned by a legal order, claiming monopoly of the legitimate use of force. |
| Nationhood | A people within a territory making up a community in the *Gesellschaft* and the *Gemeinschaft* sense, involving a high level of cohesion, binding nation and state together. |

Economy          Segregated national economy, self-sustained in the sense that it
                 comprises the main sectors needed for its reproduction; major
                 part of economic activity takes place at home.

The modern state emerged from the transformation of the absolutist state in Europe. The liberal, industrialized countries of Western Europe, North America, Japan, and Oceania are the countries closest to the modern ideal type during the early period after the Second World War. Several countries in East and Southeast Asia and in Latin America are predominantly modern. Furthermore, the Soviet Union, as well as the other centralized-socialist states Europe, exhibited some features of modern statehood as identified here.[9]

As already indicated in the 'outside-in' analysis in previous chapters, there are two additional main types of state in the present international system, the postcolonial and the postmodern state. They are further discussed below.

## The postcolonial state

It was emphasized in Chapter 4 that a large number of the 'new' states that were granted formal, juridical independence in the context of decolonization, were not modern states in any meaningful sense. Decolonization set up a new framework for the formation of sovereign states. In Europe and elsewhere, modern statehood had emerged out of a long process of violent struggle where stronger rulers swallowed weaker competitors. The normative framework around decolonization, by contrast, gave the right of independence to ex-colonies, no matter what level of actual weakness that they displayed.

It is tempting, then, to see this very process of decolonization as the basic reason for the emergence of the weak, postcolonial state; certainly, in many cases colonial rulers had done little to prepare the territories for independence. But a colonial past can only be part of the explanation because we know that a number of ex-colonies, including Taiwan and South Korea, have done quite well in terms of substantial development. In case of states that remained weak or even deteriorated further into state failure, a number of different factors appear to have been in play: rulers that hastily gave up any project of state building and started aiming primarily at personal gain; societies split up by cultural, ethnic, religious and other divisions, and economies incapable of sustaining even a very moderate level of welfare for the population. I shall briefly touch upon each of these aspects; the ideal type of weak, postcolonial state developed here draws much on the situation in Sub-Saharan Africa, the area with most of the weak states, but it will be claimed that the ideal type has more general relevance as well.

Around independence elites and popular groups rallied around the common goal of getting rid of the colonizers, but once independence was achieved there was little left to create unity. A number of leaders attempted to launch nation-building projects that would help develop a common idea of the state, for example, Nyerere's *Ujamaa* socialism, Kenyatta's *Harambee*, and Mobutu's *authenticité* (Laakso and Olukoshi 1996). There was some measure of success in a few countries, but in general the project was a huge failure: it was extremely difficult to knit together diverse ethnic groups with different languages, beliefs, and ways of living. And the state elites quickly gave up trying; in most cases they had more urgent items on their political agendas. Administrative and institutional structures were generally weak, lacking capacity, competence, and resources. Colonial rulers had often concentrated on maintaining a relatively strong set of repressive institutions, including military and police forces, whereas other parts of the state apparatus were clearly underdeveloped, including institutions having to do with welfare and economic development (Alavi and Shanin 1982). Post-independence rulers often confronted potentially strong domestic opposition; at the same time, they faced little pressure from the outside to keep their house in order.

It was in this context that the system known as 'personal rule' or 'the strongman' developed (Jackson and Rosberg 1982; Sandbrook 1985). The most important positions in the state apparatus, whether it be in the bureaucracy, military, police or in the polity, are filled with the loyal supporters of the strongman. Loyalty is strengthened through the (unequal) sharing of the spoils of office. The strongman thus controls a complex network of patron–client relationships. The functions of the state only in a very limited sense has to do with producing public or collective goods. The state apparatus is a source of income for those fortunate or clever enough to control it. Such a state is by no means a basis for security, order, and justice for its citizens; it is more of a threat, an apparatus against which the population must seek protection.

A proper designation for this type of situation is 'captured autonomy'; these fragile states are autonomous in the way that they are not significantly constrained by forces outside of the state apparatus; yet the state is captured in the sense that the elite controlling the state is exploiting that control for the benefit of its own narrow interests. The long rule of Mobutu Sese Seko in Zaire is a frequently used example of this situation. What gave Mobutu an extreme measure of autonomy? The peculiar external situation of postcolonial independence has already been noted: continued existence was guaranteed by the international society. Domestically, a strategy of coercion and cooptation, of divide and rule, soon made sure that there were no social groups outside of the state sufficiently strong to challenge Mobutu's position. Yet Mobutu's neopatrimonial state was not about development; it was about enriching himself and a small group of followers. His state services were up for sale to the highest bidder; it is sometimes said that the state autonomy required for development is especially autonomy from classes and groups involved in zero-sum activities, that is, speculation, corruption, usury and the like, in other words, 'classes which derive wealth from unproductive activities or which are otherwise hostile to industrial development' (Hamilton 1987:1243). But in Zaire those groups were exactly Mobutu and his clique, the state elite was thus part of the development problem and not at all part of the solution. When the political elite is itself the strongest zero-sum group in society, one can hardly expect it to act as provider of order, welfare, security, and justice in any meaningful way.

Against this background there has to be a lack of legitimacy. The legitimacy of the state is low because large parts of the population have no reason to support the government and the institutions it represents; and the government has no authority in the sense that people follow its rules or regulations. This is the reason why weak states have been characterized as 'balloon states', suspended in the air with no firm connections to their underlying societies (Hyden 1983). The material aspect of citizenship, the state's provision of valuable service to the population, is to a very large extent absent. The other material aspect, the provision of resources by the population for the sustenance of the state in the form of taxes and other revenues is little developed also, because people are generally poor and the state's collection apparatus is wanting. With the material aspect of citizenship largely missing, the non-material aspects of legitimacy and solidarity suffer as well. Instead of the state, people turn to their local communities, their clans or their ethnic groups for support. The bonds of community and solidarity that exist in postcolonial states are to a large extent directed toward the local/ethnic group; this is where people can turn to for material assistance and moral support. When the state is captured by specific groups instead of being a state for the whole of the people, the *Gemeinschaft* aspect of nationhood gets in trouble as well; as Christopher Clapham has emphasized, such systems comprehensively lack 'the capacity to create any sense of moral community amongst those who participate in them, let alone among those who are excluded' (Clapham 1996:59).

The lack of community in the *Gemeinschaft* sense is clearly evidenced in the context of early processes of democratization. The existence of a political community is a necessary precondition for democratization. As spelled out in Rustow's classic model, national unity simply indicates that 'the vast majority of citizens in a democracy-to-be ... have no doubt or mental reservations as to which political community they belong to' (Rustow 1970:350). Against this background it is easy to understand why early democratization frequently creates more, not less conflict in weak states. Individuals do not perceive of themselves as citizens who are members of a political community. They see themselves as representatives of specific local/ethnic groups whose interests they are obliged to promote. In sum, the communities that prevail are different ethnic sub-groups competing for access to state power and resources, sometimes building frail alliances among each other.

In ideal typical terms, the postcolonial state is economically deficient. There is a lack of a coherent national economy, capable of sustaining a basic level of welfare for the population. Two characteristics can summarize the major aspects of this kind of economy. The first is a system of reproduction fundamentally dependent on the world market. Postcolonial states are often mono-economies based on the export of one or a few primary goods and the import of more sophisticated, technology-intensive products. In Sub-Saharan Africa, for example, primary products accounted for 92 per cent of total export production in both 1970 and 1991. The second characteristic is structural heterogeneity, meaning that different modes of production co-exist in the postcolonial economic space. They include elements of a modern sector, but also feudal or semi-feudal structures in agriculture. In both urban and rural areas large parts of the population are outside of the formal sectors, living in localized subsistence-economies at very low standards.

The major features, of the weak, postcolonial state[10] have now been identified. They can be summarized as follows:

| | |
|---|---|
| Government | 'Captured autonomy', based on weak administrative and institutional structures. Rule based on coercion rather than the rule of law. Monopoly of the use of legitimate violence not established |
| Nationhood | Predominance of local/ethnic community. Low level of state/nation cohesion. Low level of state legitimacy. |
| Economy | World market dependence and structural heterogeneity. Coherent national economy not developed. |

Real-world cases need not contain all these aspects in the way that they are presented here and some countries may exhibit several of the aspects without being ex-colonies. Not all economically wanting states are weak in political-institutional terms as demonstrated by China or Egypt. These countries may be Less Developed Countries (LDCs) economically, but they are not weak states (although they may feature some elements of weak statehood). The reverse also holds; not all states that are weak in political-institutional or nationhood terms are LDCs. Yugoslavia earlier and Bosnia today, for example, are weak in these latter respects. At the same time, the ideal type is premised on the idea that there will be an overlap in many cases, so that states which are weak in political-institutional and nationhood terms are also LDCs. This is the case with most states in Sub-Saharan Africa, but also the least developed Central American states and the Central Asian states coming out of the former Soviet Union, and even some states in Asia and Europe (for example, Albania) share several of the ideal type characteristics outlined here.

## The postmodern state

The modern, liberal states that emerged from the Second World War had several incentives to intensify their cooperation. The strongest power in the system, the United States, pushed for such cooperation in face of the East–West confrontation. West Germany was set on a course of European integration from a very early point and Japan became reconstituted as a liberal 'trading state', as mentioned in Chapter 4. Furthermore, increasingly intense cooperation fed on itself in the sense that processes of uneven economic globalization, as surveyed in Chapter 5, have made states much more dependent on each other. The very success of organizing transnational economic and other relations has helped create significant welfare gains for some groups in the participating countries, but it has also led to much increased mutual dependence. In a number of fields, modern sovereign states are less capable of regulating efficiently what goes on within their own borders, because such areas as levels of welfare, economic activity, employment, culture, and so forth, are significantly affected by external forces (for a succint analysis, see Zürn 1998).

To a considerable extent, modern liberal states have responded by increasing their levels of cooperation, partly through the creation of various types of institutions with a universal reach, partly through regional arrangements, the most ambitious of which is the European Union. In combination, these developments have changed both state and society in modern liberal states, to the effect that a new type of sovereign statehood has emerged which is qualitatively different from the modern state as it was identified earlier (for a first presentation of that view, see Holm and Sørensen 1995:204–5; see also Cooper 1996). For the lack of a better term, I shall call this new ideal type the 'postmodern' state. Some sociologists distinguish sharply between 'postmodern' and 'late modern'; no such attempt is made here where the aim is merely to argue that several modern states have changed in new directions and that these changes are important for international relations. The changes concern all three main aspects of sovereign statehood; government, nationhood, and economy.

The change in government is connected with the emergence of multilevel governance, that is, the growth of regulative powers 'above' and 'below' the level of the nation-state. The most ambitious forms of multilevel governance evolve at the supranational level; this is best known from the EU. Rules are binding for Member States, overseen by supranational institutions and superior to national law (Moravcsik 1998). Some observers point to the WTO as containing elements of a supranational institution (Victor 1999; Godt 1998); Michael Zürn provides additional examples and argues that 'the extent to which institutions with supranational elements have emerged in global politics is much more than expected ten years ago' (Zürn 1999:25).

At the interstate level, international regimes, that is, set of rules governing state action in particular fields, have developed to cover new issue-areas, and domains already covered are frequently subject to more elaborate regulations. At the transnational level, governance develops in context of transnational organzations prompted by a host of actors including transnational corporations and NGOs.[11]

Because multilevel governance is most developed within the EU, the following remarks focus on that institution. The EU does not fit well into conventional schemes of cooperation between states.[12] On the one hand, it is not state–state cooperation in the conventional form of intergovernmental organizations (IGOs); it is clear that EU cooperation goes much further than that. On the other hand, it is not a federal state either, although there are some federal traits. In other words, It is a hybrid, qualitatively changing some aspects of sovereign statehood, while retaining the single Member State as the key player, albeit within an increasingly strong cross-national policy network. The role of Member States as central actors is retained especially as regards the 'big bangs' of decisionmaking, such as setting up the basic framework of treaties, the most recent of which were the Amsterdam and Maastricht treaties.[13] In day-to-day decisionmaking, the EU is more aptly described as a system of multilevel governance between various groups of actors in three interconnected political arenas: supranational, national, and subnational (Marks *et al.* 1995).

Multilevel governance can be characterized as 'plurilaterialism' (Cerny 1993:27), because it indicates a diffusion and decentralization of power, both upwards to the supranational and downwards to the subnational level. The process involves both a strengthening and a weakening of states. They are strengthened to the extent that they acquire fresh regulative powers over a vast range of issues that would otherwise have been outside the scope of their influence. They are weakened to the extent that the regulation of domestic affairs is now heavily dependent on bargaining with a host of other actors, especially the other Member States. In sum, postmodern states are deeply involved in multilevel governance; the supranational elements of such governance being the most far-reaching. It has primarily developed in the regional context of the EU but appears to be in the process of emerging elsewhere also.

Let me turn to the nationhood dimension. Intense cooperation also involves changes in the material aspects of citizenship, as demonstrated by the EU. A status of 'citizen of the community' was created in context of the Maastricht treaty. The possession of citizenship in one of the EU Member States awards rights in all other Member States. These rights include the following (summarized from Soysal 1994:148): (a) free movement, gainful employment, and residence within the boundaries of the community; (b) discrimination based on nationality among workers of the Member States with regard to employment,

social security, trade union rights, living and working conditions, and education and vocational training is disallowed according to Community law; (c)
states are obliged to facilitate teaching of the language and culture of the
countries of origin within the framework of normal education; (d) full political
rights in the long run are recommended for Community citizens living in other
Member States. At present, they have the right to vote and stand as candidates
in local and European elections.

The tendency to break up the link between national territory and citizenship
rights is not confined to the European Union, although this is where such
developments have gone farthest. Yasemin Soysal (1994:127) argues that
there is a general tendency for the erection of 'postnational membership'
where 'universal personhood replaces nationhood; and universal human rights
replace national rights', especially in modern, liberal states in the period since
the Second World War. It is clear however, that 'universal personhood' is only
in the very early process of emerging. By no means is it on par with the
formulated citizenship rights in the EU.

In sum, postmodern statehood involves a situation where citizenship rights
are no longer exclusively connected to a national territory. What are the
implications for the *Gemeinschaft* aspect of nationhood? There is no simple,
unilinear relationship between the material changes in citizenship and the
ideas about community, the identity affiliations of citizens. The populations
of EU Member States are not automatically switching their loyalties to the
supranational level. This may have to do with the way in which European
integration has progressed; former head of the European Commission, Jacques
Delors, ventured that it was 'difficult to fall in love with the domestic
market'; that is, as long as the EU does not exhibit a higher profile as an
international actor, a strong EU-European popular identity will not emerge.
Yet there is a clear tendency toward less emphasis on identity singularly
based on nationhood towards a broader conception of 'we-ness' which includes
supranational and subnational levels. The statement by Lombard leader
Paul Friggerio: 'We are Lombards first and Europeans second. Italy means
nothing to us' (quoted from Rosenau 1994:255) may not be entirely representative, but it does give indication of the opening toward non-national identities.[14]

The economic aspect of postmodern statehood has already been introduced
in Chapter 5. A number of arguments were made there for the existence of a
'global economy' so only a few remarks are necessary here. Postmodern states
are not based on segregated national economies; they are increasingly integrated in a globalized economic framework. The economically advanced states
in the OECD area are those most heavily involved in the process. The relationship between economic globalization and closer political cooperation cuts both
ways: economic globalization increases the demand for political cooperation

and more intense cooperation paves the way for further expansion of economic transactions. Such a two-way process has been at work in an increasingly liberalized world in general and in the regional networks of cooperation in particular.[15]

Uneven economic globalization has thus intensified economic relations between countries, especially between developed states, both in the old 'economic interdependence' and in the new 'global economy' (see Chapter 5) sense. For most of these countries, 'the material base of the economy has become so internationalized that there would be significant costs in attempting a strategy of national autonomy' (Piccioto, 1991:45).[16] Given these changes the traditional image of a modern state national economy has become inappropriate, and this carries important implications for international relations.

The postmodern state can be characterized as follows:

| | |
|---|---|
| Government | Multilevel governance, based on supranational, international, national and subnational institutions (in various combinations). |
| Nationhood | Supranational and international institutions are sources of citizenship rights. Collective identity also tied to levels above and below the nation. |
| Economy | Major part of economic activity embedded in cross-border networks. 'National' economy much less self-sustained. |

## Conclusion

This concludes the 'outside-in' analysis. We began with the theoretical ideas concerning the possible effects of international forces on domestic structures. One main group of theories stressed the forces of homogeneity, leading to the emergence of states that were 'like units'. Another main group of theories stressed the forces of heterogeneity, leading to states that were highly dissimilar. In order to settle this issue, three aspects of international forces were identified, and their effects on statehood structures were subjected to empirical analysis. The result was the identification of three main types of state in the present international system, the modern, the postcolonial, and the postmodern state. Their features are summarized below, in Table 6.1.

The next chapter will commence the 'inside-out' analysis on the basis of these three state types. It will be argued that security dilemmas do not have only 'international' (anarchy) preconditions, but also 'domestic' preconditions. That is to say, different types of state (different 'domestic' structures) condition 'international' structures in different ways. The three types of state exist in different forms of anarchy in context of different patterns of cooperation and conflict. Specifically, these state types confront different security dilemmas and they play different sovereignty games. Chapter 7 outlines the general argument in context of the modern state. Chapters 8 and 9, respectively, analyse the postcolonial and the postmodern security dilemmas, and Chapter 10 identifies the peculiar sovereignty game pertaining to each type of state.

*Table 6.1*  Three types of state in the present international system

|  | Modern | Postcolonial | Postmodern |
|---|---|---|---|
| Government | A centralized system of rule, based on a set of administrative, policing, and military organizations, sanctioned by a legal order, claiming monopoly on the legitimate use of force. | 'Captured autonomy' based on weak administrative and institutional structures. Rule based on coercion rather than the rule of law. Monopoly of the use of legitimate violence not established. | Multilevel governance, based on supranational, international, national, and subnational institutions (in various combinations). |
| Nationhood | A people within a territory making up a community in the *Gesellschaft* and in the *Gemeinschaft* sense, involving a high level of cohesion, binding state and nation together. | Predominance of local/ethnic community. Low level of state/nation cohesion. Low level of state legitimacy. | Supranational and international institutions are sources of citizenship rights. Collective identity also tied to levels above and below the nation. |
| Economy | Segregated national economy, self-sustained in the sense that it comprises the main sectors needed for its reproduction; major part of economic activity takes place at home. | World market dependence and structural heterogeneity. Coherent national economy not developed. | Major part of economic activity embedded in cross-border networks. 'National' economy much less self-sustained. |

# 7
# The Domestic Dimension of Security Dilemmas

This chapter will argue that the different types of state face different security dilemmas. That is, the classical security dilemma in international relations is not merely based on the existence of an 'international' anarchy. It is also based on specific 'domestic' statehood structures. I first explain why this must be the case. Next, security dilemmas in context of the modern state and its history are addressed. The security dilemmas of postcolonial and postmodern states respectively are discussed in the two following chapters.

The focus on security dilemmas is a way of moving from the 'outside-in' analysis pursued in Chapters 2 through 5 to the 'inside-out' analysis undertaken in Chapters 7 to 10. The first part of the book was concerned with the effect of 'international' on 'domestic'; that led to the identification of three types of state in the previous chapter. This and the following chapters will demonstrate how different structures of statehood have implications for forms of anarchy, for patterns of cooperation and conflict, and for sovereignty. Focus is on security dilemmas, for two reasons. First, the security dilemma has been an emblematic way of expressing the core predicament of the sovereign state. Therefore, the variation in security dilemmas across different types of state is a way of bringing home the significance of the changes in statehood analysed here. Second, the security dilemma is well suited to tie together 'international' and 'domestic' because it is based on particular configurations of the two. It follows that the investigation in coming chapters is not an 'inside-out' study in the traditional sense because such a view presupposes a sharp distinction between 'domestic' and 'international'. The examination here, by contrast, argues that different types of state display dissimilar configurations of 'domestic' and 'international'. Instead of a conventional 'inside-out' analysis, focus is on the ways in which peculiar 'domestic' structures of statehood help condition different forms of anarchy, distinct games of sovereignty, and typical patterns of cooperation and conflict.

The term 'security dilemma' was first set forth by John Herz (1950). Sovereign states taking measures to make themselves more secure may well increase their level of protection, but given the existence of international anarchy – the absence of centralized authority – that very activity will lead to greater insecurity of other states. In a self-help system, the creation of more security for one state is inevitably the creation of more insecurity for other states:

> Striving to attain security from attack, [states] are driven to acquire more and more power in order to escape the power of others. This, in turn, renders the others more insecure and compels them to prepare for the worst. Since none can ever feel entirely secure in such a world of competing units, power competition ensues, and the vicious circle of security and power accumulation is on.
>
> (Herz 1950:157)

Herz's reasoning is directly related to a way of thinking about national security that goes back to Thomas Hobbes (1946). Hobbes's major concern is security of the human being, that is, personal or individual security. He imagines what life would be like without the state by using the abstraction of a 'state of nature'. Because people are self-regarding and egoistic, they will constantly be at each others throats; in the state of nature there can be no security for human beings, only continual insecurity, a 'state of war' of 'every man against every man' (1946:82). Hobbes's vivid description of that situation is well-known:

> In such condition, there is no place for industry, because the fruit thereof is uncertain; and consequently no culture of the earth; no navigation, nor use of the commodities that may be imported by sea; no commodious building . . . no arts; no letters; no society; and which is worst of all, continual fear, and danger of violent death; and the life of man, solitary, poor, nasty, brutish, and short.
>
> (Hobbes 1946:82)

In order to escape their mutual fear, people are driven to create the sovereign state. Only by handing over all power to the Leviathan, a centralized, autocratic state, set up 'by terror . . . to form the wills of them all to peace at home and mutual aid against their enemies abroad' (1946:101) can individuals avoid the perils of the state of nature.[1] With the creation of states, the domestic anarchy of the state of nature is moved to the international level: 'In all times, kings and persons of sovereign authority, because of their independency, are in continual jealousies, and in the state and posture of gladiators; having their weapons pointing, and their eyes fixed on one another' (Hobbes 1946:101).

According to Hobbes then, security derives from the state. The state must be able to provide a sufficient level of protection of the population, from external as well as from internal threats. The means of such protection is, in the final analysis, power. But with coercive power at hand the state is not only a source of protection of the population: it is also a source of threat. That creates a problem not sufficiently analysed by Hobbes: *without* the state, there can be no protection; people will live in the nasty and brutish state of nature where egoistic humans will always get at each other's throats. But *with* the state, why would there be protection and thus security? Why would the state elite not be as self-interested and power-loving as anyone else?[2] This problem has been called the 'Hobbesian paradox' (Wight 1991:35) or 'Hobbes's Dilemma' (Keohane 1995:168).

Unfortunately, Hobbes assumes away the problem through a strict specification of demands on the sovereign for protection of people and property. That is, a Leviathan in Hobbes's terms by definition honours the terms of the social contract in creating the basis for the good life of the citizens. The state must provide safety from threat as well as possibility for community and welfare. States are valuable because they produce political goods, such as security, order, justice, and welfare (Jackson and Sørensen 1999:3). There is no doubt that Hobbes gave highest priority to domestic peace; but he was also quite clear in indicating how this would pave the way for other values.

Following the notion of high politics, the realist tradition in IR has focused most directly on the value of security; the protection that the state must supply is protection from outside threat, from the armed might of competing states. John Herz characterized the 'peculiar nature' of the modern, territorial state by the fact that it was 'surrounded with what may be called its 'hard shell' which protected it from foreign penetration. It is this factor which rendered it defensible and, at least to some extent, secure in its relation with other units' (Herz 1959:40). The identification of values other than security is most pronounced in the liberal tradition. John Locke argued that states existed to underwrite the liberty of their citizens and thus enabled them to live their lives and pursue their happiness without undue interference from other people. The state for liberals is basically a constitutional entity that establishes and enforces the rule of law that respects the rights of citizens to life, liberty, and property. The liberal tradition thus opens up to the idea that states do not merely exist to create domestic peace and order. They exist to provide the political goods needed for the 'good life' of their citizens.

But, to repeat the question above, given the egoistic nature of humans, why would the sovereign meet these demands of providing political goods for the citizens? According to Martin Wight, one possible solution is to hope; when power is concentrated 'in the hands of a single authority' we can 'hope that this despot will prove a partial exception to the rule that men are bad and should be regarded with distrust' (Wight 1991:35). But as already indicated, such hopes have not been met in a large number of cases historically and are not being met today in many cases either. Hobbes's thinking is based on the idea that measures to increase the security of the state must produce more security for human beings; if such a connection did not exist, the social contract would make no sense. If the social contract made no sense, the security dilemma would be of a very different nature, because the increased power of states that is the driving force of the dilemma would not be connected to protection and security of people in an unambiguous way. Increased state power would either mean more insecurity all around, in the international as well as in the domestic sphere,[3] or it would mean that increased protection of people from external threat would be accompanied by a perhaps even more serious increase in the domestic threat presented by the state. It will be demonstrated in Chapter 8 that this is exactly the case in postcolonial states. Another peculiar security dilemma, pertaining to the Soviet Union, is discussed below.

Regrettably, this question of the domestic basis of the security dilemma has not been much addressed by international relations theory, with a few notable exceptions (Berki 1986; Buzan 1991); that omission is of course a consequence of the sharp division between international and domestic. When this division is rejected, the issue turns up immediately. The actual shape of the security dilemma is directly related to the domestic structure of states. It cannot merely be assumed, as Hobbes did, that states provide political goods for their citizens. An examination of the domestic structure of states is therefore necessary in order to fully appreciate the shape of any concrete security dilemma.

The classical Herz–Hobbesian security dilemma is clearly relevant for the modern state. The modern state provides the context for the good life; the centralized system of rule – sanctioned by a legal order and claiming monopoly on the legitimate use of force – creates the basis for domestic peace and order as well as protection from external threat. Nationhood provides community that binds nation and state together; and the national economy provides the basis for welfare as well as the resources necessary to defend the realm. The existence of government, nationhood and the national economy are the cohesion parameters that combine to forge the link between national security and the security of individual citizens. Modern states are characterized by a high level of social cohesion; in that sense they are 'strong states' (Buzan 1991:97). The classical security dilemma is readily applicable to strong states. But strong states in this sense emerged relatively late, as we have seen. The security dilemma in previous forms of state, as well as in contemporary postcolonial and postmodern states is different, because their domestic structures are different.

To sum up so far: security dilemmas have domestic as well as international preconditions. The classical Herz–Hobbesian security dilemma must rest on the assumption that sovereign states provide political goods for their citizens, primarily security and order. It is against this background that the Herz–Hobbesian security dilemma can be singularly focused on external threat from other states. When states do not provide those political goods, the security dilemma takes on a different shape. That points to the need to examine the extent to which these political goods are provided in different previous and contemporary types of state, because the concrete shape of the security dilemma rests on such investigation. Those domestic preconditions have not been sufficiently analysed in current theories of international relations who have tended to focus singlemindedly on relations between states, not on their domestic structures.[4] The next section briefly examines security dilemmas before the modern state.

## Security dilemmas before the modern state

Before the advent of centralized rule and domestic pacification, there was no 'hard shell' of the state; consequently it is not possible to speak of a security dilemma in the classical Herz–Hobbesian sense. In the absence of a monopoly of violence, security was provided by knights, nobles, and other local rulers who had sufficient power to protect their towns, castles, or fiefs. There was frequently fierce power competition between local rulers in context of complex alliances with other holders of power, including emperors, kings, and popes. But most of the time, such competition did not translate into more security for people at the bottom; more often than not, it would increase their insecurity. Charles Tilly has described the process of state formation as seen from the perspective of ordinary people in vivid terms; it included 'the imprisoning of local leaders as hostages to the local community's payment of overdue taxes, the hanging of others who dared to protest, the loosing of brutal soldiers on a hapless civilian population, the conscription of young men who were their parent's main hope for comfort in the old age' (Tilly 1990:99).

   As indicated above, we are used to consider the protection of people, especially the protection of human life, as the core of security. Domestic peace and physical safety is what the 'hard shell' of the state affords. In broader historical terms, this is a relatively recent view, partly because the 'peace within', the reduction of violence in the domestic sphere and its clear separation from external war, also came relatively late. Patterns of punishment reflect the difference. In post-medieval times, even 'quite trivial' crimes could fetch capital punishment, whereas killing someone could be absolved by paying a fine. 'Regarding murder as the peak of the scale of crimes ... and separating murder unequivocally from the killing of alien populations in times of war, are attitudes peculiar to the past two centuries or so' (Giddens 1992:187). In a similar way, peace was no core value, quite to the contrary; the elite was always a warrior class in traditional societies and war was 'the central purpose of its existence' (Porter 1994:25). The primary aspiration of traditional elites was aggrandizement with the clear knowledge that this might involve glorious death; security may have had a role in that equation but it was not a very important one. That is, in earlier days of statemaking war was an activity that elites were always getting ready for rather than trying to avoid; and violence, including violent death, was nothing out of the ordinary.

At the same time, extraction via control and repression could lead to rebellion; successful rulers had to bargain with people and local powerholders over the concrete terms of their relationship. It was through such bargaining that the foundations for citizenship rights were formulated; these processes increased in strength after 1750, when kings went from indirect rule via intermediaries to direct control over their subject populations while also advancing their control over the means of violence (Tilly 1990:103–26). Under absolutist rule, then, emerging between the sixteenth and the eighteenth centuries, the 'hard shell' began to take shape. Domestic pacification followed centralized control over the means of violence. For example, the likelihood of dying of unnatural causes, such as murder or robbery, was tenfold higher in thirteenth-century England compared with the eighteenth century.[5]

Is it then possible to apply the idea of the classical Herz–Hobbesian security dilemma to absolutism and the early modern state? The answer appears to be yes: absolutist rulers faced an international anarchy; most of their efforts went into war and the preparation for war. Seventeenth-century great powers were at war for 94 per cent of that century and then eighteenth-century powers for 78 per cent (Tilly 1990:72). Domestically they were centralizing rule, that is, constructing a hierarchy, a pacified space beginning to be under the rule of law. Strength in war began to increasingly be dependent on the extraction of resources from society; therefore, the security of rulers and the well-being of their societies became increasingly closer related.

But there are also problems with the application of the conventional security dilemma. Ordinary people under absolutism continued to be subjects more than they were citizens. There were no strong political ties constraining the monarch; this was especially the case in the area of foreign policy, which kings continued to consider their private prerogative (Mann 1993:413). As far as resources were concerned, societal extraction could be replaced by credit obtained elsewhere (Tilly 1990:85). In pursuing such possibilities, monarchs would often act on calculations of short-term gain rather than long-term benefits; that is 'their time horizons were shorter than those of the states that they controlled' (Keohane 1995:170). For some rulers, indeed, war was considered little more than a game, an attractive and exciting play, a proper stage for demonstrating bravery, daring, gallantry. Therefore, the conduct of foreign policy including war had no clear relationship to the production of security for the subjects. These activities depended much more on the personal whims and predilections of the monarch. Frederick II of Prussia's account from 1740 is instructive in this regard:

At my father's death, I found all Europe at peace...The minority of the youthful Tsar Ivan made me hope Russia would be more concerned with her internal affairs than with guaranteeing the Pragmactic Sanction [the treaty allowing a woman, Maria Theresa, to succeed to the Austrian throne]. Besides, I found myself with highly trained forces at my disposal, together with a well-filled exchequer, and I myself was possessed of a lively temperament. These were the reasons that prevailed upon me to wage war against Theresa of Austria, queen of Bohemia and Hungary...Ambition, advantage, my desire to make a name for myself – these swayed me, and war was resolved upon.

(quoted from Mann 1993:413)

The monarch's quest for increased power might have devastating consequences for the subjects. The seven year's war which followed Frederick's first challenge to Theresa completely destroyed significant parts of Prussia. The conduct of war, in other words, was much tied to what could be called cost-benefit calculations of individual rulers without any close links to the fate of their subject populations. Later in life, Frederick formulated that calculation in explicit terms:

Armaments and discipline being much the same throughout Europe, and alliances as a rule producing an equality of force between belligerent parties, all that princes can expect from the greatest advantages at present is to acquire...either some small city on the frontier, or some territory which will not pay interest on the expenses of war, and whose population does not even approach the number of citizens who perished in the campaign.

(quoted from Herz 1959:64)

It is not surprising, then, that subject populations would continue to resist fiercely the burdens of war in terms of revenue and manpower that states attempted to place on them, even to the point of seeking the protection of another sovereign, as did Catalonia in a tax conflict with Spain in the 1640s when Louis XIII of France was called upon to assume sovereignty over the area (Tilly 1990:101).[6]

What these examples demonstrate is that there was still no fully unified realm with a well established hierarchy behind the emerging shell of the early modern state. Rulers would seek increased power for reasons that had little to do with the security of their citizens. Groups of citizens or entire regions, as in the case of Catalonia, would resist such efforts to the point of defection. In the absence of any firm connection between the power of the monarch and the security of the realm, groups of subjects always had reason to believe that the hardships imposed upon them in the name of increased central power was not worth their while in terms of increased security and that it was possible to get a better deal somewhere else. This is a domestic version of Rousseau's stag-hunt parable. That is, even though the 'shell' of the state was beginning to emerge, the distinction between an 'anarchy' on the outside and a 'hierarchy' on the inside was much less than firm. Consequently, people could not consistently count on the state to provide security. It did so sometimes, but the state was also frequently the major source of threat to people's security.

In sum, early modern statehood did produce a distinction between inside and outside, but in important ways it continued to be a domestic structure in which there was no clear link between the security of the ruler and the security of the population. On the one hand, subjects would continue to rebel against the hardships coming from the state, which could include mortal threats to their security. On the other hand, rulers had sufficient autonomy to undertake cost-benefit calculations concerning the possible profits from war against their rivals. People and groups, by contrast, had to calculate whether the protection afforded by the ruler was sufficient to warrant the hardships and insecurity imposed in return.

## The security dilemma of the Soviet Union

Different types of state face different security dilemmas. It follows that the shape of the security dilemma must vary between the two major contenders of the Cold War, the United States and the Soviet Union. The United States was a modern, liberal state. In security terms, that type of state functions as expected by Herz and assumed by Hobbes: its accumulation of power is meaningfully related to the security of the realm and the general protection of the citizens. In general, it seeks to provide political goods for the population. The Soviet Union was a totalitarian[7] society; as noted in Chapter 3, it did develop some basic elements of modern statehood, but it remained qualitatively different from the Western, liberal version of the modern state. What was the shape of the security dilemma in the Soviet Union during the Cold War?[8]

From the beginning, Stalin's security concerns were both international and domestic; the external threat from hostile capitalist powers and the domestic challenges from 'enemies of the state'. With the capitalist powers in economic and political crisis during the 1930s, Stalin concentrated on the domestic threat. The main instrument in that context was a regime of terror, with the arrest, torture, imprisonment, and very frequently killing of real as well as imagined adversaries. Seen from below, from the ordinary members of society, the state was undoubtedly the most acute threat to their security; at the same time, provided they complied with everything, the state was a provider of the 'security' of a basic standard of living. The latter element pointed to accommodation, the former to rebellion. The extent of the terror under Stalin combined with the peculiar historical past of the Russian state (Bahro 1977) are no doubt the most important elements in understanding how the rebellious challenges to the totalitarian regime could relatively easy be held under control by the rulers.

But seen from Stalin's chair, there continued to be domestic enemies everywhere, and the advent of the Cold War led to an intensification of terror at home. Possibly as much as another ten million people were sent to the labour camps and the party was purged once again (Druve 1991). According to Khruschev, 'after the war, Stalin became even more capricious, irritable, and brutal; in particular, his suspicion grew. His persecution mania reached unbelievable dimensions. Everything was decided by him alone...' (quoted from Aspaturian 1984:59).

The extreme regime of terror was discontinued after Stalin's death; what took its place was a police state under the complete control of the state elite with the communist party at its centre. That provided a little more room of manoeuvre, a 'pluralism only for and among the elite' (Aspaturian 1984:76). But it was always clear that the basic rules of the game, including the leadership and control of the party, were to remain unchallenged. Much like feudal rulers, local party leaders held unrestricted power within their respective realms as long as they did not undertake any actions that would threaten the overall structure of power. Boris Yeltsin's 1991 account of his role as first secretary in Swerdlowsk is instructive in this regard: 'the opinion of the first secretary is law; hardly anyone would dare not to comply with his requests or follow his instructions; cynical party functionaries and their underlings exploited this power beyond any limitation' (Yeltsin 1990:79).

The term 'bureaucratization' is frequently used about this system, but it is misleading in two respects. First, the system was not rule-governed, it did not function according to a formulated legal and normative framework. It pretended to do so, as evidenced in the huge number of plans, instructions, and directives that were exchanged between its different units. But to make the system work even at low levels of efficiency, ad-hoc measures, including bartering, haggling, and negotiating were always necessary. Second, the ruling elite, the *Nomenklatura*, was not a bureacracy in the formal sense but a socio-political elite that had monopolized political, economic and social power. Everybody knew that the system did not function according to the formal rules which were in place; cynicism and retreat into the private sphere was the natural reaction of many citizens (Hoffer 1992).

The ruling elite thus faced an external security problem of competition with the West and an internal security problem of challenges from below which could threaten their privileged position. Several types of relationship between these challenges are of course possible (Lebow 2000); my argument is that the domestic challenge (that is, preserve the power and position of the *Nomenklatura*) severely constrained the ways in which responses could be made to the external challenge of competition with the West. With its superior economic capacity that could in turn provide for a leading position in the arms race, the West set the standards of the competition. The Soviet Union would always be in a position of having to catch up; that called for domestic reform. But domestic reform always had to take place within the narrow limits set by the need to preserve the privileged position of the state elite; domestic security for the elite was as important as international security in this respect. Post-Stalin Soviet politics play out against this background. Where Krushchev engaged in attempts at domestic reform, his successors in the 1970s instead attempted to improve the efficiency of the economic system by increasing external ties with the West; in that sense the domestic constraints can be seen as a backdrop for external attempts at cooperation and peaceful coexistence (Ticktin 1976; Carlo 1976).

As recounted in Chapter 3, Gorbachev went to work both on the international front (ending the Cold War) and on the domestic front (*glasnost* and *perestroika*). Unintentionally, he thereby dismantled the power of the *Nomenklatura*, a development consummated by the rise of Boris Yeltsin. The peculiar domestic security problem which characterized the Soviet Union between the end of the Second World War and the late 1980s has therefore ceased to exist. It remains unclear what is going to take its place, because the structures that shape the domestic substance of the security dilemma continue to be in flux in today's Russia.

In sum, the security dilemma in the Soviet Union is very different from the security dilemma pertaining to modern, liberal states. In the Soviet Union, the communist elite was as concerned with domestic, popular threats to its position as it was worried about external threats. That domestic threat severely constrained the possibilities available for reacting to the external threat. For example, the creation of increased efficiency through emulation was not seen as a viable strategy, because that would undermine the position of the elite. From the viewpoint of ordinary people, the Soviet state was undoubtedly the most acute threat to their security; at the same time, the state also offered some basic security rewards for popular compliance and support. In order to appreciate fully the concrete shape of any security dilemma, the domestic structures of the states involved have to be taken into account.

## Conclusion

The classical Herz–Hobbesian security dilemma is predicated on the assumption that sovereign states produce political goods for their citizens, first and foremost security and protection. Therefore, that dilemma is easily applicable to modern liberal states that actually cater for such values. But in a large number of cases, both historically and in the contemporary world, states have not provided these values for their citizens. That points to the need to investigate the domestic aspects of security dilemmas; only by doing so can we discover how the variation of domestic statehood structures shapes the security dilemma in different ways.

There was no clear connection between the security of the ruler and the security of the population in early modern statehood; nor was such a link clearly present in the Soviet Union. States with vastly different domestic structures exhibit great variation in the ways in which they confront the problem of security.

The claim is that the analysis of domestic structures provides a substance of security dilemmas which is required in order to understand what is going on in international relations. In other words, it is not possible to reduce those relations to a power-play between different states, because the concrete shape of that power-play is also predicated on the domestic structures of the participating states. Furthermore, given that states are not 'like' but 'unlike' units increases the urgency of examining the domestic aspects of the security problem.

A casualty of the approach recommended here is the trans-historical idea that the essence of international relations has changed little between, say, Thomas Moore and Woodrow Wilson, a viewpoint which Arnold Wolfers has set forth (1962:249). If domestic structures are to be taken seriously as an important basis for international relations, such a view has to be abandoned. That in turn would lead to better appreciation of how, for example, the classical balance of power from the mid-seventeenth to the late eighteenth century could only have been shaped the way it did because the participating states were absolutist monarchies;[9] or of how the bipolar confrontation between the United States and the Soviet Union was shaped by the specific domestic structures of the contenders.[10]

Previous chapters have demonstrated how various types of international forces shape different types of state. This chapter has begun to demonstrate how different types of state are entangled in different types of security dilemmas. The next chapters focus on the postcolonial and the postmodern states respectively.

# 8
# The Security Dilemma in Postcolonial States

The peculiar features of postcolonial statehood create a security dilemma radically different from the security dilemmas of modern and postmodern states. The security dilemma is based on the distinct features of postcolonial statehood. Chapters 4 and 5 demonstrated how postcolonial sovereign statehood had been significantly shaped by international forces. This chapter will clarify how 'domestic' and 'international' are combined so as to create a security dilemma which most often spell acute insecurity rather than security for the people in postcolonial states. What is the substance of the security dilemma in postcolonial states? I shall argue that the security of postcolonial state elites depends much on the norms of the international system; the norms that paved the way for decolonization in the first place. For that reason, postcolonial state elites strongly support those norms; they help provide protection for the elites both in the international and in the domestic sphere. Unfortunately, this protection did not pave the way for significant development progress. People and groups in society suffer not only social and economic insecurity, but often also severe physical insecurity. In the 1980s and 1990s this situation provoked a reaction from international society, which involved itself in the government of postcolonial states to a hitherto unprecedented degree, including taking responsibilities for economic policy, political transformation, and the strengthening of civil society. The most far-reaching of such measures have been humanitarian intervention in so-called failed states. But the security for people and groups has not been considerably improved and self-regarding state elites continue to dominate in many countries. I briefly explain why that is the case. That leads up to some concluding observations on the future prospects for postcolonial statehood and the security dilemmas faced by people and by state elites.

## International norms and postcolonial statehood

The structural features of the postcolonial ideal type of state as set forth in Chapter 6 can briefly be reiterated:

| | |
|---|---|
| Government | 'Captured autonomy', based on weak administrative and institutional structures. Rule based on coercion rather than the rule of law. Monopoly of the use of legitimate violence not established. |
| Nationhood | Predominance of local/ethnic community. Low level of state/nation cohesion. Low level of state legitimacy. |
| Economy | World market dependence and structural heterogeneity. Coherent national economy not developed. |

The immediate question: how can such weak entities survive at all in a competitive international system? was briefly addressed in Chapter 4: because international society accepted a new set of norms which rejected colonial empire and established the right of self-determination of peoples. This included persistence of colonial borders; the straight lines on the map remained in place; the right of 'peoples' was not the right of individuals or groups to self-determination, but the right of pre-existing colonial units to sovereignty. In 1958 the first assembly of African independent states agreed, '... that in the interests of that Peace which is so essential, we should respect the independence, sovereignty and territorial integrity of one another' (quoted from Young 1991:23). The Organization of African Unity, founded in 1963, confirmed colonial borders in 1964 by explicitly committing itself to preserve existing boundaries. In short, the newly independent, weak states were sustained by international norms, backed by the African state elites who endorsed the inviolability of colonial borders.

It has been claimed that the OAU's commitment to colonial precincts was primarily pushed by smaller states who suspected the intentions of the larger ones (Touval 1967:104). But there were no severe confrontations between African states on the issue. This probably had to do with the general weakness of those states, large and small. The lack of an economic resource base, of any developed sense of community binding state and nation together, and of a capable apparatus of government, created a profound scarcity of mechanisms that could create coherence in the new states. In that situation it was not difficult for the elites to agree on the persistence of borders, the one remaining tangible element of cohesion (Clapham 1996a:46).

The international recognition of sovereignty based on existing borders is therefore a vital condition of strength for weak state elites, both domestically and internationally. It constrains domestic opposition, partly because any radical territorial claims to autonomy in the form of secession can not expect to gain international support; and partly because it entails the principle of nonintervention, leaving supreme legitimate power in domestic affairs to the government. In the international sphere, sovereignty means recognition as an equal player in the international system, on par with any other state, as basically reflected in the equal membership (one member state, one vote) of the United Nations. The OAU Charter explicitly confirms its commitment to the principle of non-intervention and also emphasizes the right of the state to regulate the domestic economy.

It is not surprising that the weak postcolonial states have embraced 'the dominant values of the Westphalian system' (Ayoob 1995:3) to an exceptional degree. Juridical equality helps compensate for substantial inequality (cf. Jackson and Rosberg 1982). But the existence of such norms does not make substantial inequality disappear of course. That situation made postcolonial governments push for changes in the international norms of sovereign equality; specifically they sought economic assistance from the rich countries, including their previous colonial masters. Such aid was quickly forthcoming, probably due to a combination of factors: the new strong ideology of anti-colonialism (Jackson 1993a) which came to dominate Western public opinion created a moral basis for giving aid to former colonies; national interests on part of the donors for sustaining influence in the newly independent countries pointed in the same direction; most importantly, postcolonial countries came to dominate in international fora, including the UN, where they could push for economic assistance and other forms of special treatment (Jackson 1993a; Krasner 1985). In the course of a relatively short period of time, more than two-thirds of UN funds went to areas having to do with development.

Postcolonial states, then, were in a situation where they strictly demanded to be treated as *equals* in the international system, enjoying the same principles of legal equality, nonintervention, and rights to participate in international affairs on par with everybody else; and with no less rigidity they demanded to be treated as *unequals*, with the entitlement to receive special benefits and privileges in the international economic and political system. The clearest expression of this awkward state of affairs is the Charter of the Economic Rights and Duties of States adopted by the UN General Assembly in the mid-1970s; on the one hand, the charter emphasizes that all states are 'juridically equal', with 'the right to participate fully and effectively in the international decisionmaking process'; on the other hand, developed countries are requested to provide a 'system of generalized and nonreciprocal . . . tariff preferences' and to 'give serious consideration to the adoption of other differential measures' in order to meet the 'development needs of the developing countries'.[1]

According to Mohammed Ayoob, both the commitment to upholding the Westphalian rules of the game and the commitment to change them derive from the 'deep sense of insecurity from which Third World states and regimes suffer domestically and internationally' (Ayoob 1995:3); but this statement needs qualification. Postcolonial states and regimes were not in mortal danger; no matter how they behaved, the international society had confirmed their right to sovereign statehood. It is precisely because of this 'morally and legally unassailable' (Jackson 1992:89) political independence that state elites can increase the stakes and seek the establishment of international norms, however self-contradictory they may be, which can help pave the way for less substantial vulnerability and dependence.

The lack of sustained protest from other members of international society against this stringent promotion of double standards suggests that postcolonial states enjoyed favourable conditions of operation during this period. Those conditions were in part a reflection of the new normative regime; the post-colonial states enjoyed a high moral standing in international society and that creates an insulation from external threat (Jackson 1992:88). But they were also connected to the relations and interests of the great powers. The East–West confrontation created a situation where postcolonial states could, to some extent, play on the fact that the global competitors were looking for partners elsewhere in the world; at the least they were anxious not to see too many countries line up on the side of the opponent (David 1991). Christopher Clapham notes how some postcolonial states were able to 'play off the global superpowers against one another, in order to strengthen their control over their domestic populations' (Clapham 1998:145). The point should not be misunderstood; few postcolonial states could be active power-players in the East–West confrontation; they were much too weak for that. If great powers decided to interfere in their domestic affairs or even to intervene, there was little they could do about it. But the new norms combined with superpower competition virtually guaranteed that there would be no old-fashioned, imperialistic take-overs of weak states, even though the mere differentials in power would seem to point in that direction.

In that way, the East–West confrontation helped strengthen the new norms of the right of ex-colonies to sovereign statehood. The weakest postcolonial states, in Sub-Saharan Africa, were not of considerable interest to the great powers anyway. Africa was a marginal area, a 'pole of indifference' (Wolfers, quoted from Jackson 1992:88). The United States left involvement to the former colonial powers of Britain and France and became active herself only in the areas of perceived importance, where independence created turbulence. The major case of this was the Congo, where the CIA helped in getting Lumumba murdered and later in the taking over of power by Mobutu. The Soviet Union took up the role of the most important arms supplier to the region, with Ethiopia and Angola as the primary customers (Chazan *et al.* 1988:362–83). African states did get into conflict with each other on occasion, but the sources of such conflict were mostly related to internal breakdown, that is, they were 'overwhelmingly domestic' (Clapham 1996a:109). At the same time, given their sharply limited military and economic resources, these weak states could not do severe harm to one another anyway.

In sum, the classical security dilemma is not directly applicable to weak postcolonial states, because these states do not face external threats that are a matter of life and death for the state. In general, both states and regimes are protected from outside threat by strong international norms, backed by the great powers. During the Cold War, intervention by the global superpowers did take place in some cases where the Soviet Union and Cuba came to the aid of 'progressive' forces and the United States supported anti-communist rulers. But most rulers could feel secure that no matter what they did, there was no external threat of wiping them out. Therefore, state elites could be self-seeking predators in postcolonial states to the extent that domestic chaos and violent conflict could go to any extreme without paying the ultimate price: termination of the state.

## Popular insecurity in postcolonial states

The classical Herz–Hobbesian security dilemma assumes that the state provides political goods for its citizens; this assumption does not hold true for postcolonial states. What is it that decides whether state rulers strive to take care of themselves ruthlessly rather than to provide security, order and law for their citizens?[2] We saw in Chapter 7 that Hobbes does not address the issue. International theory provides two solutions to the problem, one liberal and one realist. Unfortunately none of them have worked in the weak, postcolonial states. That is why popular insecurity has been increasing rather than decreasing.

The liberal solution involves constitutional government with check on the power of rulers (Keohane 1995). Ideally, democracy assures that state elites turning predatory will not remain in power and it assures that elites in power are subjected to the rule of law. Evidently, early successful development of stable constitutional government took place only in a small minority of postcolonial states, including Costa Rica and to some extent India. For most postcolonial states, the liberal solution to the Hobbesian problem was not readily available.

The other answer to the Hobbesian problem comes out of the realist tradition in IR. Realism posits that state elites are rational and self-seeking actors who seek security for their state as well as for themselves, that is, their regime. The latter depends on the former; without state security there can be no regime security; the state is a necessary precondition for the regime. The international system is anarchic; system-wide government is absent. It is a self-help system where states will have to rely on their own means of protection. The use of force is always a possibility, because that is the ultimate means of settling discord among states. States unable to provide protection for themselves risk their own survival.

That puts pressure on state elites; they are compelled to provide for domestic order, because without it the state will be disabled and powerless when it comes to facing external enemies. Domestic order is a precondition for bringing about the resources needed for protection of state and regime in the face of perennial external threat. States without efficient means of protecting themselves put their very existence at risk in an anarchical international system.

This, then, is the realist answer to the Hobbesian paradox: because of the constant external threat in an anarchic international system, state elites will seek to create such domestic order and civility that the state – and thus the regime – will be able to weather external threat. It is clear that the realist solution to the Hobbesian paradox is most efficient when there is a high degree of external threat, and least efficient at low levels of external threat. At very high levels of external threat, the state elite has few options but to get its act together in pursuing a domestic order which creates a sufficient level of efficiency and legitimacy. Without it, state survival, and thus regime survival, is in peril. At very low levels of external threat, domestic degrees of freedom are considerably larger and there is much more room for state elites to pursue their own narrow interests.

It was evidently the latter situation of low external threat which characterized most postcolonial states at independence, as explained in the previous section. For most postcolonial leaders, the situation at independence was one of no severe external threat against the state and the regime, combined with few domestic institutional constraints. It was under those circumstances that a large number of leaders chose the path that led to formation of the weak, postcolonial state ideal type identified earlier.

The element of choice must be emphasized; it was not predetermined that the newly independent states would come to match the weak, postcolonial ideal type of state. Some of them didn't and there is great variation in concrete cases. But it is clear that both the domestic and international conditions prevailing at independence were conducive to the formation of weak states, frequently under personal rule. Christopher Clapham has aptly summarized the situation:

> Confronted by weak administrative structures [and] fragile economies... political leaders sought to entrench themselves in power by using the machinery of state to suppress or coopt any rival organization...Rather than acknowledging the weakness of their position, and accepting the limitations of their power which this imposed, they chose to up the stakes and go for broke.
>
> (Clapham 1996a:57)

The insecurity of people and groups in weak postcolonial states then, is basically related to their being members of states that produce political bads more than they produce political goods. These political bads can in turn be related to each of the main aspects of postcolonial statehood as summarized in Figure 8.1. Each of these aspects, and the relationship between them, has been demonstrated in a large number of analyses (for example, Sandbrook 1985; 1993; Bayart 1993; Clapham 1996a; Evans 1989; Hyden 1983; Jackson and Rosberg 1982; Ergas (ed.) 1987; Bates 1981); they summarize the features of weak, postcolonial statehood outlined in Chapter 6. In the present context, therefore, only a few additional, and highly schematic remarks about recent developments are necessary; they refer mainly to Sub-Saharan Africa, the continent with most of the weak, postcolonial states.

Why has insecurity for people and groups in postcolonial states been growing rather than declining over several decades? The lack of legitimacy of state elites basing themselves on patron–client relationships created the need for coerced compliance; 'some governments command so little legitimacy and are so ineffectual at handing out the spoils that they depend heavily on force' (Sandbrook 1985:84). The need for coercion led to authoritarian forms of rule. In Africa, military, quasi-military, or one-party state regimes thoroughly dominated the political scene by the early 1980s. Rulers in such systems do not give up power easily. On the African continent, there is not a single example before 1990 of an opposition party actually coming to power after having defeated the incumbent regime in an election.

The lack of public services, poor administration and corruption creates an unfavourable climate for economic growth. It is difficult to attract foreign investment unless companies are given monopolistic advantages or complete control over attractive natural resources (Sørensen 1983). But in spite of this marginalized position in the modern world economy, postcolonial states remain highly dependent on export of a few primary products or raw materials (Clapham 1996a:163–9). The bulk of government revenue comes from import–export taxation. That leaves the economy very vulnerable to price fluctuations on the world market. From the late 1970s, increasing energy prices and decreasing

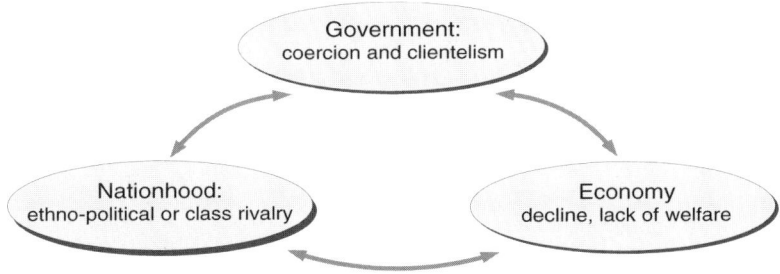

*Figure 8.1*  Salient aspects of postcolonial statehood

prices for the major export items created fiscal crises in many postcolonial states. That in turn increased the pressure on farmers when governments attempted to create additional revenue by squeezing producer prices to artificially low levels. As indicated in Chapter 6, the result is frequently withdrawal into subsistence farming; producers of primary products for exports also withdraw, by increasing the level of smuggling or by shifting into other products.[3]

The link to ethnic conflict is relatively straightforward. Patron–client relationships favour certain ethnic groups, or coalitions of groups, over others. Both 'insider' and 'outsider' access to material benefits is then to a large extent connected to ethnic identity. This increases the competition between ethnic groups. 'The greater the *competition and inequalities* among groups in heterogeneous societies, the greater the salience of ethnic identities and the greater the likelihood of open conflict' (Gurr 1994:348).[4] Of course other dividing lines between groups, perhaps most importantly class divisions, can also form the basis for these conflicts.

Given this political, social and economic context of weak, postcolonial statehood, a high level of domestic conflict, including violent conflict, must be expected. Furthermore, the claim that large-scale violent conflict in postcolonial states is a feature of the post-Cold War period should not hold up; according to the present account, these conflicts should rather have increased from the early 1960s, following the dramatic increase in the number of independent postcolonial states. This latter expectation is confirmed in Ted Gurr's comprehensive study of ethnopolitical conflict: 'The increase in serious ethnopolitical conflict since the late 1980s is a continuation of a trend that first became evident in the 1960s... The principal issue of the most intense new conflicts is contention for state power among communal groups in Third World societies' (Gurr 1994:364).

'Sixty coups in Thirty Years' was the title of a 1986 study of tropical Africa (McGowan and Johnson 1986). Violent domestic conflict has indeed characterized that region since independence. Close to four million people perished in such conflicts between 1960 and 1987. They include the following cases (with the largest death tolls first): Nigeria 1967–70 (Biafra); Ethiopia 1974–87 (Eritrea); Mozambique 1981–87 (Renamo); Sudan 1963–72/1984–87 (North vs South); Angola 1975–87 (UNITA); Uganda 1981–87 (various opponents); Zaire 1960–65 (Katanga); Burundi 1972 (Hutu/Tutsi); Chad 1980–87 (various opponents); and Zimbabwe 1983 (Ndebele) (Sivard 1987, quoted from Sandbrook 1993:51).

Ted Gurr's data from 1993–94 confirm that Africa has the highest number of serious ethnopolitical conflict. By that time, 'serious and emerging'[5] ethnopolitical conflict in Africa included: Ethiopia, Angola, Chad, Senegal, Sudan, Nigeria, Uganda, Burundi, Somalia, Liberia, South Africa, Mali, Niger, Rwanda, Djibouti, Kenya, and Zaire. But there were similar conflicts in a number of other weak (or semi-weak) states, including Azerbaijan, Russia, Georgia, Croatia,

Moldova, Bosnia, Iraq, Morocco, Iran, Burma, India, Pakistan, Bangladesh, Sri Lanka, Bhutan, Afghanistan, Papua-New Guinea, Guatemala, Peru, and Mexico (Gurr 1994:369–74).

Infringements on basic human rights, including political abduction and disappearances, undertaken by governments or by their opponents, took place in the following countries in 1985: Angola, Argentina, Bolivia, Brazil, Central African Republic, Chile, Columbia, Cyprus, Dominican Republic, El Salvador, Ethiopia, Guatemala, Guinea, Haiti, Honduras, Indonesia, Iran, Iraq, Lebanon, Mexico, Morocco, Nepal, Nicaragua, Paraguay, Peru, Philippines, Seychelles, South Africa, Sri Lanka, Syria, Togo, Uganda, Uruguay, Vietnam, and Zaire (Commission on Humanitarian Issues, quoted from Jackson 1993a:139). By 1986, such events has generated a refugee population of more than 13 million, about half of which originated in Sub-Saharan Africa.

In sum, postcolonial states and regimes have enjoyed a high degree of protection from external threat, in spite of their substantial weakness. That protection stems from strong international norms backed by the great powers. No matter how deficient they are in substantial terms – Somalia is a case in point – they are secured continued legal existence. Given the lack of substantial external (and internal) constraint, state elites frequently chose to pursue their own narrow interests. That led to the creation of state structures which provided insecurity instead of security for ordinary people and groups. The 'hard shell' of the state takes on an entirely different meaning in this context; for John Herz it was the security container that protected people from mortal external danger. For postcolonial peoples it is the *in*security container that exposes them to mortal domestic danger.

## Responses from international society

These serious problems of postcolonial states did not go unnoticed in international society of course. Aid organizations and relief agencies had to deal with the consequences of domestic conflict from very early on. Yet there was a belief that the creation of 'stability', meaning the establishment of enduring government within ex-colonial jurisdiction, would eventually lead to modernization and socioeconomic development; that in turn would create positive feedback to political and institutional development. There was also the additional consideration that governments should respect the interests of their external benefactors. In any case, both France and Britain held a record of protecting incumbent governments from domestic 'enemies', including British support for the Nigerian government in the civil war against Biafra in 1967–70 (Clapham 1998:147).

By the early 1980s, however, there were indications that this attitude was at least partly changing. In face of the postcolonial states' demand for a New

International Economic Order, donor countries had already responded by moving decisions away from the 'one country one vote' UN system, to organizations where power was distributed according to economic capability, such as the IMF and the World Bank. When the debt crisis demanded the creation of economic relief programmes, these organizations took on significant economic responsibility in postcolonial states. As a condition for the provision of urgently needed foreign exchange the organizations demanded a series of radical economic reforms intended to make the postcolonial economies less statist and more market-oriented. Typically, these Structural Adjustment Programmes (SAPs) contained the following main elements: (a) reduction of the role of the state in the economy through the decrease of public ownership and through cutbacks in public expenditures and interventions; (b) liberalizing measures to make the economy market-oriented, including currency devaluation, deregulation of prices and wages, and trade liberalization; (c) expansion of the export sector emphasizing postcolonial countries' comparative advantage in raw materials and primary products (Toye 1987; Callaghy 1991).

In context of implementing the programmes, expatriate advisors have become heavily involved in postcolonial countries. By the mid-1990s, according to the World Bank president, the number of these advisors in Africa exceeded the number 'at the end of the colonial period...some $4 billion a year is spent on technical assistance' (Barber Conable, quoted from Callaghy 1991:50). In several states, the IMF came to be known as the 'International Ministry of Finance', reflecting the new level of direct involvement in the economic affairs of postcolonial states.

The results of these efforts have been mixed, with economic progress in some countries and further setbacks in others. SAPs could claim some success in tropical Africa, notably in Ghana, but in general adjustment has not been successful in the weak African states. Per capita incomes declined by 30 per cent in the 1980 to 1988 period; averaged across Sub-Saharan countries, GNP has fallen one per cent annually over the last three decades (1960s to 1990s). This not merely has to do with the lack of success of SAPs of course, but as the World Bank itself admitted (World Bank 1994; Hoogvelt 1997:170; Callaghy 1991:51), the programmes faced substantial difficulties.

What was the problem? The answer is linked to the importance of juridical sovereignty, which has been emphasized earlier. At the moment of independence a new political, economic, social, and cultural sphere is created which has some substantial amount of autonomy. This new 'inside', the domestic sphere of the postcolonial country, can still be much influenced by external forces, but the conditions of operation are very different from before. In so far as they want to accomplish anything, outsiders are always dependent on relations with insiders; there is very little they can do entirely on their own. In other words, outsiders cannot do anything they want; they have to negotiate with insiders.

That situation immediately provides bargaining power for insiders. At the same time, outsiders are very rarely freewheeling idealists; they are actors representing interests and promoting ideologies. It is this combination of international and domestic forces that have achieved little progress in postcolonial states.

In concrete terms, the outsiders that were the IMF and the World Bank wanted to promote neoliberal reforms in the weak, postcolonial states. During most of the 1980s, the institutions were driven by the conviction that the state itself was the essential impediment to development in these countries and that a sharp reduction in the role of the state would create new, market-driven economic dynamics. Specifically, the international financial institutions wanted to promote export-led growth because it would increase foreign exchange earnings and so improve the capacity of postcolonial states to meet their financial obligations in terms of debt repayment. Both elements in this strategy has serious flaws, as demonstrated by several analyses (Schatz 1994, 1996; Mosley *et al.* 1995; Adams 1992). The point to emphasize in the present context is that these measures had to be negotiated with and implemented by representatives of the very institution that was seen as part of the problem and not at all part of the solution: the postcolonial states.

State elites, in turn, had their own agenda, with two basic components: first, securing as much additional external funding as possible; and second, accomplishing that in such a way as to preserve the largest possible autonomy in terms of political and economic control over domestic affairs. Faced with the external demands of economic reform, that led to a peculiar combination of exit, voice, and loyalty (Hirshman 1970). Exit was rarely used in full; Kenneth Kaunda of Zambia tried it in the mid-1980s, rejecting adjustment; the result was an even deeper economic and political crisis and his successor eventually had to accept an adjustment programme. Voice was used to protest against external demands and to launch an alternative programme of action: an 'alternative framework', set forth by the Economic Commission for Africa. The proposal rested on the contradiction mentioned above (that is, 'treat us as equals' and 'treat us as unequals'); on the one hand it demanded more aid from developed countries; on the other hand it called for more self-reliance and autonomy in economic affairs (Callaghy 1991:54–5). Few donors were ready to take such demands seriously, so what happened in most cases was 'loyalty' in the sense that adjustment programmes were nominally adopted, combined with 'exit' in that implementation was not pursued to any serious degree. To the extent implementation did take place, regimes were frequently able to carry out the measures in ways which transferred the cost away from the state elite and its clients.[6] The very large number of external advisors appear to have made little difference in that regard (Clapham 1996a:174).

In short, state elites continued to have substantial possibilities for making their own special kind of adjustment to increased external economic demands, even if they were now faced with less room of manoeuvre in economic affairs. The lack of actual economic progress has of course also led to programme modifications on part of the international institutions. The World Bank began to emphasize 'adjustment with a human face' in the late 1980s, indicating the need for more emphasis on social welfare in combination with liberalizing reforms. By the early 1990s focus shifted towards reform of the state itself; instead of doing away with the state, it was now admitted that efficient and democratic states are indispensable for economic development (World Bank 1997). That led to new demands for democratization and good governance.

Weak postcolonial states cannot boast a record of promoting democracy and human rights. As indicated earlier, incumbents would rather ignore the rules of the democratic game than step down. Given the lack of social, economic, and institutional development in these states, the prospects for any solid demo-cratic form of regime are slim. Richard Sandbrook, for example, found in 1985 that democracy did not have 'any real prospects in the limiting conditions of contemporary Africa'; what could be hoped for was 'decent, responsive and largely even-handed personal rule' (Sandbrook 1985:157).

The difficulties of democracy promotion inside postcolonial states were put into relief by the ways in which external forces pushed for more democracy. Just as the Western promotion of economic adjustment does not take place in an interest-free vacuum, the promotion of human rights, democratization, and good governance is also connected to specific interests and values. One recent analysis accuses the West of promoting 'low intensity democracy', 'as a way to relieve pressure from subordinate groups for more fundamental political, social and economic change' (Robinson 1996:6). A similar charge has been put for-ward against France in context of that country's policies in Francophone Africa (Monga 1997). But the Cold War conscious support for autocrats is largely a thing of the past. Current Western policies appear to be based on the support for administrations (i) that are liberal on economic policies including the support for economic openness toward the world market; (ii) that respect private property including setting up an effective system of commercial law; (iii) whose leadership is oriented towards cooperation with the leading Western countries. In that sense there is an elite-orientation in Western support for democracy in postcolonial countries.[7]

Western focus has been on the notion of holding free and fair elections rather than on the broader political, cultural and institutional transformation con-nected with a process of democratization. There is no doubt than holding free and fair elections is an important element in a transition to democracy. But as an isolated event, the election is only the tip of the democratic iceberg. If it is not closely connected with deeper rooted changes it does not mean very much. There is ample evidence on this from the African scene. With the introduction of multiparty systems, swarms of political parties have been formed. They are most often separated along ethnic lines and led by individuals with no clear ideological visions but with ambitions of becoming strongmen in their own right, controlling their own political patron–client networks.[8]

Against this background, one may speculate whether the current pressure from Western donors for multiparty systems and political democracy in post-colonial countries can have counterproductive effects. The Western countries themselves are examples of the fact that democracy cannot be installed over-night; it is a long-term process of gradual change. When quick fixes of imposing multiparty systems, for example, are substituted for the long haul of patiently paving the way for a democratic polity, the result may be that a thin layer of democratic coating is superimposed upon a system of personal rule without major changes in the basic features of the old structure (Ottaway 1995:245; for a similar view, see Dahl 1992 and Elklit 1994). In any case, the holding of elections have presented a number of possibilities for postcolonial state elites to hold on to power under new circumstances. Opposition groups are divided and control few resources; incumbents, by contrast, control not only the state apparatus and most of the means of violence, but also most of the media. In addition, rulers have the possibility of coopting rivals by offering them attractive government positions. All these possibilities have been put to use in postcolonial elections ( Joseph 1998; Clapham 1996a).

Therefore, it is less surprising that by 1995 one could count 21 multiparty elections in Sub-Saharan Africa which had not been followed by a transfer of power ( Jost 1995; see also Murphy 2000). Undeniably, there has been some democratic progress in weak postcolonial states; but in a significant number of cases, incumbents have managed to remain in power through a combination of divide and rule tactics which have often involved repression and the use of violence against political opponents. Rulers engage in 'a balancing act in which they impose enough repression to keep their opponents weak and maintain their own power while adhering to enough democratic formalities that they might just pass themselves off as democrats' (Carothers 1997:9). One observer has termed this 'virtual democracy', meaning that democratic institutions and practices are more a facade to satisfy current international democratic norms than they are indications of substantial political change ( Joseph 1998:4). A consequence of this situation is that political openings have been accompanied by more political violence.

Western countries, meanwhile, have come full circle in their attempts to find strategies that will help foster socioeconomic and political development in postcolonial states: after having relied on the market in the context of struc-tural adjustment and on the state in the context of democratization and good governance, emphasis is now on civil society with strategies of poverty reduc-tion and decentralization (World Bank 1999). It must be expected that these new strategies will have to confront the same dilemmas as the two previous ones: external forces can accomplish nothing on their own; they need domestic allies. The terms under which alliances with domestic groups can be produced are always subject to substantial influence by the strongest and most resourceful group in society, that is, incumbent state elites. These elites may face a situation of less autonomy in economic and in political affairs compared to earlier. But it is also a situation of access to fresh resources and rulers have been clever to play off external actors against each other, to roll with the punches and make the most of it. In political terms this means acceding to demands for a more competitive polity while using the available instruments to remain in power. This game is facilitated by the gradual lowering of international expectations. The current threshold for a competitive polity is extremely non-ambitious: 'All that is required is the presence of opposition parties that can contest for office, even if they are manipulated, hounded, and robbed of victory at election time' (Diamond 1996:30).

Instead of producing political goods for the population in terms of economic welfare and political freedoms, the economic and political reforms recorded here have often led to more instead of less conflict. Violent domestic conflict is nothing new in postcolonial states; the very definition of that ideal type included that the state has not established a monopoly of the use of legitimate violence. But armed opposition movements against the state have been a marked feature of both the 1980s and the 1990s, the reform periods discussed above. Especially in the present decade, state decay has, in a number of cases, led to state failure involving immense human and social cost. The next section will address the problems of state failure.

In summary, international society has attempted to mitigate the problems of security, order and welfare experienced by the people of postcolonial states. It has done so by increasing the demands made on postcolonial state elites in return for economic and other aid. But demands for structural adjustment programmes, for the promotion of democracy and human rights, and most recently for civil society empowerment and decentralization, have all had to face the need of dealing with the very state elites that were part of the problem rather than part of the solution. At the same time, donors have also looked after their own interests. Given the fact of continued substantial bargaining power for incumbent state elites and the character of demands made by international society much too little progress has been achieved. There continues to be a serious security problem for people in weak, postcolonial states.

## Political violence, state failure, and humanitarian intervention

Violent conflict in the world is increasingly domestic conflict inside weak postcolonial states. The number of armed conflicts[9] *between* states has been extremely low, varying between three and zero in the 1989–98 period. In 1998 there were two such conflicts, and even they could be related to postcolonial statehood; they were the conflict between India and Pakistan over Kashmir and the conflict between Eritrea and Ethiopia. During the 1989–98 period there were between 52 (1992) and 30 (1997) *instrastate* armed conflicts; the figure for 1998 is 32. During the ten-year period, intrastate *war* has taken place in Colombia, El Salvador, Guatemala, Peru, Algeria, Angola, Burundi, Chad, Congo, Ethiopia, Guinea Bissau, Liberia, Mozambique, Rwanda, Sierra Leone, Somalia, South Africa, Sudan, Uganda, Afghanistan, Cambodia, India, Indonesia, Myanmar, the Philippines, Sri Lanka, Tajikistan, Iraq, Lebanon, Turkey, Yemen, Azerbaijan, Bosnia and Herzegovina, Russia, and Yugoslavia (Wallensteen and Sollenberg 1999). The relationship between weak statehood and intrastate conflict ought to be clear.

The most dramatic domestic violent conflict is state failure or state collapse. State failure means that a state breaks down in decisive respects. Compared to weak postcolonial states, breakdown – again, in ideal typical terms – is a matter of degree: the problems related to weak statehood magnify. That means the distinction between weak and failed states is blurred: failure is when weakness intensifies. William Zartman describes failure as 'a situation where the structure, authority (legitimate power), law, and political order have fallen apart' (Zartman 1995a:1).[10]

State failure has attracted the attention of international society in a different way from what is the case with weak states. That is partly connected with the level of casualties; four domestic conflicts alone have each cost the lives of 500 000 to one million people; they were/are in Sudan, Ethiopia, Mozambique, and Rwanda. It is also connected to the fact that possibilities for response by the international society have been vastly improved with the end of the Cold War. No longer are UN Security Council decisions completely blocked by the East/West confrontation. Together with an increased attention to human rights as a universal value, this has led to humanitarian intervention (Donnelly 1993b),[11] not in all, but in a number of cases, including Rwanda, Haiti, Somalia, Liberia, Iraq, Bosnia, and Serbia/Kosova. Whereas the economic and political conditionalities discussed earlier are of the negotiated variety, that is, they require the consent of the governments exposed to the measures, humanitarian intervention can take place without such consent. In other words, humanitarian intervention involves setting aside the protective barriers of international norms, the defence device which allowed postcolonial state elite a free reign in domestic affairs, as explained earlier. The question must then be: has this change added to the security of peoples in weak states and if not, why not?

A first relevant observation is that in terms of looking after human security in weak states, humanitarian intervention always takes place after the fact. It follows upon a situation where the population, or substantial parts of it, have already been exposed to violent threat. The chain of events leading to humanitarian crisis are difficult to predict with great certainty, even though the number of organizations involved in 'early warning'[12] efforts have increased over the last decade. Even when such early warning is successful in terms of relaying information to the international society about impending humanitarian disasters, the international society, and especially the great power members of it, is slow to react. That is because intervention involves cost for those undertaking it, material cost as well as potential human cost in that intervention forces are exposed to violent threats themselves. Therefore, the humanitarian crisis in question must have developed to a certain stage, which includes that of having caught the attention of Western public opinion ( Jakobsen 1996), before humanitarian intervention becomes a realistic possibility. Reaching that stage entails that significant human cost has already been incurred.

Nowhere has this lack of willingness to react quickly been more clearly demonstrated than in the case of the 1994 genocide in Rwanda. It came against the background of conflicts between the Hutu majority and the Tutsi minority which go back to before independence in 1959 (Prunier 1995). The sequence of events leading up to the genocide began in 1990, when Tutsis in exile commenced a civil war in Rwanda in attempt to oust the Hutu rulers. The confrontation first led to a negotiated settlement in 1993, and a multilateral UN force of 2,500 was assigned to supervise the implementation of the agreement. But it was clear from early on that the agreement did not satisfy the Hutus (Clapham 1996b). After a period of mounting tensions, the Hutu president was killed when his plane was shot down in April 1994. That signalled the beginning of systematic killing of Tutsis by radical Hutus unwilling to give up or share state power as stipulated in the agreement; between 500 000 and 800 000 people were butchered in less than a hundred days (Prunier 1995). The UN forces had reported about impending ethnic killing already in January 1994; the Security Council was informed when the genocide began, but did nothing for two weeks. Then it decided to *reduce* UN presence in Rwanda to a token force of 270 troops to act as 'intermediaries'. Four weeks later, it was decided to deploy a force of 5,500. But the great powers continued to be unwilling to commit themselves to the operation. The actual intervention was basically undertaken by French troops and came only three months later (Knudsen 1999; Des Forges 1999). 'We all must recognize that . . . we have failed in our response to the agony of Rwanda' commented UN Secretary General Boutros-Ghali (United Nations 1994:11).

A second relevant observation is that any humanitarian intervention will always involve considerations that are non-humanitarian; power and interest are the most important additional factors. Power is reflected in the rules of the game of international society; the great powers play a special role in that game, evidenced by their special position in the Security Council. As a consequence, humanitarian intervention cannot be conducted against the great powers themselves even if there may be good humanitarian reasons for doing so in places such as Chechnya or Tibet. It also means that given the level of necessary resources to conduct humanitarian interventions, such undertakings rely on the willingness of the great powers to shoulder most of the burden. That willingness, in turn, is connected not only to the humanitarian issue, but also to considerations concerning perceived national interest. In other words, behind the innocent label of humanitarian intervention is a much more mixed palette of motives and purposes (Roberts 1996).

Three examples will suffice. The *French*-led intervention in Rwanda, *Opération Turquoise*, was not undertaken out of purely humanitarian concern. France had a history of supporting the Hutu government, economically and militarily. The intervention came very late, when the genocide was basically over and the forces of that government had been put on the defensive by the Tutsi rebels. French intervention allowed the government forces to 'retreat in relative security' (Knudsen 1999:266; see also McNulty 1997). When *Nigeria* led an ECOMOG intervention force in Liberia in 1990, it was not out of purely humanitarian concern either. The collapse of Liberia accelerated when Charles Taylor invaded the country in late 1989 to challenge the rule of Samuel Doe. Doe had an association with Nigerian military leader Babangida; he requested the intervention at a point where Taylor was winning the civil war. Nigeria had reason to believe that Taylor's coming to power would be out of line with its interests. Because Taylor immediately attacked the intervention force, the early results of the undertaking was more rather than less bloodshed (Adeleke 1995). The relatively large *American* engagement in the interventions in Somalia, by contrast, appear to be sustained primarily by humanitarian concerns, even though some observers have pointed to additional national interest considerations (Mazarr 1993). But the US was not prepared to conduct intervention at any significant human cost. When 18 American soldiers were killed by warlord Aideed's forces in October 1993, president Clinton announced the withdrawal of American forces and declared that a political instead of a military solution to the humanitarian crisis had to be found.

A final consideration concerns the operational problems involved in humanitarian intervention. Even with the purest of motives, concrete operations can come upon practical difficulties that run counter to the achievement of humanitarian aims. A number of such difficulties have turned up in the interventions mentioned here. The first UN intervention in Somalia had no clear long-term aims and lacked knowledge of local conditions; it was difficult to find out which clans were the perpetrators and which were the victims (Clarke and Herbst 1996). The intervention thus provided some short term relief but was not able to help construct a political framework for sustaining order. The second intervention became entangled in military confrontations with the clans, especially the one led by Aideed; the reason for that was understandable;

23 Pakistani UN troops had been killed in an attack for which Aideed was assumed responsible. But partly as a consequence of this trail of events, the UN force was no longer a neutral player and it never succeeded in the planned disarmament of the clans. In Liberia, the intervention force was too small to undertake the planned disarming of the contending groups. And the original plan, according to which the intervention force should only take up arms in self defence, quickly had to be abandoned (Howe 1996/97).

The above reflections are not meant to detract anything from the positive aspects of humanitarian intervention; there is no doubt that the operations saved lives and that there would have been less human security without them. But in terms of the general security problem for people in weak states, humanitarian intervention can never be a satisfactory solution; it can merely sometimes mitigate the worst consequences of violent domestic conflict. It cannot easily deal with the root causes of such conflict and therefore it cannot present a solution to the problem of popular security in weak states. Three reasons why that is the case were discussed here. First, humanitarian intervention must take place after, not before, humanitarian disaster; in that sense it is in the nature of such intervention to be undertaken too late. Second, humanitarian intervention always involves considerations that are non-humanitarian; power and interest may severely limit what can be done in purely humanitarian terms. Third, humanitarian intervention must confront operational problems that put further limitations to what can be achieved in terms of enhanced human security.

In sum, there is no reason to expect that humanitarian intervention can deal effectively with the problem of popular security in weak states. It may be that by setting aside the principle of nonintervention (albeit not in all cases), such intervention removes part of the normative protection shield around weak states, but this happens in such a way that there are no certain positive payoffs in terms of sustained improvements in popular security. Furthermore, the norm change associated with humanitarian intervention has not led to a decrease in domestic wars in weak states, indeed the number of such wars increased from seven in 1997 to 13 in 1998, eight of which are in Sub-Saharan Africa.

## The search for alternatives: secession and post-sovereignty

Given the poor record of weak states in producing even the most basic political goods of order and safety, the conservatism of international society is being increasingly called into question. The logic is the following: why continue to underwrite weak entities that appear to be part of the problem more than part of the solution? Why not attempt the creation of new, more viable entities, capable of delivering political goods to the population?

It is true that the international society of states in basic respects is a staunch champion of the status quo. This is particularly the case as regards the persistence of sovereign borders. New members of the society of sovereign states are accepted only when two conditions are met: (1) the states in question can point to previously existing jurisdictions; and (2) all the states affected by the promotion of such entities to independence consent to it (Jackson 1994). This has been the principle[13] behind the formation of new independent states, including the states that came out of the former Soviet Union. In tropical Africa, these standards have meant that the recognition of a new state is a very rare occasion; Eritrea could point to a previously existing jurisdiction, but it took thirty years of guerilla warfare including capture of the national capital of Addis Abeba to get the 'consent' of Ethiopia. Only then was Eritrea internationally recognized. Another aspect of the international society conservatism can be seen in the context of failed states. States that collapse completely still retain formal international recognition, as in the case of Somalia, Sudan, Sierra Leone, and Liberia. Nor has the increased concern for human rights including minority rights been allowed to get in the way of the respect for existing sovereign borders. The deliberations of the international organizations on this issue are firmly based on the respect for state sovereignty (Jackson-Preece 1999).[14]

What are the alternatives to the politics of status quo? The most radical proposals suggest to increase the pressure on postcolonial state elites in order to push the formation of viable states with domestic order and legitimacy. In operational terms this means that international society accepts secession and the creation of new states in a much more radical manner than has been the case so far. It also means acceptance of warfare as a means of creating capable states. Hence the proposal to 'Give War a Chance' (Luttwak 1999) and the statement that there is 'very little evidence that African countries, or many others in the Third World, will be able to find peaceful ways to strengthen the state and develop national identities . . . war may not seem such an undesirable alternative' (Herbst 1989:691–2; see also Herbst 1990).

The recreation of such a Darwinian design would require that the international society should disregard the human cost involved; that is the very logic of 'giving war a chance'. It would also require a willingness to abandon any practice of recognizing existing jurisdictions and begin a fundamental redrawing of borders. Both of these requirements are highly unlikely to be accepted by the international society because they run directly counter to the current practices. But if for a moment we disregard such 'practical' considerations, what would be the consequence of this reinvention of war?

There is no reason to expect that established great powers from the North would begin recolonizing weak states. The latter would be left to struggle among themselves. In view of the weakness of these states, large and small, any productive Darwinian payoff in terms of effective state building should surely not be expected in the short and medium run. A certain outcome, by contrast, would be a much larger number of collapsed states. Given the substantial human cost of current state failures, such a development would definitely involve extremely high human cost.

If the war option is neither realistic nor desirable, are there more productive ways of recreating external threat in ways that can promise rapid effective state building and less human cost? A number of different proposals have been put forward; they include changing the rules of secession, making the formation of new states easier; the decertification of states by the international community, that is, highly ineffective states should then 'no longer be considered as sovereign' (Herbst 1996–97:142); and circumventing sovereignty by giving aid to regions instead of to states, thereby making a connection to precolonial African conceptions of overlapping jurisdictions not based on control of territory but on power over people (Herbst 1996–97).[15] These proposals attempt to evade the 'slavish devotion to the sovereignty of existing states' (Herbst in Joseph and Herbst 1997:182) that characterizes present practices of the international community; for the time being such evasion appears unlikely, but in the present context the speculation about them is relevant anyway.

To simplify, let me focus on secession. The suggestion is that better possibilities for secession would lead to a larger number of viable states better capable of protecting and providing other political goods for their populations. Who should be allowed to secede? At present, for example, there are evolving secession conflicts in the following weak states in Sub-Saharan Africa: Somalia, Ethiopia, Senegal, Cameroun, Angola, Sudan, and Congo. Which of these cases should benefit from a policy change? Sceptics argue that secession most often will create more problems than it solves. Both in the former Soviet Union and in ex-Yugoslavia, secession has been accompanied by massive acts of so-called 'ethnic cleansing' (Bennett 1995). In Sub-Saharan Africa, the human cost would probably be even higher. The question is also where to stop; which groups should be allowed to create new states following which specific criteria? A recent study on state collapse in Africa is very cautious on this point:

> except for the current case of Ethiopia, there is not a case in this book for which a change in boundaries or secession of a territory is a necessary condition of state restitution. Moreover, even in those cases where secession has been posed as a possibility... the potentially seceding members are likely to be worse off and the remaining core no better off as a result... The logic of secession works against seceding states, threatening an infinite regress of self-determination.
>
> (Zartman 1995b:268)

It appears to be a genuine dilemma: the old borders are holding together groups that fight against each other because they cannot agree on forming a political community. The result is insecurity and underdevelopment. Splitting them up appears to create more problems than it solves; they cannot stay together and they cannot split up. The very different views on the possible benefits of secession are tied to different calculations concerning short term as well as long terms benefits of the undertaking. Proponents are rather optimistic, opponents very pessimistic. One way of addressing the dilemma would be to favour secession in cases where the benefits are clearly deemed to outweigh the cost, and to reject secession in other cases. That would appear to speak more in favour of independence for Somaliland than for the other cases mentioned above. At the same time, even such moderate changes would increase the incentives for potentially seceding groups to seek control of their own state because of the potential benefits of such control (Bartkus 1999:206–15); that in turn, will spur violent domestic conflict perhaps to the extent of requiring a new basis for the calculation of costs and benefits of secession.

The considerations in this section demonstrate how difficult it is to increase external pressure on postcolonial state elites in a way which will both (a) avoid excessive human cost and (b) lead to the creation of effective states with capacities for delivering security and other political goods to their citizens. In contrast, consider a case where external pressure has worked well: Taiwan under Guomindang rule. In mainland China, and even on Taiwan between 1945 and 1947, Guomindang rule had every attribute of the archetypical predatory state; it was violently repressive, inept, reactionary, and corrupt. Yet it turned around in a surprisingly short time and began seriously promoting economic development on Taiwan (Gold 1986; Sørensen 1991a).

External pressure was a vital factor in this process. Jiang Kaishek emerged from the utter humiliation of defeat by the communists with the realization that for the Guomindang Nationalists to stand up to the communists and even entertain the idea of reconquering the mainland, a solid basis had to be built on Taiwan; 'the party had to be fundamentally cleansed and the people of Taiwan given an incentive to support it' (Gold 1986:57).[16] Another kind of external pressure came from the United States. During his last years on the mainland, the Americans had propped up Jiang with increasing disgust; now they demanded an efficient state machinery and structural reforms pushing economic and social development on Taiwan in return for their continued military and economic support. These demands were followed up by a very substantial constructive engagement on Taiwan, both economically and otherwise (Jacoby 1966).

The contrast to present-day weak states is clear: (a) there is no comparable external pressure from a significant power; (b) there is no comparable external pressure in the form of a high level of constructive engagement from donors. Both of these missing elements derive from the same source: the lack of substantial interest, negative or positive, on the side of capable, developed countries to get involved with the weak postcolonial states. In short: these countries are not interested taking over the weak ones; neither are they interested in providing substantial resources to help their development – aid as a percentage of GNP is at around 0.3 per cent for OECD countries.[17]

Seen from the leading, substantial states in the system, the strong international norms upholding the existing borders of weak states acquire a different import; they are the containment barriers behind which problems of violent conflict, disintegration, and fragmentation are held in check, if not always completely then at least sufficiently to avoid serious threats to the international order. Unfortunately, that same barrier continues to be an insecurity container for very large groups of postcolonial peoples.

## Conclusion

This chapter has identified the peculiar security dilemma in weak, postcolonial states and analysed it in detail. Postcolonial states display highly unusual features compared with modern states and that makes for a radically different security dilemma. State elites in weak postcolonial states are not facing severe external threat. Such states can collapse completely and still retain formal membership of the society of states. Weak states and regimes are protected by strong international norms, backed by the great powers.

Given the lack of external and internal constraint, state elites often chose to pursue their own narrow interests. That led to the creation of state structures which provided insecurity instead of security for very large groups of people. International society's attempt to address these problems began in earnest in the 1980s and were further expanded during the 1990s. Economic and later political conditionalities were aimed at disciplining state elites with the intention of creating more effective and responsive forms of governance. But because such efforts cannot succeed without domestic allies, the incumbent elite, as the most powerful group in society, has substantial possibilities of influencing the bargains made with insiders. State elites have been clever to adjust to new economic and political demands while holding on to their power positions. The spin-offs in terms of increased security for the populations have been miserably inadequate.

Nor has the setting aside of the non-intervention norm in context of addressing state collapse or failure produced significant improvements in human or popular security in weak states. A combination of operational problems, non-humanitarian considerations, and the fact that humanitarian intervention must always take place after and not before serious security problems have emerged, explain why that is the case. Several scholars have reacted by producing proposals that attempt to go beyond sovereignty or at least advance the formation of more effective states. It was demonstrated that there are no simple ways of introducing external threat in ways that will avoid excessive human cost and – with any great certainty – lead to the creation of such improved states. Apart from a number of special cases, the developed Northern states are not terribly interested in getting involved in the weak, postcolonial states. The lack of involvement reflects the logic of sovereignty: take care of your own people. Denmark, for example, takes pride in spending more than one per cent of its GNP on development aid, because that is much more than most other countries spend; but it is nowhere near the resources spent on internal redistribution from the Danish rich to the Danish poor which amounts to some 30 per cent of GNP or more than a hundred times the OECD average spent on external aid. The sovereign state first and foremost takes care of itself; that means there must be some perceived national interest if the 'less than one per cent'-logic is going to be set aside. Such interest is rarely present when it comes to dealing with weak, postcolonial states.

The claim made here is by no means that state building and development cannot happen in weak states. The measures taken by the international society during the 1980s and 1990s have not been useless. There has been some social development progress in weak states during this period (Gaile and Ferguson 1996). Some states which looked as classical candidates for weak statehood have done rather well, including Botswana and Mauritius (Carroll and Carroll 1997). The claim made here, by contrast, is that development and state building does not always happen; it requires certain preconditions, domestic and international. Given the present domestic and international situation of many weak states, such preconditions are not easily produced. In other words, domestic popular insecurity, often combined with perennial threat of violent domestic conflict, will continue to characterize a large number of weak, postcolonial states. The measures taken by international society are bound to be constrained in such a way that they are not capable of effectively addressing the problem.

There are many defenders of the status quo: in several ways, the sovereign border is convenient for state elites on both sides of it: seen from the outside, it helps contain desperate problems of security and development; seen from the inside, it helps provide resources and autonomy to incumbents. But seen from the people in weak states it often provides insecurity rather than security. Good intentions to the contrary notwithstanding, dramatic change to the better in that regard is not likely.

This examination of the peculiar security dilemma of postcolonial states emphasizes how the specific features of postcolonial statehood creates a distinctive security dilemma. An analysis focusing only on states as 'like units' would miss out entirely on the conspicuous characteristics of postcolonial statehood and its associated security dilemma. It is not be possible fully to comprehend 'international' relations without reference to different types of state. The distinct sovereignty game tied to postcolonial statehood will be addressed in Chapter 10; the implications for international theory of postcolonial (and postmodern) statehood is the subject of Chapter 11.

# 9
# Postmodern States: from Security Dilemma towards Challenges to Effective Governance

Focus in this chapter is on postmodern states. The traditional security dilemma has been overcome in the sense that large-scale violent conflict between postmodern states is out of the question. The standard neorealist picture of states in a Hobbesian anarchy no longer applies to the relations between postmodern states. The alternative image suggested here draws on the liberal tradition in general and the work of Karl Deutsch in particular; postmodern states, it is argued, are members of a coordinated security community. Consequently, external military threat from each other is no longer a worry of postmodern states. In security terms this is most certainly a huge accomplishment, because the major threat to the physical safety of postmodern countries and populations has been removed.

What has emerged instead are a number of different challenges to effective governance that spring from the distinct features of postmodern statehood. These challenges are related, not to traditional security, but to other aspects of the political goods that capable states are expected to supply: order, justice, welfare, and freedom. They are connected to the fact that the framework for the state's provision of political goods to its citizens is substantially transformed in postmodern states. That transformation concerns the levels of economy and government, as well as the level of nationhood and identity.

The economic cohesion of postmodern states has been significantly reduced compared to modern states, because postmodern economies are not neatly segregated along national–territorial lines. That creates two new issues concerning economic security. The first concerns the identification of the relevant object that is being threatened; if it is no longer the national economy, what is it? The second problem concerns the supply of welfare, the political good most directly related to the economy.

Political cohesion has been reduced as well in postmodern states. When multilevel governance is established, the protection of the political institutions of the state is logically no longer a concern of threat to purely national institutions, because the relevant organizations are found at different levels, including supranational ones. Three issues emerge as a result. First, what is the object of threats to political institutions? Second, how is the political good of effective governance supplied in the new context? And third, what are the consequences for democratic participation and legitimacy?

Finally, the changes in nationhood and identity raise the issue of threats against the 'idea of the state' (Buzan 1991:69) in a new way. When identities develop in ways that challenge the cohesion between the state and the nation, the strengthening of such identities may weaken rather than strengthen the idea of the state.

In sum, the traditional security dilemma has, to a considerable extent, been replaced by governance challenges concerning the effective supply of the political goods of the 'good life', that is, order, justice, welfare, and freedom. Important as these challenges are, they should not detract from the fact that postmodern statehood offers an unprecedented opportunity for peace and cooperation towards mutual benefit.

## Out of raw anarchy: a coordinated security community

The basic features of the postmodern ideal type of state as set forth in Chapter 6 are the following:

| | |
|---|---|
| Government | Multilevel governance, based on supranational, national, and subnational institutions. |
| Nationhood | Supranational and international institutions are sources of citizenship rights. Collective identity also tied to levels above and below the nation. |
| Economy | Major part of economic activity embedded in cross-border networks. 'National' economy much less self-sustained. |

The notion of perennial danger of war between states stems from the observation that sovereign states exist in a condition of anarchy. As observed in Chapter 7, according to the Hobbesian logic the creation of sovereign states provided domestic hierarchy that created order; but the consequence was that the domestic anarchy of the state of nature was moved to the international level. That is the basis for the well-known realist dynamic of states as self-help systems creating security dilemmas and balances of power that may lead to war.

Against the background of postmodern statehood the realist premise of anarchy as lack of government is put into question. The relations between postmodern states involve elements of legitimate and effective international and supranational authority, as exemplified in Chapter 6. The development of governance structures in context of postmodern statehood thus creates a significant measure of order and government in the relations between postmodern states. A case can be made that postmodern states have incorporated those elements of order and government in their 'national' identities.[1] To the extent that is the case, 'national' interests have themselves been changed under the influence of the substantial changes from modern to postmodern statehood.[2] In short, the combined development of various forms of governance structures and changes in interests mean a move away from Hobbesian ('raw') anarchy.

These developments are underscored by the changes in the economic sphere.[3] The conventional neorealist view is that states may well be economically interdependent, but they continue to basically take care of themselves economically. And they strive to keep it that way: 'Nations pull apart as each of them tries to take care of itself and to avoid becoming dependent on others' (Waltz 1979:143). In context of postmodern statehood that view is misleading. Under present conditions, growth and welfare requires participation in economic globalization.[4] During the formation of modern states, national markets were created from more localized economic contexts. Economic globalization in turn, creates a new economic framework, on a transnational level.[5]

The transformation of relations between postmodern states has created what will be called a coordinated security community. Deutsch and his collaborators defined a security community as 'a group of people which has be come 'integrated'. By integration we mean the attainment, within a territory, of a 'sense of community' and of institutions and practices strong enough and widespread enough to assure, for a 'long' time, dependable expectations of 'peaceful change' among its population' (Deutsch *et al.* 1957:5). Two types of security communities were identified by Deutsch: 'pluralistic' which 'retains the legal independence of separate governments'; and 'amalgamated' with 'a formal merger of two or more previously independent units into a single larger unit, with some type of common government' (Deutsch *et al.* 1957:6). The security community among postmodern states is not amalgamated, but it is not pluralistic either, because multilevel governance has created some measure of common government, thus the label of 'coordinated security community'.[6]

Seen from the viewpoint of liberal theory, the coordinated security community is based on four main elements of liberalism: republican liberalism, institutional liberalism, interdependence liberalism, and sociological liberalism (Zacher and Matthew 1995). The republican element builds on the fact that the members of the community are consolidated liberal democracies (Sørensen 1992); the institutional element is based on the dense network of institutions facilitating cooperation (Keohane and Hoffman (eds) 1993); the interdependence element is the high level of economic interdependence and general interconnectedness across states and societies (Keohane 1995); the sociological element emerges from the transnational networks of a variety of substate actors (Risse-Kappen (ed.) 1995; Deudney and Ikenberry 1999).[7]

There is no precise empirical overlap between these different elements. The institutional network within the EU is more developed in scope and depth than other networks, so are economic connections; relations between America and Europe are more institutionalized than relations between these areas and Japan; some countries may be part of most of the institutional and economic networks without being fully consolidated liberal democracies (for example, Turkey); other countries are consolidated democracies without being fully integrated in the institutional networks (for example, Switzerland). The coordinated security community of postmodern states, in other words, is blurred at the edges, because the aspects of postmodern statehood have been developed to different extents in various countries. The inner circle is EU-Europe, followed by Western Europe and Western Europe/North America, and Western Europe/North America/Japan. The outer circle is the 29 members of the OECD with some of the recent members (Mexico, South Korea) as borderline cases. The present argument is of course most applicable to the inner circles.

These reflections leave one important question unanswered: what are the minimum requirements for the emergence of a coordinated security community? The question is not easily answered and Deutsch was not at all clear about the necessary and sufficient conditions for security communities. It is clear that the postmodern coordinated security community is overdetermined, simply because 'all good things' tend to go together: consolidated democracy; dense networks of cross-national institutions; integrated economic structures; common values and outlooks; and so on. Consequently, it is difficult to say how much regress that could take place on one or several of these dimensions for the coordinated security community to be endangered. That important question cannot be pursued here[8] where focus is on identifying the specific features of the security dilemma in postmodern states.

So far, it has been established that postmodern states are not concerned with external military threat from each other. Elements of the conventional security dilemma are still in place, however, because postmodern states may be exposed to conventional security threats from modern states, or from turmoil in weak, postcolonial states. In the present context, however, I am interested in the new challenges connected with postmodern statehood. If it is not external military threat, what is it? The first part of an answer concerns the changed structure of the economy and the provision of economic well-being.

## Challenges to the economy in postmodern states

For the modern state is was reasonably straightforward to define economic strength and economic security. This state is based on a national economy;

because such an economy is not autarkic, it needs external access to inputs and markets. When such access is attained there is economic security. A conventional definition of economic security thus runs as follows: 'access to the resources, finance and markets necessary to sustain acceptable levels of welfare and state power' (Buzan 1991:19).[9] In the case of postmodern states with economies less 'national' and much more integrated in cross-border networks, the definition of economic security is more troublesome. The reason is mainly that economic globalization underscores the tension between vulnerability and efficiency hich is at the core of all areas of economic security (Buzan 1991:237). When 'national' economies are integrated to an extent where opting out of the world market is no longer a viable option, there must be substantially higher vulnerability.

At the same time, that vulnerability cannot easily be managed by traditional mercantilist strategies of increasing the state's economic strength, for two reasons. First, in a globalized economy, there is no simple relationship between measures favouring the 'national' economy on the one hand and 'national' economic strength on the other. That is because the 'national' producers may very well be foreign firms, and the 'outsiders' may be 'national' companies.[10] Second, the effectiveness of traditional instruments to defend the national economy, including trade policies and measures concerning regulation of financial activities, are significantly reduced.[11] In so far as national economic autonomy is no longer a viable option because the level of economic welfare and economic strength depends on continued successful economic integration across borders, there must be a corresponding shift in the object economic security, away from the purely 'national' economy, towards the regional/global economic framework in which the so-called 'national' economy is now irrevocably embedded. To the extent that is the case, the basis for talking meaningfully about strong states in the economic sense has undergone definite change.[12]

Such qualitative changes take place over an extended period of time and even if postmodern countries have moved in this direction, there is great variation between them. The discussion here will proceed in more general terms, addressing the governance of the OECD economies during the postwar period in the context of looking after economic security. What are the new challenges in the economic sector, compared to earlier, when these countries were modern rather than postmodern?

The problem in 1945 was the establishment of a multilateral system which avoided the protectionist unilateralism of the 1930s while at the same time giving countries political space for setting up stable social welfare systems at home. The Bretton Woods system accomplished that task. It created embedded liberalism: economic liberalization in relation to other countries combined with social cushioning provided by interventionist governments at home (Ruggie 1982). For quite some time, national systems of economic welfare and management could be combined with a liberalized international system which fostered more intense economic integration between countries. The promotion of global markets, cultivated by liberalization of regulations, has undoubtedly created benefits for both public and private economic actors. But the new, economically integrated context posed a number of challenges to traditional instruments of economic policy. A basic precondition for effective governance severely challenged by globalization is the overlap between the territorial reach of political regulations and the socioeconomic space at which these regulations are aimed. In due course the very process of globalization to which the embedded liberalism compromise opened up reached a level where the territorially limited governance instruments of 'national' economic security that were the other main aspect of embedded liberalism were themselves undermined.

Arguably, that undermining concerns all the main areas of state activity in economic affairs, as emphasized by Phil Cerny (1995). His analysis singles out three such areas: (1) the provision of a 'market framework' such as property rights, a stable currency system and a legal framework for economic activity; (2) industrial policies, including subsidies and infrastructural support for private firms; and (3) welfare procurements or economic redistribution. The 'market framework' is affected because counterfeiting, copyright violations, transnational capital flows, tax havens, and intra-firm trade undermine property rights; the currency system is challenged by the global financial market where currency and interest rates are increasingly difficult to place under political control. Industrial policies are affected because they can no longer discriminate between national and foreign firms; the option is one of providing an environment basically conducive to private companies, whether they are of foreign or domestic origin. Welfare procurements and high social standards are undercut by the improved exit opportunities of firms; this also entails negative affects on employment and salary levels (Cerny 1995:608–12).[13]

The embeddedness of states in a globalized economic context creates a pressure towards policy measures acceptable to the markets. Some scholars find that the state then becomes a 'residual state' or a 'competition state', whose effective action is restricted to providing 'a relatively favourable investment climate for transnational capital' (Cerny 1995:611; also Ruggie 1997; Zürn 1999; Strange 1996). This does not mean that states are left powerless (cf. Sørensen 2000), but there are higher incentives to pursue such policies, because insulation from the market has become more costly. These developments may in turn challenge the states' provision of the welfare aspect of economic security. Economic inequality has risen sharply, both within and between countries in context of globalization (UNDP 1999).[14]

The 'state power' aspect of economic security is also challenged by the new framework of globalization. The key industries that provide for the state's defences also participate in the process of globalization. Analysing the European experience in this area, Theodore Moran drew the following main conclusions:

> First, there are dangers hidden in the global nature of industries crucial for the functioning of modern nation-states that pose unacceptable risk to those states, even in peacetime relations among allies. It is not prudent to dismiss the problem of industrial dependency as the liberal economic tradition is wont to do, by advocating that governments simply allow markets to work. Second, the threat of foreign control...cannot be remedied merely by establishing national companies or insisting on local production by foreigners...Third, the impulse to self-sufficient autarky...carries its own perils not only in terms of higher cost, fewer units, and delayed deployment, but also from being locked into performance unacceptable for national security requirements.[15]

In sum, the context for economic security is significantly different under conditions of postmodern statehood. While economic globalization creates significant opportunities for gains in growth and welfare, there are also new challenges. First, intense economic globalization opens up the issue of what the object of economic security really is. If previously national economies are now permanently integrated in a larger economic space upon which they crucially depend for their growth and prosperity, it can be argued that the object of economic security is that larger economic space and not merely the national slice of it.[16] Second, the governance measures related both to the provision of the 'growth and welfare' aspect and to the 'state power' aspect of economic security are challenged because territorially limited regulations can not effectively cover the relevant, larger socioeconomic space. One important consequence of this is increased demand for international cooperation.[17] In that way, states attempt to compensate the decreased ability to autonomously control activity within their own borders with an increased capability of regulation at the regional/international level. The new problems emerging in that situation are addressed in the next section.

## Challenges to the polity in postmodern states

Multilevel governance creates a new context for politics. This is most easily observed in the case where such governance is most developed: the EU. For a number of reasons explained earlier, Member States cooperate in order to obtain regulative powers they would not otherwise have had. Intense cooperation creates a supranational level of governance where – in a number of areas – a majority of states or supranational institutions can define rules applicable to all Member States. This goes squarely against the standard way of protecting the state: fend off any outside interference. Outside interference is the logical consequence of multilevel governance: states allow other states a measure of influence on (some of) their domestic affairs – in return, of course, they achieve a measure of influence on (some of) the domestic affairs of other states. These developments are not easily grasped through the standard definition of political security which emphasizes 'the organizational stability of states, systems of government and the ideologies that give them legitimacy' (Buzan, 1991:19). Multilevel governance, by contrast, indicates that the organizational stability of states, indeed their whole system of government, is undergoing significant transformation.

What can then be the meaning of political security in the new context? One way of making sense of these developments is to see them as containing a change in the objects of (political) security. National security comes to include a supranational level of governance, because such a level is now part of the system of government and the political institutions that characterize Member States. The consequences of this are potentially dramatic, because a shift from anarchy to governance implies that 'the entire framework of the security problematique would have to be redefined' (Buzan 1991:23). What the final outcome will be of such redefinition remains unclear. In the case of the EU, Member States did commit themselves to more cooperation in foreign affairs in context of the Maastricht treaty and in the Amsterdam treaty of 1997 the EU Council Secretary-General was given the additional charge of 'High Representative for the common foreign and security policy'.[18] But foreign policy and defence continues to basically remain under control of the single Member States. Compared to classical modern statehood, postmodern countries are in a permanent 'in-between' situation: they are not autonomous 'self-help' entities, but they are not integrated parts of a federal state either. The definition of 'national security' in that situation remains troublesome.[19]

In short, the notion of (a) what is state strength in the political sector? and (b) how is it defended? has changed away from its earlier straightforward content to something more complex. The standard definition of political security no longer applies; a new operational definition of political security in a context which clearly includes multilevel governance is only in the process of emerging.

The core of politics arguably concerns the provision of the political goods deriving from effective governance. To which extent is such provision possible under the conditions of postmodern statehood? It was established earlier that postmodern states are not concerned with external military threats from each other. But in the context of postmodern statehood a number of different threats have emerged. They are linked to the fact that postmodern societies are densely interconnected, not merely with each other, but also with other countries. That is to say, postmodern countries are embedded in a globalized social context;

that creates a globalized risk environment, in which risks are 'largely without boundaries, not limited in space, and because they are also likely to affect future generations, not limitable in time either' (Lash 1993; Lash and Urry 1994). An influential sociological analysis has termed this state of affairs 'Risk society' (Beck 1992), indicating that sovereign borders provide little in terms of effective protection in the new environment. Social problems and risks emerging from single societies can therefore quickly be transmitted to other societies. Disease, pollution, terror, ecological imbalances, crime, drugs, migration, and economic crisis are relevant examples. Effective governance under these conditions is the ability to manage this complex risk environment.

Are postmodern states capable of effectively confronting this challenge? On the one hand, it can be argued that states and individuals not only face a new and more complex set of risks; they also have within reach a new and wide-ranging set of opportunities. People are better educated than ever; individuals and institutions have access to highly effective means of communication, of storage and dissemination of information, and of all varieties of expert systems. The possibilities for effective monitoring and action are unquestionably better than ever. In short, new risks are more than matched by new opportunities.

On the other hand, it has already been indicated that the conventional governance instruments of economic security are being increasingly ineffective under the new conditions. Maybe current instruments of governance are relatively ineffective in other areas as well? Susan Strange has argued that the current system of sovereign states is a 'Westfailure' system because of its demonstrated inability to 'satisfy the long term conditions of its sustainability'. Three such conditions are identified in her analysis: environmental damage ('that threaten[s] the survival of not only our own but other species of animals and plants'); financial infrastructure ('the institutions and markets that create and trade the credit instruments essential to the "real economy"'); and social inequality ('between the constantly growing power of the...transnational capitalist class and that of the "have-nots", the social underclasses...immigrants, unemployed, refugees, peasants...') (Strange 1999:346). The implicit core of Strange's argument is that government organized along the lines of sovereign statehood is increasingly ineffective and has not been replaced by any capable system of governance at the supranational level in any of the three areas. It is not necessary to agree with everything in this analysis[20] in order to accept its main thrust: that government organized primarily along national lines faces new and serious challenges in a globalized world, challenges to which effective responses have not yet been found.

Another way of putting this is to say that the multilateral governance of the Bretton Woods embedded liberalism system is no longer effective and that no new, effective system has taken its place. In other words, there is multilevel governance but it is too limited in content and geographical scope. In that sense, a new version of the 1945 problematique is on the agenda: how to devise compatible forms of international liberalization and domestic stability (Ruggie 1997)? If such a new social compact is direly needed as a part of effective governance under new conditions, why is it not forthcoming? In order to answer that question a number of basic differences between 1945 and today should be appreciated. First, the number of players has increased dramatically. The old system of embedded liberalism was for the West only and by the West; the South and the East did not play any important role. Today, there are a large number of players with very different interests and at very different levels of development. Second, there are a larger number of relevant issues to address, including economic, social, and environmental affairs; that is, the agenda is much more complex. Third, the United States is much less interested in taking the lead than she was in 1945. Back then, effective multilateralism was extremely high on the American agenda. Today, the US appears more inclined to regionalism, bilateralism, or even unilateralism. And neither the EU nor Japan are strongly in favour of a genuine multilateralism. In short, multilateralism is needed in the face of the challenges of globalization and postmodern statehood, but it has no strong enforcer. Fourth, even if leading states were more willing to take initiatives, they have arguably lost power to the leading economic players in the marketplace, as recorded earlier. Fifth, there is no real agreement on the content of multilateralism. Embedded liberalism in 1945 made room for the free market as well as for the interventionist welfare state. How to strike such a combination today? To the extent that we know it, liberal free marketeers, social democrats, and mercantilist conservatives certainly cannot agree on how to put it together. Sixth, it can be questioned whether the proper institutional framework for an effective multilateral governance is in place. There are no international institutions in the economic, social, and environmental fields of governance which can compare with the institutions in the security field proper, including the UN Security Council and NATO. There has been much talk about creating a UN Economic Security Council, about a strengthening of G7/G8, and about new possible roles for the OECD, but so far little has changed.[21]

In sum, effective governance under postmodern conditions faces a number of challenges to which clear responses have not been formulated so far. In the meantime, to the extent governance of the globalized realm is taking place, it happens primarily in two ways: the first is 'bottom-up' multilateralism in the form of various regional arrangements, of which the EU stands out as the most ambitious attempt. That may be effective regionally but it does not solve the governance problem for the larger context. What dominate here are much less stringent patchwork forms of 'global legal pluralism'[22] or networks of 'transgovernmentalism'[23] combined with scattered attempts by existing international institutions to create regimes in various issue-areas. It is by no means certain that effective governance will be the result of those processes.

The final aspect of politics under postmodern conditions to be addressed here concerns the legitimacy of governance and the democratic link between rulers and ruled. The problem is relevant here because the democratic legitimacy of government provides a solution to the Hobbesian dilemma discussed in Chapter 7. In the absence of democratic government, the link between the actions of the state and the general well-being of the population can be weakened or even severed.

Postmodern statehood challenges two fundamental assumptions of mainstream democratic theory. The first concerns the overlap between the political community of citizens within a defined territory on the one hand and the group of people affected by the political decisions taken by those citizens' representatives on the other.[24] The second concerns the room of manoeuvre of the sovereign, democratic state; the assumption is that such states enjoy a high degree of national autonomy, allowing them to a large extent to be in control of their own future (Held 1991:201). The first assumption is challenged because a large number of 'national' decisions in one state has significant implications for citizens of other states in context of postmodern statehood. The second assumption is challenged because economic and other integration significantly narrows the policy options in individual states; several examples to that effect have been given above.

In other words, postmodern states have a problem with democracy because their political systems are constructed on the basis of modern statehood on core assumptions that do not apply to postmodern statehood. In so far as reverting to modern statehood is not a feasible option, new solutions have to be found. The most elaborate suggestion in this regard is probably the model for multilevel governance in the form of 'cosmopolitan democracy' set forth by David Held (Held 1995). But such models require far-reaching changes in the structure of international governance. So far, the most elaborate model of multilevel governance is the EU; does that model solve the democracy problem in context of postmodern statehood? Most observers agree that it does not, because the system contains serious deficiencies seen from a democratic point of view. They concern three major areas (Corydon 2000:8): first, the question of proper, balanced representation of *demos* in the supranational institutions; second, the degree of ultimate control by *demos* over the decisionmaking of those institutions; and finally, there is the question of a (lacking) democratic, political community at the transnational level. The problems in these areas are the basis for talking about a 'democratic deficit' in the EU; these problems are briefly discussed in what follows.

In a broad sense, the democratic deficit of the EU means that powers of rulemaking and rule adjudication are moved away from the national context to a supranational level which has no 'widely legitimated constitutional framework' (Marks *et al.* 1995:41). The problems of representation are reflected in the (limited) roles played by national parliaments on the one hand and the European Parliament on the other, compared to the powers of the Commission, the European Council and the Councils of Ministers on the other (Dinan 1994:228). If political elites are considered strategic actors seeking maximum autonomy for themselves, this problem is exacerbated. In the national, democratic polity, such autonomy is severely constrained by domestic groups; by pushing more decisions and influence upwards towards the supranational level, political elites can enhance their autonomy from domestic actors, especially when the supranational realm is not constrained by developed democratic structures.[25] To the extent this is a valid line of reasoning, the liberal solution to the Hobbesian problem identified in Chapter 7 is severely weakened in the new context of multilevel governance.[26]

The problems of control by the *demos* is heightened because the sheer number and complexity of cases on the tables of elected representatives compels them to relinquish increased powers to the Commission and especially to the administrative Council of Permanent Representatives (Coreper). In effect, very substantial portions of what later becomes national law and regulations is made up in close bureaucratic circles outside any significant democratic control.

The problem of political community refers to the lack a developed transnational sphere of public debate and the formation of public political opinion. Habermas has analysed the importance of such a sphere for the development of democracy in context of the sovereign state; that process of creating political community must now be repeated on a supranational level. The future of Europe, says Habermas, must be discussed 'throughout Europe in interlinked public spheres; that, is, the same issues must be discussed at the same time, so as to foster the emergence of a European civil society with its interest groups, non-governmental organizations, civic initiatives, and so forth'. (Habermas 1999:58). This will take time; it will require school systems that provide a 'common grounding in foreign languages' (*loc. cit.*), and the construction of a European party system.[27]

But the EU has also improved democracy in a basic respect. Regional processes of development have been brought under political control; seen from the single state that means an increasing scope of democracy. There are new possibilities for harnessing external influences over which states and societies had little control earlier. Furthermore, the three problems mentioned above can be seen as temporary obstacles that can be overcome, just as national obstacles were overcome in the development of democracy in the national realm. On balance, supranational cooperation creates new constraints on democracy, but is also opens new possibilities. At the present time, it is the constraints that stand out; therefore the debate about a democratic deficit. Yet several observers are optimistic that the problems can be successfully confronted (Zürn 1998).

These remarks on politics and governance can be summarized as follows: first, postmodern statehood requires a redefinition of political security which addresses the core questions of what is state strength in the political sector and how is such strength defended? The old definition of political security emphasized the organizational stability of states. But postmodern statehood requires anything but stability; it calls for far-reaching transformation of existing (national) systems of governance. The exact meaning of political security in the new context has not been precisely spelled out so far. Second, postmodern statehood creates new problems for the effective provision of political goods. The close interconnection of postmodern societies creates a new, globalized risk environment. Six reasons were given above, why it is difficult to provide effective governance in response to these new challenges. Finally, postmodern statehood means that basic preconditions for a democratic polity as spelled out by mainstream democratic theory are no longer in place. That creates a democratic deficit problem which is exacerbated if political–administrative elites are seen as strategic actors seeking maximum autonomy. In sum, the meaning of political security, the provision of effective governance, and the democratic link between rulers and ruled are all challenged in the new context. There are presently no clear and definite answers as to how these issues are confronted under conditions of postmodern statehood.

## Challenges to nationhood and identity in postmodern states

It was emphasized in Chapter 6 that the modern state is characterized by a high level of cohesion; nation and state is bound together by a set of rights and obligations. Community, legitimacy, and solidarity are important aspects of this relationship. A high level of cohesion thus means that there is a strong sense of national identity which in turn strengthens what Barry Buzan calls the idea of the state (Buzan 1991:69–82). That is, state strength derives in large measure from legitimacy; legitimacy, in turn, requires a strong national identity. The term 'national security' itself points directly to the nation; the term would not make much sense if it did not refer to a group of people sharing a strong national identity.[28]

Collective identities change in the context of postmodern statehood. Increasingly, they are also tied to levels above and below the nation. What does postmodern statehood mean for national identity and cohesion and what are the implications for the strength of the state?[29]

It should be noted right away that different collective identities need not be mutually exclusive. It is clear that people living in closely interconnected societies are exposed to a large number of possible systems and symbols of identification and that they can take on a number of them simultaneously. A local identity (Munich), a regional identity (Bavaria), a national identity

(Germany), a supranational identity (Europe), and a global identity as a world citizen can coexist in the same person; and they can be combined with an additional number of religious, sexual, and class identities. At the same time, the very process of identity creation involves emphasizing some symbols and values at the expense of others. People are not Protestants and Buddhists at the same time; and when they are Danes and Europeans, they have ideas about the extent to which they are what. As sociologists have noted, the interconnected plurality of postmodern statehood be no means eradicates difference; it rather invites a much more individualized and sophisticated construction of personal identities (Giddens 1990; Jameson 1991). Globalization involves a process of breaking up the 'traditional link between "physical setting" and "social situation"' (Held 1995:23). As a consequence, identities are no longer firmly embedded in 'particular times, places and traditions' (Held 1995:124).

In this complex landscape, there appears to be two different main tendencies concerning collective identities under postmodern conditions. One could be labelled integrative; the other fragmenting. The former is an expression of how the perception of identity changes in an integrating direction, in an interplay with the changes taking place on the political and economic levels. There has developed a common 'civic identity' (Deudney and Ikenberry 1999:192–5) among the populations of postmodern states which is cohesive in the sense that it supports a number of core values and norms, including constitutional government, political democracy, civil and political liberties, human rights, and a liberal market economy supervised by the state. In context of these values, elements of a transnational civil society is in the process of emerging, facilitated by improved means of communication and exchange. Some of the most successful organizations, including Amnesty International and Greenpeace, derive great strength from addressing on a global level the promotion of common core values, such as human rights and environmental safety. Educational exchange, travel, political and economic cooperation, and a host of other factors help create support for a common value system. An important element in this context is the growth of a popular mass culture based on 'the commonality of commodities and consumption practices' (Deudney and Ikenberry 1999:193; Featherstone (ed.) 1990).

The other main tendency is fragmenting. Ironically, it is in part directly connected with the unifying elements of mass culture just mentioned. The levelling-out of difference also helps create a demand for further emphasizing difference, what Freud called 'the narcissism of the tiny dissimilarity' (Zürn 1998:269; Beck 1993:121–2; Hassner 1993:131). Such psychological tendencies are easily reinforced in context of a process of uneven globalization. That process is bound to create winners and losers. Unskilled, less educated groups at the lower rungs of the social ladder are poorly prepared to face the challenges of a 'Risk society'. They may be further pressured by the competition from larger groups of immigrants. Outbursts of violence in urban riots or the growth of right-radical movements which emphasize a much more exclusive definition of 'community' and 'nation' are two well-known consequences of these developments (Horsman and Marshall 1995:172–83). A part of this picture is the declining effectiveness of national governance discussed above.[30]

A different aspect of the fragmenting tendency concerns the demands for regional autonomy in Canada (the Quebecois), Britain (Scotland, Wales), Belgium (the Flemish) and elsewhere. In economic terms, these regional areas may be winning or losing; the common element is that they experience uneven development compared with the country of which they are a part. This is then combined with the cultural tendency mentioned earlier, to emphasize difference (Anderson 1994:11). Furthermore, regional groups in Europe now have new possibilities for linking up directly with a supranational centre ('Scotland in Europe'); to the extent that such groups find that they enjoy too little autonomy within their nation-states, this may appear to be the more attractive arrangement.[31]

Both the integrative and the fragmenting tendencies identified here demonstrate that collective identities may very well be strengthened under postmodern conditions in ways which go against rather than support the state.[32] As for the integrative tendencies, the development of a civic identity does entail increasing adherence to common values; but the very process behind this creation is also an expression of more autonomous and self-assertive individuals whose complete loyalties to states can no longer be taken for granted. This is the point made in a series of analyses by James Rosenau (1990; 1993; 1997). He argues that individuals have greatly extended their activities owing to better education and access to electronic means of communication as well as foreign travel. Furthermore, states' capacity for control and regulation is decreasing in an ever more complex world. The consequence is a world of better-informed and more mobile individuals who are far less tied than before to 'their' states. Rosenau thus sees a profound transformation of the international system that is underway: the state-centric, anarchic system has not disappeared but a new 'multi-centric world has emerged that is composed of diverse "sovereignty-free" collectivities which exist apart from and in competition with the state-centric world of "sovereignty-bound" actors' (Rosenau 1993:282).

The point to be made here is a bit less dramatic: the strengthening of collective identities need not strengthen the idea of the state. This holds true for the fragmenting tendencies as well. The whole idea behind the regionalist movements is a disengagement from the state; in the case of right-radical movements they most often tend to develop defensive-nationalist strategies which seek exclusion from social, political, and economic networks of integration and cooperation.[33] In a postmodern context, this creates severe divisions towards those groups that vie for more, not less, supranational integration. In effect, the group that is the nation is increasingly divided among itself.

These brief remarks can be drawn together as follows: in the modern state, the identity of the nation was strong; a major aspect of national security was therefore the security of the nation. Strengthening collective identity with reference to the nation meant strengthening (the idea of) the state. Under postmodern conditions, by contrast, collective identities are to a larger extent differentiated and they develop in ways that may weaken rather than strengthen the idea of the state. Two consequences follow: first, the definition of 'national' security in identity terms is much more difficult under postmodern conditions because the dynamics of change in identities turn them into a moving and more complex target; second, collective identities are no longer linked to the socio-political cohesion and thus to the strength of the state in any well-defined way. Strengthening of collective identities may lead to weaker rather than to stronger states. The idea of the state is arguably 'the most central' (Buzan 1991:69) component of the state. Postmodern statehood puts that component on the agenda in ways that are not at all foreseen in most of the current analyses of 'national' security.

## Summary: old and new threats under postmodern conditions

Postmodern states are not heavily concerned with external military threat. They make up a coordinated security community and in that limited sense they have moved out of anarchy. They face no urgent military threats from modern states either, so their current military considerations to a significant extent have to do with setting up units that can operate 'out of area', in the case of collapse of weak, postcolonial states. While conventional security concerns have receded, different sets of challenges have emerged. They are not primarily threats to the physical safety of countries and populations. They rather concern new questions about what the relevant objects of security really are and they concern challenges to the provision of effective governance in key areas.

The first set of problems concerns the objects of security. When economies are deeply integrated across borders and different 'national' economies very significantly depend on each other for their reproduction, what is then the object of economic security: the larger economic space or merely the national segment of it (to the extent that that segment can be singled out)? When the national political systems are parts of a complex of multilevel governance, what is then the object of political security: the entire structure of that governance including the supranational level, or merely the national and lower levels? When collective identities change and are increasingly tied to levels above and below the nation, what does 'national' security mean in terms of identity and what are the consequences for the strength of the state? These questions emerge because under postmodern conditions the economies, the polities, and the collective identities of citizens are no longer neatly confined behind sovereign, territorial borders to nearly the same extent as is the case with modern states. Therefore, the standard way of protecting the state – by strengthening the hard shell behind which the good life can be pursued – is no longer a feasible security strategy. And because postmodern statehood does not simply involve the amalgamation of states to larger units,[34] the hard shell cannot be established at any higher level either. The objects of security therefore remain suspended in a space that is not easily territorially demarcated and confined. That is a challenge to all conventional security strategies, because they are predicated upon such demarcated and confined spaces as their objects of security. Here lies probably the root cause as to why the questions at the opening of this paragraph have not been given clear and satisfactory answers.

The second set of problems concerns the supply of effective governance. In the economic sector, the traditional governance instruments connected both with the 'growth and welfare' aspect and the 'state power' aspect of economic security have been undermined by globalization. In discussing the political sector, it was demonstrated that the problem of effective governance pertains to other areas as well. Government primarily organized along national lines have only limited possibilities of responding effectively to the challenges posed by a global 'Risk society'. For a number of reasons outlined above it is difficult to establish effective multilevel governance in the new context.

A third set of problems concerns legitimacy, democracy, and nationhood. This is partly connected to the problems with effective governance; it was emphasized in Chapter 6 how modern states derive legitimacy from their capability to deliver the political goods connected with effective governance; in the absence of effective governance such legitimacy can be undermined. In broader terms, postmodern statehood have political systems which do not meet basic preconditions for a functioning liberal democracy. One answer to this problem is multilevel governance; but the multilevel governance developed in context of the EU contains a democratic deficit, intensified to the extent that political–administrative elites are strategic actors seeking maximum autonomy. At the same time, collective identities are being strengthened in ways which create divisions in the community that is the nation. If collective identity is the glue which holds a community together, postmodern statehood reopens the issue about to which community individuals primarily belong. If the nation is weakened in that process it is not clear what combination of identifications is going to emerge instead.

The problems concerning governance and democracy are certainly not evenly distributed across postmodern countries and among the people of postmodern states. As regards countries, the large and resourceful are relatively less dependent on the new globalized economic and political context whereas such dependence is higher for smaller and less resourceful countries. As regards people, there is a real sense in which effective governance and democracy is for the weak; the strong can take care of themselves. The resourceful groups can seize the opportunities created by postmodern statehood; the less resourceful groups face the risk of marginalization or exclusion.

Such different groups also faced uneven chances in modern states. But the successful modern state provided a clear framework within which everyone could seek the 'good life'. In the postmodern context, such a clear framework is missing; as a consequence, the supply of effective governance is challenged, the identification of relevant objects of security is more troublesome, and there are problems concerning legitimacy and democracy. This is not a security dilemma in the traditional sense of safety from external threat to physical safety. It is rather a dilemma related to the other political goods that capable states are expected to supply: order, justice, welfare, and freedom. The trans-formation from modern to postmodern statehood undoubtedly brought a number of economic, political and other benefits. But that same process also ushered in new threats and challenges to effective governance as well as to democracy and legitimacy.

## Conclusion

How is security provided in an insecure world? The conventional answer has been the creation of strong states, not merely in terms of military strength, but primarily in terms of states with a high degree of socio-political cohesion. Such cohesion concerns three main aspects of statehood: the idea of the state; the institutional expression of the state; and the physical base of the state (Buzan 1991:65). In other words, the concept of state behind the notion of 'strong state' is that of the highly cohesive and largely autonomous modern state.

When the state is strong, national security 'can be viewed primarily in terms of protecting the components of the state from outside threat and interference. The idea of the state, its institutions and its territory will all be clearly defined and stable in their own right' (Buzan 1991:100). The link between national security at the level of the state and individual and group security ought to be clear: 'the creation of stronger states is a necessary condition for both individ-ual and national security' (Buzan 1991:106). For weak states 'the idea of national security borders on nonsense unless they can make the transformation to strong state structures' (*loc. cit.*).

The prescriptive dimension in Buzan's analysis thus concerns the movement from weak to strong states. Strong states substantially enhance individual and national security. The problem is that current developments in the inter-national system work against the creation of strong states in this sense, both in the South as demonstrated in the previous chapter, and in the North as demonstrated in this chapter. As especially regards postmodern statehood, current changes point towards processes which may well increase state strength in some respects, but this happens in a way which also creates new threats and challenges. Postmodern states have overcome the military threat from each other. They have created a coordinated security community; in that area, they meet the expectation of strong states enhancing individual and national security. But in other areas new challenges emerge in the context of changes in statehood. In sum, changes in statehood must require revisions in the underlying ideas of what a strong state is.

The problems related to postmodern statehood must not be overstated. The creation of a coordinated security community is a real step ahead because it removes the threat of war and it is not impossible to find solutions to the challenges to effective governance. But the analysis serves to emphasize that the transformation from modern to postmodern statehood not merely creates new opportunities; it also creates new problems. The distinctive characteristics of postmodern statehood requires a redefinition of the concept of a 'strong state' and it requires a rethinking of security in a context that is much more difficult to define in precise territorial terms. What exactly does it mean to pursue 'national security' under these new conditions? The point made earlier bears repeating: the specific features of postmodern statehood create a distinctive framework for the provision of security. It is therefore not possible to fully comprehend 'international' relations without reference to different types of state. The distinct sovereignty game tied to modern, postmodern and postcolonial states will be addressed in the next chapter; the implications for international theory of different types of statehood is the subject of Chapter 11.

# 10
## Sovereignty and Changes in Statehood

Previous chapters have analysed changes in substantial statehood in the areas of government, economy, and nationhood. Three main types of state were identified and the security dilemmas pertaining to weak postcolonial and to postmodern states have been examined in detail. This chapter will investigate the consequences for sovereignty of the existence of different main types of state in the international society.

There is a passionate debate about what happens to sovereignty as a result of the changes in statehood; it includes assertions about 'the end of sovereignty' and going 'beyond sovereignty'; the argument here is that sovereignty is a remarkably flexible institution which has adapted to the transformations of statehood. Therefore, the notion of an 'end of sovereignty' is misleading. But in the context of such adaptation, the relationship between 'domestic' and 'international' is redefined. Since it was the sovereign border which created that distinction in the first place, as explained in Chapter 1, this redefinition is of course crucially relevant for the 'international–domestic–international' connection which is the main focus of the present study. The typical 'international' relations of postcolonial and postmodern states respectively are predicated on different, specific combinations of substantial statehood and rules of sovereignty. These combinations are only understandable when both 'domestic' and 'international' aspects enter the analysis. That is, we should not seek to explain relationships between fixed realms of 'domestic' and 'international'; we should rather identify different modalities of that relationship in context of different main types of statehood.

Against this background, the final part of the chapter will consider the future of sovereign statehood. The argument will be that modern statehood, the state model underlying all the major theories of international relations, may well turn out to have been a temporary phenomenon that characterized the major part of the twentieth century, but is now in a process of decline. At the same time, the new major types of state identified in this study do not appear to be of very long-term historical importance either. Consequently, the study of IR will have to face up to a situation where sovereign statehood and the relationships between 'domestic' and 'international' are variables that always undergo redefinition over time, simply because there is no such thing as a final destination where states sit back, relax and exclaim: 'We are finally there! We have made it to perfect statehood, let's go no further.' The development of statehood is an ongoing process; both juridical and substantial aspects of statehood change continuously in response to 'domestic' and 'international' challenges.

Only a few years ago, sovereignty used to be taken for granted in the study of world politics. J. D. B. Miller expressed the prevailing opinion in simple, but clear terms: 'Just as we know a camel or a chair when we see one, so we know a sovereign state. It is a political entity which is treated as a sovereign state by other sovereign states' (Miller 1981:16). Today, few would be satisfied with Miller's summation. Sovereignty is being intensely debated among scholars and practitioners of world politics. The intense scholarly interest in sovereignty is most clearly evidenced in the very large number of recent books and articles on the subject.[1] A central issue in most of these contributions concerns the question of change. Is sovereignty a stable and unchanging institution or has it undergone dramatic change, both in present times and in earlier periods? If there is dramatic change, is the institution in the process of disappearing or at least losing much of its significance? What follows makes an attempt to resolve the 'continuity versus change' debate by arguing that both positions have a point; there are core aspects of the institution of sovereignty which remain unchanged and there are other aspects of the institution which have changed dramatically over time. In making that argument, I employ a distinction between constitutive rules of sovereignty (which remain unchanged) and regulatory rules of sovereignty (which have changed in several ways), and I introduce the notion of different sovereignty games played by different types of sovereign states.

## Continuity of constitutive rules

It will be recalled from Chapter 4 that sovereignty is an institution, that is, a set of rules. In order to find out whether the institution of sovereignty is changing or not it is helpful to look at the rules of sovereignty as making up a special kind of game played by a special type of player, the sovereign state.[2] We may distinguish between two qualitatively different kinds of rules in the sovereignty game: constitutive rules and regulative rules.[3] Constitutive rules are foundational;[4] they define the core features of what sovereignty is. Constitutive rules 'do not merely regulate, they also create the very possibility of certain activities' (Searle 1995:27). This type of foundational rules, says Searle, comes in systems which characteristically have the form 'X counts as Y in context C'.

When this reasoning is applied to sovereignty, the first relevant question is: what are the features of the entities that satisfy the X term in the game of sovereignty? Not any association can become sovereign; transnational corporations, churches, or football clubs do not satisfy the X term. Only a certain type of player does, the one we label 'state'. Which features must the state have to satisfy the X term? It is commonly agreed that three elements are necessary: territory, people, and government (James 1999). Georg Schwarzenberger and E. D. Brown put it in the following way: 'The State in quest of recognition must have a stable government ... it must rule supreme within a territory – with more or less settled frontiers – and it must exercise control over a certain number of people. These features have come to be taken as the essential characteristics of independent states' (quoted from Jackson 1993a:53). That is to say, the emergence of the constitutive rules of sovereignty (the Y term) is predicated upon the previous existence of states with a delimited territory, a stable population, and a government. A well-known study of international law published in 1968 makes the point in the following way: 'The international legal order does not provide foundation for the State; it presupposes the State's existence. Recognizing the appearance on a territory of a political entity showing the characteristics generally attributed to the State, it merely invests it with personality in the law of the nations' (de Visscher 1968:174–5). The consequence of that view is that classical international law is 'the child and not the parent of states' (Jackson 1993a:53).

Once we have the X term we can proceed to the constitutive rule of sovereignty (the Y term). What is the definitorial content of sovereignty that is bestowed on some (but not all) states? It is recognition of the fact that the state entity possesses constitutional independence. As emphasized by Alan James, sovereignty 'in this fundamental sense, amounts to constitutional independence'. Constitutional independence, according to James is 'a legal, an absolute, and a unitary condition' (James 1999:462). That it is a legal condition means that sovereignty is a juridical arrangement under international law. The sovereign state stands apart from all other sovereign entities, it is 'constitutionally apart' (*loc. cit.*) That means that the sovereign state is legally equal to all other sovereign states. Irrespective of the substantial differences between sovereign states in economic, political, social, and other respects, sovereignty entails equal membership of the international society of states, with similar rights and obligations. The fact mentioned earlier, that every sovereign member state, irrespective of differences in substantial powers, has one vote in the UN General Assembly is a concrete expression of this legal equality.

Constitutional independence is also an absolute condition; it is either present or absent. Other juridical categories share that quality; a person is either married or not, there is no legal status of being 75 per cent married. A person is either a citizen of a particular country or not, there is no legal status of being 75 per cent German. The same goes for sovereignty; a state does either have it or it does not have it. There is no half-way house, no legal in-between. (Some will object that the EU is exactly such an in-between condition, but that is misleading as will be argued below.)

Finally, sovereignty as constitutional independence is a unitary condition. That means that the sovereign state is of one piece; there is one supreme authority deciding over internal as well as external affairs. Such is the case even in federal states with a high degree of political decentralization; powers may have been delegated, but there is one supreme authority.

To sum up so far: the constitutive content of sovereignty can be seen as a foundational rule in the form of 'X counts as Y in context C'. The X term are states with territory, people, and government. The Y term is constitutional independence which is a legal, absolute, and unitary condition. Context C is of course the international society of states, the domain where states have 'established by dialogue and consent common rules and institutions for the conduct of their relations, and recognize their common interest in maintaining these arrangements' (Bull 1995:13). As noted in Chapter 1, the international society involves acts of recognition and mutual obligation between states. Such recognition confers a special status on states. The sheer physical features of the X term (territory, people, government) are not in themselves sufficient to guarantee the status and function specified by the Y term;[5] as emphasized by Searle, 'collective agreement about the possession of the status is constitutive of having the status, and having the status is essential to the performance of the function assigned to that status' (Searle 1995:51).

It is necessary to emphasize, even if the formulation is awkward, that the constitutive rule content of sovereignty is constitutional independence in the sense discussed above. It is this constitutive content which has remained fundamentally unchanged since it became the dominant principle of political organization in the seventeenth century. In that sense there is continuity, not change, in the institution of sovereignty. The history of sovereignty from then to now is a history of the victorious expansion of the principle of political organization embodied in sovereignty: constitutional independence. Several authors have recorded the history of that expansion; Hendrik Spruyt has argued that there was nothing inevitable about the process and he traces the complex interplay between actors and structures in the triumph of sovereign statehood (Spruyt 1994b). Charles Tilly also notes how the sovereign state has outcompeted a large number of rival forms of political organization since its first establishment in Europe (Tilly 1990). None of this needs to be covered here. We may note that 'once the system of modern [sovereign, GS] states was consolidated, the process of fundamental transformation ceased: "[states] have all remained recognizably of the same species up to our own time"'.[6]

The sovereign state remains the preferred form of political organization; no serious competitor has emerged (Jackson 1993b:346–69).

In sum, there is a stable element in sovereignty which marks the continuity of that institution. That stable element is the constitutive core of sovereignty: constitutional independence possessed by states which have territory, people, and government. The comprehensive talk about changes in sovereignty should not ignore this vital element of continuity. This does not mean that there have been no changes in the instution of sovereignty. There have been very substantial changes in sovereignty's regulative rules, the rules that the sovereignty game is played by.

## Changes in regulative rules

Changes in sovereignty pertain to changes in sovereignty's regulative rules. Regulative rules 'regulate antecedently existing activities' (Searle 1995:27). The freeway speed limit is an example of a regulative rule, regulating the antecedently existing activity of driving. The regulative rules of sovereignty regulate interaction between the antecedently existing entities that are sovereign states. How do states go about dealing with each other in war and peace, who gets to be a member of the society of states on what qualifications, are examples of areas of regulative rule. Such regulative rules would not be meaningful or necessary without the prior of existence of the special type of player which is subject to regulation: the sovereign state. In other words, the constitutive rules come first, the regulative rules second; without the former there would be no object of the latter.

The regulative rules of the sovereignty game have changed in several ways over time. One important area of change concerns the rules of admission. For a very long time, the sovereignty game was a European game, played by a European society of sovereign states. Other would-be members were held out because the Europeans found they did not satisfy the basic criteria for statehood: a delimited territory, a stable population, and a dependable government with the will and capacity to carry out international obligations. When non-European states eventually became members, they did so by meeting the membership criteria set up by the Europeans. Consequently, the international society of states was 'based on a selective membership principle which discriminated between a superior class of sovereign states and an inferior class of various dependencies' (Jackson 1993a:61).

The precise criteria for recognition have always been a subject of debate in the society of states and for a very long period there were no clear rules supported by all sovereign states.[7] This reflects a situation where countries could to some extent be players in the sovereignty game without actually having the formal recognition by all other members. Britain attempted to block the entry of the United States into the society of states by reference to the norm of mother state acceptance – that is, the United States' recognition by other states depended on prior acceptance of such sovereignty by Britain. France did not accept this claim and recognized the United States already in 1778; British recognition did not follow until 1783.

After the Congress of Vienna in 1815 rules of recognition became clearer, but were still subject to exemptions that reflected the specific interests of the European great powers. The emergence of nationalism and ideas about the nation were also reflected in recognition practices, but it was not until 1919 that the principle of popular sovereignty – that is, the idea that nations have a right to self determination – became the official basis for recognition. Yet as James Mayall emphasizes, clear guidelines for implementation of this principle were never formulated. It proved extremely difficult to answer the innocent question: which are 'the appropriate collective selves whose right to selfdetermination must be recognized as the basis of the new political order'? (Mayall 1999:476). With the adoption of the Universal Declaration of Human Rights in 1948, the issue of human rights obtained a more prominent position on the international agenda. Yet human rights did not emerge in the principles of recognition until after the end of the Cold War and even in this recent period demands for certain human rights standards have not been consistently applied to the recognition of the new states emerging from the Soviet Union and Yugoslavia.

I cannot further pursue the discussion of recognition rules here. Even from these few remarks it ought to be clear that the rules of admission to the society of states have changed in several ways over time. Let me turn to the rule of the sovereignty game itself. Once the membership issue is decided, by what rules is the game played? Robert Jackson identifies a number of playing rules, among them 'nonintervention, making and honouring of treaties, diplomacy conducted in accordance with accepted practices, and in the broadest sense a framework of international law... In short, the rules include every convention and practice of international life which moderate and indeed civilize the relations of states' (Jackson 1993a:35).

It is immediately clear that these regulative rules of the sovereignty game have changed substantially over time. The geographical expansion of the international society of states has combined with a trend towards a more dense regulation of the relations between states. International regimes have been set up in a large number of areas; the size and number of international organizations have grown dramatically; after the end of the Cold War new practices of humanitarian intervention in weak or failed states have developed. In order to record such changes of regulative rules in detail, we would have consult diplomatic history, the development of international law, the evolution of intervention practices, and so on. This is not necessary for the present argument. What must be emphasized here is the dynamic and changing content of the sovereignty institution's regulative rules. They have developed and adapted over time in the context of a society of states which has itself undergone dramatic development and change in substantial terms; the most important developments in statehood have been recorded in earlier chapters. Given this high degree of dynamic development, is there any way of finding systematic patterns in the way which the institution of sovereignty confronts us today? The following section makes an attempt to do this by employing the notion of different sovereignty games.

## Games of sovereignty in present-day international society

The above discussion makes clear that the debate about whether sovereignty has changed in every respect or remains wholly unchanged is really not helpful. There is a stable element of continuity in sovereignty, embodied in the constitutive rule of constitutional independence. And there is a dynamic element of change in sovereignty, embodied in the institution's regulative rules. These two sets of rules must not be conflated with a third element of dynamic change, namely the development of substantial empirical statehood. Formal sovereignty, as reflected in constitutive and regulative rules, can pertain in equal measure to small, weak and to big, strong states. Irrespective of their substantial weaknesses, less powerful actors such as Ghana or Denmark have sovereignty in the form of constitutional independence and they play by certain regulative rules. The fact that there is mutual dependence between countries does not annul the existence of sovereignty as constitutional independence. The substantial, positive content of sovereignty has always been contested (Krasner 1999), the rules of sovereignty exist irrespective of the fact that many sovereign states have not always actually enjoyed the autonomy implied in the notion of constitutional independence. In that sense it is misleading to talk about the 'end of sovereignty' with reference to such substantial features as economic globalization or the like. The institution of sovereignty and the actual degree of state autonomy are two different things. This should not be taken to mean that there is no relationship at all between the rules of the sovereignty institution and these substantial developments. To the contrary, substantial developments often trigger changes in the rules of sovereignty, as will be discussed below.

In order to ascertain the development of sovereign statehood over time, we need to consider the three aspects of it identified here. That is, the constitutive rule of constitutional independence; the regulative rules of sovereignty; and the development of substantial, empirical statehood, meaning the concrete features of statehood (government, economy, nationhood). The present result of those substantial developments is the modern, the postcolonial and the postmodern state. If we take into account these three different aspects of sovereign statehood, then it is very often the case that those talking about continuity of sovereignty and those talking about change of sovereignty are really not addressing the same aspect. The 'change people' talk about the development and change of substantial statehood, or development and change of sovereignty's regulative rules, or some mix of the two (see for example Camilleri and Falk 1992 and Weber 1995). The 'continuity people' (for example, James 1999) most often talk about the stable rule of constitutional independence. Both are right, but the discussion is not very productive, because they address different aspects of the complex phenomenon that is sovereign statehood.

Is it possible to find ways of synthesizing that complex entity which is sovereign statehood in a way that respects both change and continuity and which also encompasses the three aspects discussed here? It should be clear by now that any detailed historical picture will always be flimsy instead of neat and clean. Instead of looking in vain for a synthesis that will never be empirically accurate, I develop the idea that each of the three types of state identified earlier plays a distinct, ideal typical game of sovereignty that encompasses a particular relationship between 'domestic' and 'international'. As already indicated, the raw material for these three games of sovereignty will be drawn from the three aspects of sovereign statehood identified above: (1) constitutive rules; (2) regulative rules; and (3) substantial, empirical statehood.

The first level, that of constitutive rules, is the stable element which is unvarying across the games: all three games are played by states that have constitutional independence as members of the society of states. In terms of differentiating between types of games, therefore, this first level drops out. The second level, that of regulative rules, is more difficult to handle because there are several such rules, as was demonstrated earlier. I have chosen to focus on two regulative rules which have always been considered vitally important, even *Grundnorms* or 'golden rules' (Jackson 1993a:6) of the sovereignty game: nonintervention and reciprocity. Nonintervention is the prohibition against foreign interference in the domestic affairs of other states; reciprocity is the principle of quid pro quo, the 'exchange of roughly equivalent values'[8] between the legally equal partners of the sovereignty game. The point is that these two *Grundnorms* are played out in different ways in the sovereignty games discussed below and these differences help us capture the distinct features of each game.

The third level concerns substantial statehood. All participants in the three games satisfy the X-term of sovereign statehood discussed earlier, even if one category of players does it only just barely: there is a territory, a population and some form of government. But beyond these basic aspects, the players of the three games differ substantially is their empirical statehood, on the following dimensions: structure and content of the economy, structure and content of the polity, and the relationship between nation and state, that is, the issue of nationhood. We now have the necessary tools for identifying the different ideal types of sovereignty games.

### The modern sovereignty game

The substantial features of modern statehood were identified in Chapter 6. They are:

| | |
|---|---|
| Government | A centralized system of rule, based on a set of administrative, policing and military organizations, sanctioned by a legal order, claiming monopoly of the legitimate use of force. |
| Nationhood | A people within a territory making up a community in the *Gesellschaft* and the *Gemeinschaft* sense, involving a high level of cohesion, binding nation and state together. |
| Economy | Segregated national economy, self-sustained in the sense that it comprises the main sectors needed for its reproduction; major part of economic activity takes place at home. |

The modern sovereignty game is based on nonintervention and reciprocity. For modern states, nonintervention is the right of states to conduct their affairs without outside interference. That also implies that the modern sovereignty game is one of self-help; states are individually responsible for looking after their own security and welfare: the state decides for itself 'how it will cope with its internal and external problems, including whether or not to seek assistance from others ... States develop their own strategies, chart their own courses, make their own decisions about how to meet whatever needs they experience and whatever desires they develop' (Waltz 1979:96). That situation is of course not only one of opportunity, but also of constraint: 'Statesmen are free within the situation they find themselves which consists externally of other states and internally of their subjects. That is obviously a circumstance of constrained choice...' (Jackson 1993a:6).

The dealings with other states are based on reciprocity, that is, they involve a notion of symmetry, of giving and taking for mutual benefit. In the present context, reciprocity should be seen less as a bargaining strategy employed by single actors and more as a systemic norm according to which bargains between parties are made. A game based on reciprocity is a symmetric game where the players enjoy equal opportunity to benefit from bi- and multilateral transactions. Reciprocity in this sense is expressed, for example, in the 1947 adoption of the General Agreement on Tariffs and Trade (the GATT). That organization is based on rules that are basically liberal in character. The basic norm is the 'Most Favoured Nation' rule which stipulates equal treatment in commercial relations between states, regardless of size, power, location, and any further particulars about them.

The correspondence between the substantial features of statehood and the rules of the modern sovereignty game should be emphasized: the game can only be one of self-help, as expressed in the principle of nonintervention, because modern states are capable entities that are able to take care of them-selves. They are able to take care of themselves because of the healthy and productive resource basis made up by their national economies; their efficient political institutions; and the strength and support of a population which is a community that provides cohesion and legitimacy to the state. Similarly, the game is one of reciprocity, because modern states do not expect special treatment, or assistance, from others. Nor do they, as a principle, offer it in return.

The modern sovereignty game is based on a clear distinction between what is domestic and what is international. Again, there is correspondence between substantial features of statehood and the rules of the game. In substantial terms, modern states can make very clear distinctions between inside and outside. The sovereign border is not a mere juridical construction; it expresses in real terms that the national polity, the national economy, and the national community exist within the territory demarcated by that border. Nonintervention is the recognition in formal rule terms that there is a clearly defined domestic realm; reciprocity is the defining condition on which relations between inside and outside can be established. Looking at 'domestic' and 'international' in terms of the three levels of the sovereignty game, we get the picture set out in Table 10.1.

The security dilemma of the modern state defined in Chapter 7 was based on the idea that the modern state provides the context for the 'good life', supply-ing the political goods of security, order, liberty, and welfare. The modern sovereignty game is based on the same idea: that the modern state is a capable entity, qualified to secure the 'good life' for its citizens. The sovereignty game in itself is not a guarantee that such goods will be provided, of course. The right of nonintervention is a negative right; a freedom from, not a freedom to.[9] But to the extent that sovereign states are comprehensively unable to provide those political goods, the modern sovereignty game has been modified or changed accordingly. That is the case with weak, postcolonial states as will be explored below.

*Table 10.1* 'Domestic' and 'international' in the modern sovereignty game

| Aspects of modern statehood | | Relationship between 'domestic' and 'international' |
|---|---|---|
| Constitutive rules | Constitutional independence | Segregated |
| Regulative rules | Non-intervention; reciprocity | Segregated |
| Substantial statehood | National polity, economy, community | Segregated |

## The postcolonial sovereignty game

The substantial features of postcolonial statehood were identified in Chapter 6. They are:

| | |
|---|---|
| Government | 'Captured autonomy', based on weak administrative and institutional structures. Rule based on coercion rather than the rule of law. Monopoly of the use of legitimate violence not stablished. |
| Nationhood | Predominance of local/ethnic community. Low level of state/nation cohesion. Low level of state legitimacy. |
| Economy | World market dependence and structural heterogeneity. Coherent national economy not developed. |

The *Grundnorms* of nonintervention and reciprocity both create problems for postcolonial states; they cannot fully play by these 'golden rules' because their deficiencies in substantial statehood do not allow that. As concerns reciprocity, postcolonial states cannot systematically base their relations with developed countries on reciprocity. They are too weak to reciprocate in a quid pro quo manner; they need special, preferential treatment from the developed world. That is the basis for the emergence of development assistance regimes, where economic aid flows from rich, developed countries to poor, underdeveloped countries. This is a sharp deviation from the liberal, equal opportunity principle in relations between states; what has emerged instead is a principle of special, preferential treatment of the weak party. As will be recalled from Chapter 8, postcolonial states have attempted to make the most of these principles, as reflected in the demands for a New International Economic Order and numer-ous other, more recent declarations, including calls for debt relief, preferential treatment of technology transfer, special subsidies for export items, and, in general, higher levels of economic aid.

The aid regimes and the existence of special treatment in an additional num-ber of areas, such as for example the GATT/WTO regime which has special provisions for weak, postcolonial states,[10] reflects that in some areas a change has taken place, from the classical principle of reciprocity between equals to a new principle of nonreciprocity between unequals. The system is not supposed to be permanent, but temporary. When the weak players have gained strength (that is, development), they are supposed to graduate from the special treatment of nonreciprocity to the standard treatment of reciprocity. This is an indication that there are sharp limits to the scope and depth of nonreciprocity. A compre-hensive regime of global redistribution from rich to poor has by no means replaced the classical liberal regime of equal opportunity. Postcolonial state elites can therefore invoke both principles (that is, 'treat us as equals' and 'treat us as unequals'); so can developed countries in the North, of course, as reflected in the (limited) granting of development aid on the one hand, and the (much higher) concern for domestic economic, social and related problems on the other.[11]

Even if reciprocity has not been fully replaced by nonreciprocity, it is clear that the international system is not one of self-help for postcolonial states. Neither is it purely non-self help, because the international society has not assumed full responsibility for the development and security of postcolonial states. It is sooner a self-help plus: in basic ways, postcolonial states are required to take care of themselves, but this takes place within a context where there is no severe external security threat and where donors provide some socioeconomic safety-nets in terms of various systems of preferential treatment.

Economic and other aid gives the donors an amount of influence over the domestic affairs of recipients. Chapter 8 analysed how the attitude of donors has changed, from one of refraining from comprehensive interference in postcolonial states in the 1960s and 1970s, to one of increasingly demanding specific changes and reforms as a condition for providing economic and other assistance. Such changes clearly put pressure on the principle of nonintervention. The clearest example of setting aside the principle of nonintervention is the case of humanitarian intervention. Such intervention is explicitly defined as 'dictatorial or coercive interference in the sphere of jurisdiction of a sovereign state' (Bull 1984:1). Political or economic conditionalities are not accompanied by similar dictatorial interference, but they may be difficult for weak, postcolonial states to reject anyway. If this is neither intervention, nor classical nonintervention, what is it? This new regime could be called 'negotiated intervention'. The term 'intervention' emphasizes the element of outside interference in the 'domestic' affairs of postcolonial states; the term 'negotiated' emphasizes that postcolonial state elites, because of constitutional independence, retain a significant measure of bargaining power over the concrete terms of such interference.[12]

Some will argue that this relationship is not at all exceptional, because in international society weak states have always had to deal with strong states from a disadvantaged position. Three elements suggest, however, that 'negotiated intervention' can be seen as a peculiar feature connected to weak, postcolonial states. The first is the scope of such intervention; it has developed to encompass every sphere of society, from regime forms and political institutions, over economic strategy and structure, to the construction of major aspects of civil society. The second element is the depth of intervention; election systems are set up, constitutions are rewritten, economic policies are overhauled, civil associations are set up, and so on. Finally, negotiated intervention takes place against the backdrop of aid-regimes. Donors are in special position because they supply the necessary funding. Yet state elites continue to be able to influence the terms and, perhaps more significantly, the implementation of the bargains made with outsiders.

In sum, the regulative rules of reciprocity and nonintervention have been significantly modified in the postcolonial sovereignty game. The coexistence of reciprocity and nonreciprocity creates a situation of 'self-help plus'. Similarly, nonintervention and intervention have been combined in a regime of negotiated intervention.

The weak, postcolonial states are in major ways non-capable entitites, unable to take care of themselves. Therefore, their deficiencies in terms of substantial statehood does not allow them to play a sovereignty game of complete self-help; they would be comprehensively unable to survive in a highly competitive state system. Because nonintervention and reciprocity are golden rules connected with the institution of sovereignty, they have not been completely abandoned in the case of these states. Instead, they have been modified so as to compensate for the weaknesses in substantial statehood. But 'self-help plus' and 'negotiated intervention' are unstable compromises,[13] because they encompass elements of qualitatively different systems: the classical liberal system of self-help and equal opportunity, and a very different system of non-self help and global redistribution.

It is against this background that weak, postcolonial states display a distinct modality of 'domestic' and 'international'. On the one hand, postcolonial states have constitutional independence just as any other sovereign state; therefore, the sovereign postcolonial state stands apart from all other sovereign states. In terms of legal, political authority, constitutional dependence therefore creates a clear distinction between inside (the territorial realm of the sovereign state) and outside. On the other hand, this clear distinction between inside and outside is not corresponding to the substantial features of postcolonial statehood. Behind the sovereign border are not entities that are able to take care of themselves; they are substantially dependent on the international system. The weakest states are placed under direct care of the international system, as happens in the case of humanitarian intervention. The less weak, but still highly dependent ones, must accept a very high degree of outside interference in their political, economic, and social affairs. This peculiar combination of 'domestic' and 'international' at the level of substantial statehood is reflected at the level of the regulative rules of the postcolonial sovereignty game. 'Self-help' plus and 'negotiated intervention' is an expression in formal rule terms of a similarly peculiar combination of 'domestic' and 'international'.

The situation can be summarized as set out in Table 10.2. This combination creates a tension in the sovereignty game of course, between the segregation of 'domestic' and 'international' implied by constitutional independence, and the association between 'domestic' and 'international' at the levels of substantial statehood and the regulative rules of sovereignty. It can be resolved in two ways: either the weak, postcolonial states become more capable entities through state building and development; that would turn them into resource

*Table 10.2*   'Domestic' and 'international' in the postcolonial sovereignty game

| Aspects of postcolonial statehood | | Relationship between 'domestic' and 'international' |
|---|---|---|
| Constitutive rules | Constitutional independence | Segregated |
| Regulative rules | 'Self-help plus', 'negotiated intervention' | Associated |
| Substantial statehood | Dependence, weak institutions, lack of national community | Associated |

ful entities, capable of self-help and the provision of the 'good life' for their citizens. In short, they would become modern states. It was argued in chapter 8 that in many cases such a development was not likely to happen sometime soon. The alternative scenario is that postcolonial states remain substantially very weak and that their legal standing in international society is adjusted accordingly. That would imply that constitutional independence is abandoned and international society assumes a more direct responsibility for these states in some sort of post-sovereign arrangement; that is, the decertification of states by the international community discussed in Chapter 8. But it was argued in Chapter 8 that such a development was also highly improbable. The tension in the sovereignty game between 'segregation' and 'association' is therefore likely to remain for some time, together with the peculiar combination of 'domestic' and 'international' which it contains.

## The postmodern sovereignty game

The substantial features of postmodern statehood were identified in Chapter 6. They are:

| | |
|---|---|
| Government | Multilevel governance, based on supranational, national, and subnational institutions. |
| Nationhood | Supranational and international institutions are sources of citizenship rights. Collective identity also tied to levels above and below the nation. |
| Economy | Major part of economic activity embedded in cross-border networks. 'National' economy much less self-sustained. |

The sovereignty game played by postmodern states differs in basic respects from the 'modern' and the 'postcolonial' sovereignty games. The following clarification of this will focus on the EU, because this is where multilevel governance has progressed most.[14] In that context, the rule of nonintervention is seriously modified in that a set of formal and informal channels have been created for legitimate outside intervention by Member States in national affairs. In formal rule terms, this is most clearly evident in the Single Market Treaty where a majority of Member States may define rules applicable to all members. This 'First Pillar' of cooperation as defined by the Maastricht Treaty (ratified in 1993) was set to expand to cover additional areas in coming years. By the late 1990s, the current dominant project is the European Monetary Union and the introduction of the common currency. During the past decade, institutions at the European level have gained considerable influence over areas that were traditionally considered to be prerogatives of national politics: currency, social policies, border controls, law and order.[15] An important player in this context is the European Court of Justice, which has helped push supranational governance by establishing the supremacy of Union law in important areas.[16] This is clearly not a system of nonintervention. It is sooner a system of regulated intervention that is continuously being developed. Because the political compromises made in context of the treaties (Maastricht, Amsterdam) are often unclear, it is left to future bargaining processes to determine the exact scope and content of European level governance in specific areas.

As regards reciprocity, the classical system has been modified as well. Whereas in the modern game, the rule of reciprocity is basically that of equal or fair competition, in the postmodern game it is cooperation rather than competition. For example, poor regions get special, preferential treatment. In other words, there is some redistribution of economic resources across national boundaries which is not based strictly on member countries, but also on regions within countries. This resembles the aid regime desribed in the postcolonial game, but there is a decisive difference. In the EU context, there is an institutional structure with overseeing powers. That is, EU institutions have the legal possibility of controlling whether aid for poor regions is actually used according to intentions and take corrective measures if this is not the case. A similar combination of cooperation and control is absent from the postcolonial sovereignty game.[17]

The modifications of the regulative rules of the sovereignty game described here imply that postmodern states have become integrated in the sense that they have developed standard operating procedures for the intervention in their respective 'domestic' domains. These procedures correspond in basic ways to the way in which the substantial features of postmodern statehood have developed. Their polities, economies and societies are increasingly integrated as well, as clearly reflected in the concept of postmodern statehood analysed earlier. Instead of border controls which have largely been removed, there are several cases of development of intensive forms of local cross-border cooperation (Brock and Albert 1995).[18] The development of transnational elites, it has recently been suggested, has undercut the possibility for governments to play two-level games, because 'the two audiences overlap, swap information, form transgovernmental coalitions, respond to transnational lobbies. European governance is above all governance by committee: through multilateral negotiation, mutual accommodation, intensive and extensive consultations and exchanges of information'[19] (Wallace 2000:206). European level 'international' politics has become so thoroughly integrated with 'domestic' politics that it is increasingly difficult to make a clear distinction between the two.

Postmodern states, then, have also developed a specific modality of 'domestic' and 'international'. Constitutional independence remains in place; in that basic sense also postmodern states stand apart from all other sovereign states. But in terms of substantial statehood, postmodern states by no means stand apart; they are increasingly integrated with other states. That substantial integration has developed in interplay with significant modifications of the regulative rules of the sovereignty game where a similar integration between 'domestic' and 'international' has taken place. We therefore get the following picture set out in Table 10.3.

This means that there is also a tension in the postmodern sovereignty game; it is, on the one hand, between the continued national independence (and sharp distinction between 'domestic' and 'international') that is present on the level of constitutive rules. And, on the other hand, the high level of integration (and lack of a clear distinction between 'domestic' and 'international') reflected in the regulative rules and in the development of substantial statehood. It is this tension of course, which is represented in the debates about the development of the EU. One side of the debate stresses the fact of constitutional independence and the EU as basically an instance of inter-governmental cooperation; the other side of the debate emphasizes the novelty of integration as expressed in substantial statehood and especially in the regulative rules of sovereignty.[20] But the tension in the postmodern sovereignty game stems exactly from the fact that both sides in the debate have a valid point: on the one hand, constitutional independence remains the basis for EU-cooperation; on the other hand, integration has progressed so far that constitutional independence is increasingly under pressure. The two poles of the debate are also expressed in the discussion on exit possibilities, where one side maintains that states can opt out (Jackson 1999b:453) and another side maintains that that is 'practically' impossible (Christiansen 1994).

*Table 10.3*  'Domestic' and 'international' in the postmodern sovereignty game

| Aspects of postmodern statehood | | Relationship between 'domestic' and 'international' |
|---|---|---|
| Constitutive rules | Constitutional independence | Segregated |
| Regulative rules | 'Regulated intervention', 'cooperative reciprocity' | Integrated |
| Substantial statehood | Government and society increasingly 'de-nationalized' | Integrated |

We do not know about the concrete extent to which the regulative rules can be developed in the direction of 'integration' while they continue to rest on a basis of 'segregation' as expressed in constitutional independence.[21] That is why the debate remains unsettled.

There is another aspect of this debate about sovereignty and postmodern statehood. It concerns the question of whether the EU is a *sui generis* or whether the kind of cooperation it embodies is relevant for a larger group of countries. As indicated earlier, the present analysis endorses the latter view; the substantial features of postmodern statehood are relevant for a larger group of countries, and there is no inherent reason why they would never undertake similar far-reaching modifications of the regulative rules of the sovereignty game that have taken place in context of the EU.[22]

The tension between 'segregation' and 'integration' in the postmodern sovereignty game as displayed by the EU can be solved in two ways. First, if the EU creates a federation based on a European constitution, the level of constitutive rules is changed to conform with the changes on the level of regulative rules and substantial statehood; the EU would be a new sovereign state with 'integration' on all levels of the sovereignty game (that is, constitutive rules; regulative rules; and substantial statehood). Second, cooperation may backslide to the conventional, inter-governmental level, in which case regulative rules would much better conform to existing constitutive rules, that is, 'segregation' would become the dominant feature of the sovereignty game on all levels. Given the present dynamic of EU, there is not much evidence speaking in favour of the latter development. But there is no significant evidence in favour of the former development either; the last of the great federalists, Helmut Kohl, has left the scene and there are no strong federal projects in the making; focus is rather on the expansion of membership and the debate about the institutional changes necessary in that context. Therefore, the tension, and probably the debate, will remain with us for the foreseeable future.

## Conclusion: the future of sovereign statehood

Sovereign statehood as expressed in the modern state has been an extremely successful organization. Modern states are strong states, with a high degree of socio-political cohesion. They have provided a context for the 'good life' of their citizens and they have delivered the major political goods: security, freedom, order, justice, and welfare. The idea that all states are modern states, or on the way to becoming modern states, has been a very powerful one among students of the state. Neorealism maintains that less successful states emulate the more successful ones or fall by the wayside. Liberalism envisions that less developed states undertake a process of modernization by which they acquire the same social structure as those that are already modern and developed.

Classical Marxism finds that backward states see a picture of their own future in the more developed capitalist states. In order to create optimum conditions for security analysts have called for the creation of strong, modern states, as mentioned in Chapter 9. The implication is that the modern state is a particularly stable and enduring organization.

The paradox behind these views concerns the peculiar combination of dynamic development and static non-development upon which they are based. Dynamic development is understood to be entirely possible, but only until the end point of successful, modern statehood has been reached. When that end goal is arrived at, only thoroughly epochal changes, such as the transformation from anarchy to hierarchy (neorealism); world revolution (Marxism); or cosmopolitan world order (liberalism) appear able to activate further changes. But it is clear that such epochal changes are not at all necessary in order to push further development and change of sovereign statehood. If anything, the twentieth century has demonstrated that the modern state never stands still. It develops and changes continuously sparked by a large number of factors, economic, social, cultural, and political.

At the present time, it would appear that the modern state, as conceptualized in the modern sovereignty game above, was the dominant mode of sovereign statehood in the third quarter of the twentieth century. During that time, a liberal democratic variant of the modern state in the West competed against a totalitarian state in the East which aspired to become modern. The totalitarian socialist model proved unviable; but the very condition for the success of the liberal model appeared to be its capacity for dynamic change, including change that transformed the modern state in basic ways. Embedded liberalism led to uneven globalization; uneven globalization, together with several other changes, led in the direction of the postmodern state. Success creates emulators; the role model for successful statehood today is hardly the modern state with its sharp distinction between what is domestic and what is international. The role model is sooner the postmodern state with its high level of integration with other states, as expressed in the postmodern sovereignty game. The East European countries that became free from Soviet dominance proudly declared their sovereignty and then immediately sought intense integration in context of the EU. Whether all this will lead to a world dominated by postmodern states remains to be seen; but it is clear that the modern state is much less dominant than it was only a few decades ago.

There is a second paradox behind the views presented in the opening of this section. It is the notion of uni-directional development: from weak to strong; from less to more developed; from postcolonial to modern. It was made clear in Chapter 8 that successful state building and development does not always happen; that process requires certain preconditions, domestic and international. Unless they can be created, development on a significant scale will not be forthcoming. The present combination of an international environment which insures weak, postcolonial states against extinction and domestic post-colonial elites which exploit their control of the state for personal benefit has certainly not produced impressive results in terms of development. It has rather led to processes of decay and state failure.

In the postwar era, then, sovereign statehood has developed away from the traditional model of modern statehood in the direction of two other types of state, the postcolonial and the postmodern. Each of these types is based on a peculiar combination of 'domestic' and 'international' which creates tensions in their respective sovereignty games. In that sense, they are inherently unstable types. Yet, despite these shortcomings, they are likely to stay with us for some considerable time. Changes in the postcolonial game will demand either a change in the international legal context so as to introduce forms of sovereignty that fall short of constitutional independence; or, alternatively, change in empirical statehood of weak states towards much more substantial statehood. Neither prospect is likely. Changes in the postmodern game are predicated upon either a setback towards more conventional forms of inter-state cooperation, or, alternatively, progress towards more genuine federal structures. None of those prospects is likely either. If modern statehood is in the process of being replaced by different types of state; and if those new types are in themselves unstable constructions, there would appear to be an urgent need for further study of changes in statehood and the resultant variation in the relationship between 'domestic' and 'international'. The challenges posed to IR-theory by the development of and changes in sovereign statehood are taken up next.

# 11
# Types of State and International Theory

The first part of this book demonstrated how various 'international' forces have helped shape three different types of state in the present international system. Subsequent chapters analysed the specific security dilemmas and the peculiar sovereignty games pertaining to the modern, the postcolonial, and the postmodern state respectively. The coexistence of qualitatively different types of state in the system is a challenge to IR-theory. How well can existing theories of international relations account for the emergence of different types of state? In what ways are the assumptions, the core contentions, and the strategic recommendations of existing theories challenged by an international system containing three different main types of state? These questions will be addressed with respect to five different major theories or clusters of theories of IR: realism, liberalism, the English school, neomarxist international political economy, and constructivism.

Before entering this discussion, it should be noted that the present analysis is in agreement with the major IR-theories when it comes to maintaining analytical focus on the sovereign state. As indicated in Chapter 1, a singleminded focus on states either 'winning' or 'losing' in relation to other actors tends to misconstrue the debate because the transformation of sovereign statehood means that the state can be both 'winning' and 'losing' simultaneously. Furthermore, a broader notion of sovereign statehood which includes not merely states as institutions of government, but also includes society and economy, will incorporate most of those issues that 'non-statists' want to bring in to the analysis. In sum, given that the concept of state goes beyond government institutions to include society and economy, the traditional IR-theory focus on sovereign states is warranted. The basic difference between the dominant mainstream theories of realism, liberalism, and the English school on the one hand, and the present study on the other, is that these former theories are all based on a concept of state which strongly resembles the modern ideal type identified in Chapter 6. This creates a number of problems and, it will be argued, a need for theoretical development and adjustment.

# Realism

Sovereign states exist in a realm of decentralized authority, that is, anarchy. States (that is, governments) are rational, unitary actors. The condition of anarchy means that states are self-help agents,[1] they 'must rely on the means they can generate and the arrangements they can make for themselves' (Waltz 1979:111). Anarchy compels states to be primarily focused on their security. States 'seek to ensure their survival';[2] that compels them to worry about their power relative to other states.[3] In a self-help system, states want to preserve their autonomy and freedom of action; they don't want to become overly dependent on others and they are concerned that gains of cooperation may accrue primarily to others.[4]

I believe this is a fair summary of main assumptions and claims made by most realists and neorealists. Can this starting point account for the emergence of different types of state? Let me begin with the weak, postcolonial states. According to realism, the existence of such weak entities must be understood against the background of the interests of the dominant great powers in the international system. It was noted in Chapter 4 how the old colonial mother-lands lost the ability to set the international agenda after the Second World War. The new leading powers, the United States and the Soviet Union, generally favoured decolonization. During the Cold War, those same leading powers intervened in weak states when they perceived that to be in their interest. After the end of the Cold War, the weak, postcolonial states are subject to tighter control by Western donors, but, as Chapter 8 explained, there is no substantial interest, negative or positive, on the side of capable, developed countries to get deeper involved in weak states. There are minimal aid regimes, but the dominant powers continue to basically take care of themselves; there is occasional humanitarian intervention, but none of the leading states have an interest in taking over very weak ones, probably, according to realist reasoning, because the potential costs are higher than the potential benefits. Therefore, the weak, postcolonial states persist.

What about postmodern states? A realist account would again begin from the premise of great power interests. The embedded liberalism regime was, in the main, created by the United States after the war. That is, the new leading Western power compelled the others in the Western camp to cooperate and provided them with incentives to do so. The extraordinarily intense coopera-tion in context of the EU would appear to present a special challenge to realism. Yet this can also be seen in context of national interests and relative power. Tighter cooperation in the EU reflects an interest on part of European powers to become able to balance against great powers in the system, including Japan and, eventually, the United States. At the present time, this cooperation has not reached a level where it is perceived as a competitive challenge to these latter states; therefore they don't work actively against it. Inside the EU, realists face another challenge: why are the other states not balancing against great power Germany? One realist attempt at an answer stresses 'voice opportunities', that is, 'relatively weaker states may choose to cooperate through an institution in order both to pursue balancing against an external challenger *and* to mitigate their domination by the strongest partner in the balancing coalition by ensuring that the institution is composed of rules and practices that provide the weaker partners effective "voice opportunities"' (Grieco 1997:185). But why would Germany be willing to tie itself in? Because it corresponds to Germany's economic and political interests; it is the only way for Germany to exercise its growing 'power discretely and legitimately and thereby dominate its neighbours without arousing substantial resistance' (Grieco 1997:186).

Realists have a point. In a world of constitutionally independent states, there can be a logic of national self-interest and power, and that logic may lead towards the creation of peculiar entities such as postcolonial and postmodern states. One could object that international norms also play an important role in the persistence of weak states, so that the pointing to instrumental power calculations does not exhaust the issue,[5] but this can be seen as a supplement to realism rather than a rejection of it.

The real problem not faced by realists is that the logic of power and interest may help create a world which no longer adequately corresponds to realist assumptions concerning anarchy and sovereign statehood. This is exactly what has happened. Postcolonial and postmodern states are distinct entities that play particular sovereignty games and face specific security dilemmas. These entities are not at all sufficiently analysed by realists. The standard realist answer is that these developments do not really pertain to the great powers and therefore they are less interesting for what goes on in the international system; the big and important things concern great power relations and here realist assumptions continue to be valid.[6] But this is not a satisfactory answer: first, the development of postmodern statehood does involve several of the major states in the system; second, the exceptional problems of postcolonial statehood concern so large groups of people that they do qualify as 'big and important' things.

The existence of different main types of state challenges major assumptions and contentions of realism and neorealism. Three aspects of this will be addressed in what follows: (1) the notion that an anarchical system is composed of 'like units'; (2) the security dilemma in anarchy; and (3) the relationships between 'international' and 'domestic'. The neorealist idea that socialization and competition leads to 'like units' was introduced in Chapter 2. Discussing this idea, several arguments were introduced that could severely limit the homogenizing effects of competition and socialization. Chapter 3 demonstrated some of those limitations through an analysis of the evolution of the

Soviet Union/Russia. Stalinist policies of forced industrialization amounted to an innovation which led away from sameness; nuclear weapons created a security umbrella that allowed the Soviet leadership to continue to be an 'unlike unit' because nuclear deterrence postponed the need for catch-up in other areas. Nor did Russia after the fall of communism emerge as a 'like unit'. Subsequent chapters demonstrated how international norms and economic power respectively could contain processes leading towards heterogeneity as well as towards homogeneity.

In short, the processes taking place in an anarchical international system do contain elements leading towards homogenization of states, but for several reasons the result needs not be one of 'like units'. Consequently, states need to be brought back in; the alternative is a truncated and ultimately misleading analysis, where 'like unit' states are always forced 'to behave in similar, rational, power-maximizing ways, or fail and be conquered'.[7] As demonstrated in previous chapters, this neorealist description of state behaviour and the consequences of it certainly does not begin to exhaust what is going on in the international system today.

There is a logical inconsistency in neorealism which may help explain the problems identified here. It concerns the theory's basic assumptions of self-help and autonomy. Self-help indicates that a state can pursue any policy that conforms to its self-interest. Autonomy indicates that policies which limit the freedom of manoeuvre of states will not be followed.[8] Further, when states do accept constraints on their autonomy, that can lead to a situation where the logic of self-help is severely circumscribed, as was argued in context of post-modern states in Chapter 9. We then enter a complex of relations between (postmodern) states about which neorealism does not have very much to say because its basic assumptions no longer apply.

One of the major areas that remain undertheorized – or not theorized at all – in realist and neorealist thinking concerns the peculiar security dilemmas which confront postcolonial and postmodern states respectively. According to realists, it is the 'hard shell' of the state which is to provide security in an anarchical world. But for postcolonial peoples, that shell is more frequently an insecurity container exposing them to lethal domestic danger. This takes place in a situation where state elites in postcolonial countries are not facing severe external threat. Violent conflict today is almost always taking place inside weak, postcolonial states, not between sovereign states. These dynamics of domestic insecurity and state failure in context of an international system which underwrites the continued right to constitutional independence of weak, postcolonial states is not easily analysed with the concepts and assumptions offered by realism and neorealism.

Nor does the unusual security situation of postmodern states sit well with a realist analysis. Postmodern states make up a coordinated security community;

they are not seriously concerned with external military threat from each other. At the same time, new challenges have emerged in the economic, political and societal sectors. It is not at all simple to pursue 'national security' in a context that is difficult to define in precise territorial terms. Realist and neorealist analysis appears to be comprehensively unready to confront the new context for security as it presents itself in terms of postmodern statehood.

In realist analysis, the relationship between 'domestic' and 'international' is a fixed one, following the sovereign border. Chapter 10 argued that different modalities of the domestic–international relationship can be identified when the changes pertaining to the regulative rules of the sovereignty game and to the development of substantial statehood are examined. The argument was that this provides a better way of understanding that relationship. A transhistorical distinction between 'system' on the one hand and 'states' on the other misses important elements of the dynamic evolution of the domestic–international relationship. Finally, the policy recommendations that can be drawn from realism when it comes to the creation of security are insufficient and problematic in a world of different main types of state. As will be recalled from Chapter 9, the conventional realist strategy for creating security is the formation of strong states with a high degree of socio-political cohesion. But strong states in the conventional sense (that is, modern states) are no longer easily created, neither in the South nor in the North. If that is the case, fresh analysis of the relationship between security and statehood is necessary, because simple strengthening of the 'hard shell' of the state is neither feasible, nor sufficient.

In sum, the narrow realist and neorealist focus on effective (that is, modern) states pursuing self-help and autonomy under conditions of Hobbesian anarchy does not effectively address several important issues that grow out of a world with different main types of state.

## Liberalism

For liberals, history is potentially progressive. Progress is intimately bound up with the emergence of the modern, liberal state. Human reason and rationality are driving forces of modernity. Cooperation for mutual benefit can prevail, not only within states, but also across borders, between states and between societies. The process of modernization increases the scope and the need for cooperation. This is expressed in four different main strands of liberalism: institutional, republican, interdependence, and sociological liberalism. Each of these strands help explain why peaceful cooperation between modern, liberal states can prevail even in a world of constitutionally independent states.[9]

Liberal modernization theory contains, at least implicitly, an account of weak, postcolonial states, as indicated in Chapter 2. They are the pre-modern entities which have yet to progress through the stages of modernization. Not all of them may make it however, or the process may take place over an extended period; therefore, the system contains these weak entities. Postmodern states, by contrast, are the highly sucessful modernizers that have taken the processes contained in institutional, interdependence, sociological, and republican liberalism to new, hitherto unknown levels of development.

Liberals have a point, but theirs is not a flawless account. First, most liberal thinking is based on the idea that all states have at one point been traditional and non-modern, before they moved down the road of modernization. But it can be argued that the weak, postcolonial states represent a specific trajectory which is qualitatively different from the development of modern statehood in the North.[10] Given the belief in progress, liberal thinking has not been very clear in explaining why development does not seem to arrive in weak, postcolonial states. Second, as regards postmodern states, these entities embody a development beyond modern statehood which is also insufficiently reflected upon in liberal IR-theory, as will be further demonstrated below.

Liberals face the task of explaining why the means of progress identified by various strands of liberalism have not brought more modernization cum development to weak, postcolonial states. The problem for liberals is that some of the core elements of liberal advancement to which they point (for example, democratization and economic modernization) do not work very well in weak, postcolonial states. And if the last four decades are anything to go by, this is not merely a matter of abiding time. Instead of interdependence, postcolonial states face is a high degree of socio-economic dependence. Postcolonial states are weak players in a marginalized position in the world economy, as explained in Chapter 8. International institutions are heavily involved in weak states, but they lack domestic counterparts, and in the absence of effective domestic institutions, sustained progress is difficult to achieve.[11] Furthermore, the attempt to quickly introduce democracy in weak, postcolonial states has largely failed; in that context, early elections have tended to produce more, not less, violent conflict. In short, liberals are not very clear when it comes to explain sustained lack of development.

In the case of postmodern states, liberals face a different kind of challenge. The development to postmodern statehood has brought to the fore a new set of problems which, paradoxically, can be seen as an effect of those very strands of liberalism that were supposed to contain solutions instead of problems. Intense cooperation has led to a problem with democracy, including a 'democratic deficit' problem in the EU, as explained in Chapter 9.[12] As a matter of fact, intense cooperation has undermined the basic preconditions for a democratic polity as they are set forth in mainstream liberal democratic theory. Economic interdependence in the form of globalization transforms and in some ways restricts the ability of the liberal state to provide effective governance. The growth of transnational relations theorized by sociological liberalism may strengthen identities in ways that go against rather than support the liberal state. In sum, when the modernizing elements theorized by liberalism develop beyond modern statehood, they do not merely continue to signify progress and cooperation. They also exhibit a number of problems which liberal theory has not sufficiently confronted.

These problems point to the need for further liberal analysis of the relationship between 'domestic' and 'international'. The major liberal efforts in this respect have concerned exploration of the nature of the democratic peace (Russett 1993), and the analysis of international institutions. Only recently have liberals begun to explore the relationship between changes in statehood and the development of a liberal international order.[13]

Finally, traditional liberal policy recommendations concerning the creation of security will have to be revised. According to liberals the fundamental vehicle for creation of security and for the provision of other political goods is the modern, liberal state. But that road to security does not appear to be a feasible path in many weak, postcolonial states. Among postmodern states, by contrast, new issues of political, economic, and societal security have emerged, because these states have developed beyond modern statehood. In short, a security strategy based on the achievement of modern, liberal statehood is not well suited for confronting the security problems of postcolonial and postmodern statehood.

## The English school

Relations between sovereign states can be interrogated in three different ways (Wight 1991), each of which captures a particular aspect of those relations. The first way is realist; it emphasizes power politics in an international anarchy, involving the risk of conflict and warfare. A typical theorist in this tradition is Machiavelli. The second way is rationalist; it stresses that sovereign states conduct themselves in accordance with international law; they form an international society in that they see themselves bound by a common set of rules and by common institutions. A typical theorist in this tradition is Grotius. The third way is revolutionist; it accents human beings instead of states. Human beings make up a community of humankind. Progress towards human fulfillment is possible when international relations are better organized according to human needs. A typical theorist in this tradition is Kant. While these three traditions are all relevant, most English school theorists emphasize the rationalist view. That leads to an emphasis on the study of 'the anarchical society' (Bull 1995). Bull's major focus in that study is on international order.

The study of international order black-boxes the domestic affairs of states. It proceeds on the assumption that sovereign states are capable entities that provide the framework for the 'good life' of their citizens.[14] On this basis, English school theorists are not well equipped to account for postcolonial and postmodern states; when any analysis of change and development in substantial statehood is sharply downplayed, the emergence of such states can easily be overlooked. Yet such a critique is not entirely fair. With its focus on international norms, the rationalist approach was well suited to pick up the normative changes that led to constitutional independence for weak states, including ways in which these new weak entities had to create problems for existing international norms based on the assumption on more capable states (Jackson 1993a).[15] As regards postmodern states, Bull speculated in 1977 that the EU could come to rest in an 'intermediate stage' where 'there was real doubt both in theory and in reality as to whether sovereignty lay with the national governments or with the organs of the community' (Bull 1995:256). In a way this is exactly what has happened, but Bull was satisfied that such a situation would be confined to Europe, so that it 'would not mean that the global states system had been eclipsed, only that in this particular area ... there was a hybrid entity' (Bull 1995:256).

Yet Bull's statement is not entirely accurate. The economic, political, and socio-cultural changes towards postmodern statehood are relevant for a much larger group of states, as was argued in chapter 9. The predicament of weak, postcolonial states has been addressed, but more in terms of the standing of those states in international society than in terms of their substantial development.[16] It is a major shortcoming of English school theory that the development of substantial statehood in various parts of the world is left undertheorized.

As indicated, the English school frequently stresses the analysis of international order. International order is defined as 'a pattern of activity that sustains those goals of the society of states that are elementary, primary or universal' (Bull 1995:16); these goals concern the preservation of the society of states and the independence or external sovereignty of individual states.[17] But these goals are precisely premised on the notion that states are valuable entities that provide the political goods of the 'good life' for their citizens; any other justification for preserving sovereign states would not make sense. However, the changes in substantial statehood and in the regulative rules of sovereignty have created a new situation where the major issues are not addressed by attending to the traditional agenda of international order. Preserving the society of states and the sovereignty of individual states does not begin to address the security dilemma in weak, postcolonial states; neither does it begin to address challenges to effective governance in postmodern states. International order is primary for Bull because it creates the freedom for citizens of individual states to pursue their preferred versions of the good life. That is why sovereignty is so valuable. But this view fails to capture how the distinct sovereignty games of postcolonial and postmodern states have changed the conditions for the good life in major parts of the world in such a way that the creation of political goods has acquired an explicit international dimension.

In short, we are beyond international order in the traditional sense analysed by rationalists and depicted in the modern sovereignty game. But there is no developed cosmopolitan order either, where sovereign statehood has been clearly transcended and a different, global arrangement has taken its place.[18] It is this in-between situation, which rest on types of state that are very different from the modern state, that is insufficiently analysed by English school theorists.

Finally, this has implications for the appropriate ways of achieving security. In rationalist analysis, security means the preservation of international order, that is, preserving the society of states and the sovereignty of individual states. War plays a distinct role in this context; on the one hand, it is a manifestation of disorder which international society is compelled to restrict. On the other hand, war is 'a means which international society itself feels a need to exploit so as to achieve its own purposes. Specifically, in the perspective of international society, war is a means of enforcing international law, of preserving the balance of power, and, arguably, of promoting changes in the law generally regarded as just' (Bull 1995:181). That is, war may be needed for the establishment or maintenance of international order.

But this is not how security has been brought about among postmodern states;[19] they have instead chosen to restrict their autonomous exercise of sovereignty by establishing elaborate procedures for mutual intervention in their respective 'domestic' domains. A major concern in this respect has been the preservation of peace and stability. In the postmodern realm, therefore, security is no longer defined as the preservation of sovereignty and war is not a means to that end. It is rather the other way around: the manipulation of the rules of sovereignty is a means to achieve security defined as peace and stability. In postcolonial states, by contrast, domestic wars do not at all serve to create order, neither domestic, nor international. And international order, defined as the preservation of sovereignty as constitutional independence, is not at all meaningfully related to security for people in postcolonial states. The rationalist view of security as international order and of the role of war in that context stands in need of revision.

## Neomarxist international political economy

There are several neomarxist contributions to choose from. I have in mind here the work by Robert Cox (1996). The analytical starting point is historical structures, defined as 'a particular configuration of forces' (Cox 1996:97). Historical structures are made up of three categories of forces in reciprocal interaction: material capabilities, ideas, and institutions.[20] In the next step, historical structures are identified at three different levels and the dialectical interplay between these levels is examined. The levels (Cox 1996:100–1) are outlined in Figure 11.1.

The analytical task is to identify the specific configurations of these reciprocal relationships in the present historical conjuncture. As regards world order, Cox hypothesizes that we are approaching an order which is: (a) post-hegemonic, in the sense that it is based on 'mutual recognition of distinct traditions of civilization' (Cox 1993:141);[21] (b) post-Westphalian, in that political and economic power is less and less based on territory; and (c) post-globalization in that the pure market forces of globalization are increasingly brought under some form of political control.

It appears unproblematic for the framework provided by Cox to account for the emergence of different types of state. The very idea that such different forms or types exist are built directly into the analytical starting point. The analytical accent in doing so, however, is different from the one chosen in here. In accordance with historical materialism, Cox puts most emphasis on the production of material life. That is, changes in substantial statehood are explained primarily by reference to the development of forces and relations of production. In that context, the weak states in the periphery are primarily a product of imperialism, 'the dominance and subordination of . . . center over periphery, in a world political economy' (Cox 1996:96). In general, different forms of state are primarily important because they 'condition the ways in which different societies link into the global political economy' (Cox 1993:144). The present analysis puts more emphasis on the institution of sovereignty; that leads to accentuate changes in international norms. It also leads to highlighting the autonomy and responsibility of state elites in postcolonial states.[22]

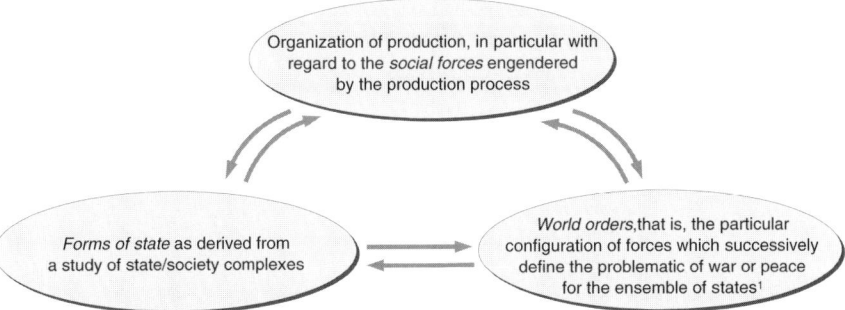

[1] 'Considered separately, social forces, forms of state, and world orders can be represented in a preliminary approximation as particular configurations of material capabilities, ideas, and institutions ... Considered in relation to each other ... each will be seen as containing as well as bearing the impact of, the others' (Cox 1996:101).

*Figure 11.1* Cox's analytical framework

The downplaying of sovereignty and the emphasis on political economy means that the study of world orders in Cox's framework is less concerned with war and peace, violent conflict, or different types of security dilemmas, and more concerned with issues of hegemony in the global political economy. Further, security problems are seen to derive directly from the development of capitalist production towards post-Fordism.[23] In that context, Cox's analysis does not speak very much to the issues of weak and disintegrating postcolonial states and there is no identification of the peculiar security dilemmas pertaining to different types of state. At the same time, his analysis is by no means a purely economistic one, and it would appear to be entirely possible to incorporate such elements in the framework. The revision that is needed for that to take place is a further move away from the traditional historical materialist emphasis on the structure of production and the accordance of a more important role to the institution of sovereignty.

The relationship between domestic and international is not a core theme in the Coxian approach. That is because the analytical framework is formulated in a way which conceives of a totality that includes 'domestic' as well as 'international' from the beginning. One can begin from the 'inside' part of the framework, that is, territorially based forms of state, and trace the effects of changes there on the 'outside' part, that is, social forces and world orders. Or one can begin from the 'outside' part and trace the effects of changes there on forms of state. The advantage of this view is that the dialectical interplay between 'domestic' and 'international' is made very clear and explicit. The potential downside, against the background of a desire to explore the international–domestic connections, is that the concept of a totality tends to eliminate this issue from the analytical agenda. Yet it appears possible to give it a more pronounced place within the Coxian framework. Again, this will require a revision that gives more emphasis to the institution of sovereignty and less emphasis to the structure of production.

The framework provided by Cox does not contain policy recommendations for the creation of security in the sense discussed earlier, because there is no explicit identification of security dilemmas. But there is a vision of a possible challenge to the existing world order by popular forces:

> The globalizing economy is polarizing advantaged and disadvantaged, while it fragments the disadvantaged into distinct and often rival identities. The challenge here is to build a coherent coalition of opposition. Such a coalition must, most likely, be built at local and national levels among groups that are aware of their day-to-day coexistence . . . Many locally based social forces will have to build transnational arrangements for mutual support . . . The macro-regional level offers a prospectively favorable terrain, most of all in Europe.
>
> (Cox 1996:309–10)

In so far as this is a call for more effective governance and democracy, it resonates with the analysis of postmodern statehood in Chapter 9[24] even if the analysis there also emphasized political and societal security; in weak, postcolonial states, however, it is difficult to conceive of this as an effective security strategy. These states contain very little of 'social forces' in the modern sense, and their main security problem is not created by capitalist globalization, but by self-interested state elites. Addressing those problems will, again, require a revised analysis with less focus on the capitalist world economy and more focus on the exceptional security dilemma in weak, postcolonial states.

## Constructivism

The constructivist approach comes in various versions. The remarks here will focus on the recent contribution by Alexander Wendt (1999). Material conditions matter in IR, but purely material factors can explain very little. The content and meaning of power and interest are 'constituted by ideas and culture' (Wendt 1999:371). The anarchy of the international system is primarily made up of a social structure, a distribution of ideas. A central element in the social structure of anarchy is the shared understanding concerning the use of organized violence. Three different ideal types of anarchical systems can be identified, each of which are based on different relationships between states: 'enemy' (a 'Hobbesian' culture of anarchy); 'rival' (a 'Lockean' culture of anarchy); and 'friend' (a 'Kantian' culture of anarchy) (Wendt 1999:ch. 6). A progressive evolution towards more cooperative forms of anarchy is not inevitable, but such progress is possible and once it has been achieved change to the worse is unlikely.[25] The dominant culture in the international system has been 'Lockean' but a number of states have created a 'Kantian' culture.

The ontological points raised by constructivism concern the nature of the social world. As recorded in Chapter 1, there are two extreme positions in this debate. At the objectivist extreme, international relations is a world shaped by the material structure of the international system;[26] at the subjectivist extreme, the social world of international relations is constituted by our language, ideas and concepts. Wendtian constructivism places emphasis on ideas as well as on material factors; so does the argument made here. Wendt's focus is on ideas shared by states; focus in this study is on material and non-material changes in statehood.

That there are different cultures of anarchy corresponds well with the ideas of different security dilemmas and different sovereignty games developed in the present analysis. But the constructivism set forth by Wendt is a systemic theory, a theory of the states system rather than a theory of the state. In developing that systemic theory, states are treated as unitary, intentional actors. In other words, the theory is not focused on the relationships between domestic and international; it is focused on the shared ideas which states develop through their interaction in the international system. As a purely systemic theory, constructivism is therefore not well suited to account for the emergence of different types of states.

Yet there are elements in the framework that can open up to such an account. Wendt identifies four variables that are causes of collective identity; that is, they can lead to changes in the culture of anarchy. They are: interdependence, common fate, homogeneity, and self-restraint (Wendt 1999:343–66). It is possible to connect those variables to the changes in statehood discussed here. That would link up the changes in postmodern statehood and the creation of a coordinated security community with the constructivist idea of a 'Kantian' culture of anarchy. Making the connection to postcolonial statehood is more difficult, because the postcolonial state violates some of the assumptions about sovereign statehood that Wendt makes in order to construct his systemic theory;[27] these assumptions do not foresee the existence of a 'Hobbesian paradox' in weak, postcolonial states. It is clear that a systemic theory tends to create a gulf between system and (state) unit, the very gulf that it is the primary ambition of an international–domestic–international analysis to overcome.[28]

It is an implicit assumption in Wendt's framework that states are valuable places that seek to create political goods for their citizens; as we have seen earlier this is an assumption shared with the dominant mainstream theories of realism and rationalism. Especially the security dilemma of weak, postcolonial states challenges that assumption. To address this issue requires that domestic factors are more integrated into the analysis. As it stands, the analysis of cultures of anarchy and of the factors that cause structural change from one culture to another says 'relatively little about domestic factors which are likely to be crucial for any pathway' (Wendt 1999:364).[29]

Finally, the security strategy implicit in constructivist systemic theory does not sufficiently address the security problems of weak, postcolonial and postmodern states. The very existence of postcolonial states is premised on a 'Lockean' anarchy where weak entities are not swallowed by stronger ones; but state elites that behave according to 'Lockean' norms externally may well be 'Hobbesian' predators domestically, as analysed in Chapter 8. The 'Kantian' anarchical culture created between postmodern states is connected to changes in substantial statehood that have also put new problems on the agenda. Neither the analysis of organized (domestic) violent conflict in postcolonial states, nor the analysis of economic, political, and societal challenges in postmodern states are sufficiently addressed through the examination of different systemic cultures of anarchy.

# Conclusion

The study of international relations has tended to insulate itself from the study of domestic politics. It has proceeded on the assumption that sovereign states are entities which seek to create the 'good life' for their citizens. In the vocabulary of the present analysis, most theories of IR have based their reflections on security, war, peace, conflict, and cooperation on a state unit that corresponds to the ideal type of the modern state identified in Chapter 6. Neorealism in particular appears to be dedicated to an analysis of international relations which conducts a purely systemic examination of the relations between sovereign states that are 'like units'. The other clusters of theory open more up to diachronic forms of analysis where the development and change of statehood and/or of 'cultures of anarchy' are a possibility. Especially the approach set forth by Robert Cox, but also to some extent liberalism, constructivism, and the English school can connect with an analysis which emphasizes the development and change of sovereign statehood. The theoretical revisions required for that to happen were indicated above.

From a broader perspective, the issues introduced by the analysis of sovereign statehood point to the need for reemphasis on the intimate connection between international political theory and domestic political theory.[30] The assumption that the international realm is not only one of power and the domestic realm is not only one of authority[31] is no longer acceptable. Coordinated security communities include authority; domestic realms of some states include (Hobbesian) anarchy. With the development of weak, postcolonial states on the one hand and postmodern states on the other hand, these elements of authority and anarchy respectively can no longer be sufficiently dealt with by introducing a simplifying assumption that does away with them.[32] The transformation of statehood and the development of new games of sovereignty require this more diverse analytical focus.[33]

In sum, the remedy required for facing the analytical challenge presented by different types of state is the (re-)marriage of 'international' and 'domestic' political theory. The result, hopefully, is a more comprehensive political theory which is dedicated to speculate about the state both in its 'international' and in its 'domestic' aspects. The great theoretical traditions in IR, including realism, liberalism, rationalism, and Marxism all grew out of theoretical endeavours that were committed to this broader agenda of political theory.[34] The need to proceed in this integrating manner was also quite clear to the political scientists writing in the early 1900s and even in the interwar period[35] (cf. Schmidt 1998). But that comprehensive agenda was somehow narrowed down during the Cold War. The development of sovereign statehood demands a restoration of the original, broader research programme. The next chapter will have more to say on this.

# 12
## Conclusion

How much has changed in international relations? The question of 'what has changed?' cannot be answered without reference to theory and history. Assessing the significance of what has happened requires prior notions of what is important and such notions can only come from theory applied to specific historical contexts. 'Change' in and of itself is not interesting. Outside of a theoretically specified research context, change is as important or unimportant as its opposite, continuity. The point was forcefully made by R. J. Vincent: 'It makes as little sense ... to write about 'change in international relations' as it would to write about 'continuity in international relations'. Neither project has a centre, a thesis, a 'research question" (Vincent 1983:68).

International relations theory contains a number of different, theoretically informed answers to the 'what has changed question' (Sørensen 1994). They range between the 'conservative' view that nothing much has changed and the 'radical' view that almost everything has changed. The major 'conservative' view is neorealist. Neorealist analysis underscores the basic continuity of the present international political system. There has been no great transformation from anarchy to hierarchy. Anarchy prevails; states will continue to have to fend for themselves. But there has been 'medium term' change in the system; we are in an altered state of bipolarity, meaning that the first steps have been taken in a transition from bipolarity to multipolarity (Waltz 1993).

The major 'radical' views are connected with differents strands of radical liberalism. Some analysts foresee the end or the disintegration of states into many small units due to the process of globalization (Ohmae 1993, Naisbitt 1994). Others perceive of a profound transformation of the system, 'from the long-standing state-centric, anarchical system to a new set of bifurcated arrangements wherein a multi-centric world composed of diverse "sovereignty-free" collectivities has evolved apart from and in competition with the state-centric world of "sovereignty-bound" actors' (Rosenau 1993).

The neorealist view sees too little change; it diagnoses continuity in that anarchy has reigned for some eleven hundred years (Mearsheimer 1995); even the transformation in the polarity of the system is an extremely rare event; we are presently in the process of the second change in that area over a period of more than three hundred years. 'Radical' versions of liberalism, by contrast, diagnose too much change; they tend much prematurely to sign off the sovereign state to the dustbin of history.

But if the glass of change is both half full and half empty how do we proceed in order to arrive at more precise assessments of what has happened? The present analysis has suggested to focus on changes in statehood and their consequences for international relations. The analysis sides with the conservative view in taking sovereign states as the basic units of the international system; it also sides with the conservative view in emphasizing the continued existence of sovereignty as constitutional independence. However, the conservative view is not sufficient. It does not capture the significant transformations of substantial statehood and of the regulative rules of sovereignty. These changes have helped create new and qualitatively different security dilemmas in weak, postcolonial and in postmodern states. They also helped create qualitatively different games of sovereignty. Indeed, the tension between constitutional independence on the one hand, and the new regulative rules of the two sovereignty games on the other hand, precisely point to the tension between 'old' and 'new', between continuity and change in the present international system.

Critics could argue that the ideal types are not really very interesting because they merely represent limited regional groupings in Africa and Europe respectively. It is clear that the postcolonial ideal type of state is modelled primarily on the experience of Sub-Saharan Africa, whereas the postmodern ideal type is modelled primarily on the experience of EU Members. But Africa and Europe are more than 'limited regional groupings', that is, what happens there is sufficiently important to be relevant for the larger international system. Furthermore, the ideal types are relevant for other areas as well. Chapter 9 made clear that the defining aspects of postmodern statehood have developed to different extents in various countries in the OECD area. In other words, while the features of postmodern statehood have developed unevenly across countries, there is no reason to believe that these developments are confined to EU-Europe alone. They are significantly present in all the most advanced states in the international system.

As regards postcolonial statehood, the distinct features of that ideal type are clearly relevant for a larger number of countries in the Third World. The more general studies of problems in what is often called 'developing countries' identify the specific traits of these countries in a way which clearly reflects the characteristics of postcolonial statehood set forth here (see for example

Martinussen 1997). The annual 'Human Development Report' from the United Nations Development Programme is most often focused on those same aspects as well. That said, it is true that a large group of Sub-Saharan African states undoubtedly make up the weakest units in the present international system. Many other Third World countries in large parts of Latin America and Asia have fared somewhat better.

The idea that the sovereign state is being transformed while it continues to be the focal entity in world politics is shared by a great number of scholars, several of which have been discussed earlier in this book. It is not a controversial position at all, because the critical devil is in the detail: to which precise extent have states been transformed and what are the results of that for the future of world order, understood as the configuration of forces that set the context for world affairs? Most of the present investigation has been devoted to answering the first part of that question. The second part of the question, about the consequences for world order, is briefly discussed here followed by considerations on the implications of the overall analysis for IR-theory.

A basic premise for present and future reflections on world order must be a rejection of the sharp division between 'domestic' and 'international'. Both postmodern and postcolonial forms of statehood contain features which transcend that sharp division because they exhibit new forms of integration between 'domestic' and 'international'. Considerable implications follow from this. As indicated in the previous chapter, political theory about the good life can no longer use an unambiguously segregated 'domestic' sphere as its analytical point of departure. Nor can speculations about violent conflict and survival be definitely consigned to an 'international' sphere of anarchy. In other words, both thinking about the good life and about survival and violent conflict requires an integrated analysis of 'domestic' as well as of 'international' because sovereign statehood has been transformed so as to contain such integration.

With this point of departure, an evaluation of future prospects for world order must include both the classical 'international' issue concerning survival, that is, the outlook for war and peace; and the classical 'domestic' issues concerning the good life, which in this context will be seen to contain two aspects. The first is the primarily material aspect of economic welfare and equality; the second is the primarily non-material aspect of identity, community and cultural values. My remarks on world order perspectives aim at emphasizing the interplay between 'domestic' and 'international'; there is no room here for a fully developed world order investigation; furthermore, focus will be on postmodern and postcolonial states.

Postmodern states, I have argued, make up a coordinated security community; they have moved out of the Hobbesian anarchy which is at the heart of neorealist analysis. Their peace is basically a liberal peace. The liberal theory of peace has most often been classified as a second image theory,[1] because it is essentially predicated upon relations between states that are 'good', that is, liberal, democratic states. On this view, we should expect the future development of the liberal, coordinated security community to hinge on the continued health of liberal democracy in the states that are members of that community. But given the context of postmodern statehood this is clearly a misleading position. Whether liberal democracy improves or deteriorates is by no means a purely 'domestic' issue anymore. It is fully as much an 'international' issue, because the major challenges to liberal democracy are connected to the cooperation that unfolds on the supranational level, as most easily seen in the context of the EU.

Supranational cooperation has furthered democracy in the sense that it enlarges the potential scope of democratic control; what was 'external constraints and influences' earlier are converted to processes that elected representatives can in principle regulate and control in cooperation with other Member States. But supranational cooperation also challenges democracy in several ways, as indicated in Chapter 9. The democratic problems related to supranational governance include major aspects of democracy: the proper, balanced representation of *demos* in the supranational institutions; the degree of ultimate control by *demos* over the decisionmaking of those institutions; and the existence of a democratic community, that is, a common sphere for public debate and the formation of public opinion. The EU-system has problems in all of these areas, especially the last one, because there is no well-developed cross-border democratic community in the EU; the formation of public opinion continues to take place in context of the single Member State. Therefore, the transformation to postmodern statehood contains challenges to democracy as well as possibilities for an improved democracy.

A precise balance sheet of the advances and the problems cannot be drawn here; it would have to take the consequences of the expansion of EU-membership in Eastern Europe into consideration. But even when the existence of a 'democratic deficit' problem is acknowledged, it is highly implausible that the liberal peace community would be put in serious jeopardy. On the one hand, EU-membership has contributed to the consolidation of democracy in the formerly authoritarian members from Southern Europe (Portugal, Greece, Spain); there is thus reason to believe that membership will have similar effects in Eastern Europe. On the other hand, the 'democratic deficit' on the supranational level is recognized and intensely debated in the EU at the present time.

What about the prospects for the larger postmodern security community? It has been slowly expanding over recent decades, in conjunction with the further development of the liberal pillars upon which it is based: republican liberalism (transitions to democracy and further consolidation of democracy in more countries); institutional liberalism (further expansion of institutionalized cooperation between states); interdependence liberalism (higher levels of economic interdependence and general interconnectedness); and sociological liberalism (extended scope and depth of transnational networks of substate actors). These liberal pillars have furthered a 'constructivist' change in 'national' identities helping further cooperation and integration. Neither profound changes in the balance of power in context of the ending of the Cold War, nor 'bad apples', such as setbacks for democracy in some countries, have seriously endangered it.

Any prospects for major inter-state war is therefore not connected with the realm of postmodern states; it rather emerges in context of those large countries that display a combination of the features of weak postcolonial, modern, and postmodern statehood. They include Russia, China, and India. A pessimistic comment on Russia was offered in Chapter 3. All that can be added here is that even the development of these large states is increasingly tied in with an inter-play between 'international' and 'domestic'. This is especially the case in Russia and China, where embryonic civil societies remain relatively weak and the ruling state elites therefore enjoy a high degree of domestic autonomy. In those cases external pressure, or the lack of it, can have a crucial influence of the trajectory of development. Whether or not the IMF continues to bail out the ruling Russian oligarchy and thereby helps postpone the day of reckoning for a sick economy and a predatory elite is then of paramount importance. Whether or not the optimum external pressure for democratization and a more open society in China is applied then becomes of paramount importance.

What about domestic violent conflict in weak postcolonial states? Are there additional state failures or breakdowns under way? The basic preconditions that sparked violent domestic conflict and state failure remain in place. They consist of states that are weak in substance and have sovereignty in the form of constitutional independence. Rapid processes of development creating states with more substance are not to be expected, as argued in Chapter 8. Nor is it likely that constitutional independence will be abandoned, as indicated in Chapter 10; in that sense the 'slavish devotion to sovereignty' will continue. The result will often be states that are ever weaker in substance, but retain the shell of sovereignty that is constitutional independence. International society will not assume anything near full responsibility for the development of post-colonial states or for the safety and well-being of their populations. It has stepped in sometimes, not in all possible cases for sure, when a situation of state failure or breakdown created a sufficiently dramatic situation of acute human suffering. But most of the time, the peoples – and the governments – are basically responsible for themselves in accordance with constitutional independence. The continued predicament of individuals and groups in weak post-colonial states is based on a formal right to sovereign statehood underwritten by international society. The domestic degrees of freedom this has provided for state elites have been exploited for predation more often than for the creation of domestic security. This is likely to continue; not primarily because it is actively supported by international society but because viable alternatives to the international and domestic conditions that produced that situation are unlikely to emerge.

Let me turn to the issue of welfare and equality. The truism that economic globalization contains new possibilities for advance towards more welfare and less inequality as well as new constraints that may involve setbacks in these areas bears repeating. In the postmodern realm, general increases in living standards have been accompanied by increasing inequality.[2] The poorest people are in the weak, postcolonial states in Africa south of the Sahara, but there are also considerable pockets of poverty in Central America and Asia (China, Burma, Nepal, Bhutan) and a relatively large part of the world's poor are in India, a country of enormous internal economic variation.

Against this background, global inequality is stark and on the increase. The richest 20 per cent of the world's population claim an 86 per cent share of world GDP compared with a one per cent share for the bottom fifth. Similar figures apply to shares of exports of goods and services, shares of foreign direct investment, of world telephone lines, and so on (UNDP 1999). The message is clear, as indicated in Chapter 5: economic globalization does not bring development to countries in and of itself. A successful process of development requires a favourable set of international and domestic preconditions. It was argued in Chapter 8 that the peculiar external security situation of postcolonial states had created an unfavourable environment for development. At the same time, the domestic situation of 'captured autonomy' must be considered primarily responsible for the lack of development progress.

These reflections point in two directions when it comes to assessment of development prospects; the first concerns the importance of state elites that are seriously interested in promoting development, that is, who are not narrowly self-seeking. The other concerns the need for development strategy and theory which contemplates the interplay between 'domestic' and 'international'. The importance of the competence and commitment of political leaders was stressed in a recent analysis of two postcolonial (relative) success-cases, Botswana and Mauritius. On independence in 1968, Mauritius was a poor sugar-economy with deep ethnic cleavages in the population; Botswana was a cattle-economy with a population divided into eleven different tribes. Botswana had the good fortune of discovering diamonds on its soil and Mauritius is favourably positioned for foreign trade, but other postcolonial countries have had similar advantages and have not been able to convert them into broader development. How could Mauritius and Botswana succeed economically and politically (in establishing major aspects of political democracy)? A recent analysis identifies several relevant factors (Carroll and Carroll 1997). In the present context it is relevant to emphasize the importance of 'talented political leaders that were personally committed to democratic government, and to economic development' (1997:470).

As indicated by Carroll and Carroll, it is reasonable to assume that success cultivates success: once a competent leadership has been established and has demonstrated a decent track record chances are good that capable leadership will continue. But what about that crucial turn-around phase, where success is by no means secure and leadership might as well turn out to be narrow-minded, egoistic, and self-serving? What is it that brings forward the Mandelas instead of the Mobutus? If it is not pure coincidence then the question merits further research. The hopeful answer that such leadership is more or less automatically created by holding elections has not been confirmed by events.[3]

From a more general perspective, there is a need for reviving a comprehensive development thinking with focus on the interplay between 'domestic' and 'international'. A case can be made for the revival and further development of dialectical dependency theory. Orthodox neomarxist dependency theory one-sidedly stressed how (the lack of) development in the weak states in the periphery was due to economic exploitation by the advanced capitalist states in the core. Dialectical dependency theory expanded this view to include a more dynamic analysis of the interplay between primarily economic 'international' and 'domestic' forces (Cardoso and Faletto 1979; Kay 1989). A revised version would put further emphasis on non-economic factors of that relationship (political, social, cultural) and also place it in context of the development of the institution of sovereignty. That would lead to a more balanced view of 'international' opportunities for, as well as constraints on, 'domestic' processes of development. Furthermore, there is a need to combine reflections on security with reflections on development.[4] Such a move would open for better based assessments of concrete development prospects in the various postcolonial states.

The final set of issues I want to address concerns identity, community, and cultural values. These issues have received growing attention in recent years, perhaps because it has become increasingly clear that the interaction between 'domestic' and 'international' in several cases led to the creation of group identities and values with a problematic relationship to sovereign states. The development and change of sovereign statehood, I have argued, sets the primary framework within which group identities and notions of community have been formed. National communities based on *Gemeinschaft* (the cultural–ethnic idea of a community of people defined by the nation) and *Gesellschaft* (the duties and obligations of individuals to the state and the rights and privileges that they receive in return, that is, citizenship) replaced completely different, feudal forms of identity and community in context of the larger set of economic and political changes which led to the formation of the modern state.[5] There was nothing automatic about the process: winning political rights and civil liberties involved protracted struggles by popular groups against elites toiling to preserve their privileged positions. The creation of national political and cultural communities based on democratic citizenship and human rights was not completed in several modern, Western states before well into the twentieth century.

Two consequences follow from this; first, it is not possible to cast the current debates about identity, community and values in the form of a 'clash of civilizations' which feature a liberalized, democratic 'West' against the ('particularist and collectivistic') 'Rest' (Huntington 1996), because such a view completely disregards the historical context. Not long ago, Europe was herself 'particularist and collectivistic' and not democratic at all. Identity, community, and the values upon which it is based, develop in interaction with the larger development of statehood; this is the case both in Europe and elsewhere. Therefore, if there is a 'clash' concerning identity, community and basic values, it takes place in an interplay where the stage is set by various 'domestic' groups on the one hand, affected by a host of 'international' influences on the other. What is frequently classified by observers as 'fundamentalist' reactions by Hindus and Moslems alike should rather be seen as contemporary discursive reactions to the challenges posed by complex processes of modernization in postcolonial societies (Senghaas 1998; Hansen 1997). By no means is this a process pitting 'civilizations' against each other.

Second, dramatic changes in statehood are likely to involve significant changes in patterns of identity, community, and values. In the weak postcolonial states, lack of success in state-building has obstructed nation-building as well. States have not supplied any benefits of citizenship; the result has frequently been a popular retreat into ethnic community which then functions both as the repository of cultural identity, and as a provider of (at least some of) the services that more substantial states offer their citizens. It was explained in Chapter 8 how that could lead to violent conflict between ethnic groups, but this is a contingent outcome, predicated on the interplay of a complex set of factors, including the trajectory of development of the state in question and the 'primordial' characteristics of specific groups. Furthermore, the formation of identity and community in postcolonial states is increasingly infused with attempts by external and some domestic forces to promote accountability, democracy, and human rights.

Changes from modern towards postmodern statehood have produced a different set of challenges, as discussed in Chapter 9. Globalization and multilevel governance have pushed fragmentation in some cases, but they have also further helped promote a sense of cosmopolitan community based on liberal ideas of democracy, liberties, and rights. Several scholars are hopeful that this will form the basis for an innovative construction of cosmopolitan citizenship and democracy (Held 1995; Linklater 1998).

There is thus a discernible trend towards the strengthening of identities and communities 'below' and 'above' the level of the state in context of the changes in statehood analysed in this book. The analysis of these developments would benefit from more focus on the necessary and sufficient conditions for the development of cosmopolitan citizenship and democracy. It would appear to be the case that such notions must have more to offer the radically excluded groups in postcolonial states than the mere possibility of presenting their views and being heard in the debate. Without substantial material improvements in context of a cooperating world polity and world economy towards better conditions of existence for these groups, there would appear to be scant possibility for the creation of a cosmopolitan community worthy of the name. This takes us back, of course, to the severe dilemmas of postcolonial development analysed earlier.

What are the implications of all this for IR-theory? The aim of the following brief remarks is not to promote any specific body of theory; I rather consider it an advantage that 'IR theory is now *irretrievably* plural', so that attempts to 'stifle debate or at least to direct it and channel it into 'appropriate' methodological forms are pointless' (Rengger 2000:189–90). The present study has certainly benefited from a number of different insights, produced by liberals, realists, English school theorists, neomarxists, international political economists, constructivists, normative theorists, and others. Continued debate between different theoretical (in the broadest sense) positions should be welcomed. What is sooner missing from many theoretical debates nowadays is any attempt to make a connection between what strikes one as extremely sophisticated epistemological and ontological positions on the one hand, and their implications – or at least their broad attachment – to substantial research agendas on the other. It would therefore be helpful, so is the present claim, for the further development of IR-theory if the concrete issue of 'what to study and why' was given a higher priority in the discussion.

The starting point for the research agenda which grows out of this analysis is the acknowledgement that 'international' and 'domestic' are intimately connected and that this requires a broad study of the development and change of sovereign statehood. That leads to the following recommendations, guiding the pursuit of more concrete questions:

1. Proceed on the assumption that the core values pursued by states, that is, security, freedom, order, justice, wealth, and welfare, each contain 'international' as well as 'domestic' aspects. None of those values can be reduced to a purely 'international' or a purely 'domestic' issue.
2. Therefore, avoid purely systemic or purely domestic analysis. Put the 'international'–'domestic' interplay at the centre of inquiry and ask questions about 'outside-in' and 'inside-out' relationships.

3. Interrogate the normative issues connected with changes in sovereign state-hood. What is the ethical standing of the sovereign state as an institution given the changes in statehood that have taken place? What are the institutional alternatives to sovereign statehood?

The modern state was fundamentally self-sustained. It was expected to uphold or furnish a series of core values for its citizens (Jackson and Sørensen 1999:3–7). In the pursuit of these values the modern state faced a number of typical problems which have made up the subject matter of IR-theory. First and foremost the problem of survival and security in an anarchic world where heavily armed states faced each other. Profound changes in statehood have created qualitatively different security dilemmas. In postcolonial states the traditional security dilemma has been turned on its head; instead of domestic order and international threat there is domestic threat and international order. In postmodern states violent external threat has been dramatically reduced because these states make up a coordinated security community. But new challenges to effective governance have emerged instead.

New research questions concerning security emerge from these changes. Some of the most significant ones are briefly spelled out in what follows. First, as regards the value of security: what are the pertinent security problems after sovereign statehood has been so radically transformed in different parts of the international system? How is security provided under the new conditions? What are the implications of this for the good life? Is it at all possible to uphold the idea that sovereign states are extremely valuable institutions or do the new conditions of statehood support the critical view that states create more problems than they solve?

Freedom was another core value upheld by modern states. Sovereignty in context of the modern state has traditionally been assumed as the appropriate framework for personal freedom, that is, the proper context for democracy and democratization. Postcolonial and postmodern statehood create an entirely different framework for the pursuit of freedom and democracy. Can freedom be realized under the new conditions? Is it at all possible to construct meaningful forms of freedom and democracy under the conditions of postcolonial and postmodern sovereign statehood? In which ways must ideas about democracy and freedom be developed in order to explicitly confront the new situation?

Order and justice make up additional major values that states are expected to uphold. Hedley Bull defined international order as 'a pattern or dispositions of international activity that sustains those goals of the society of states that are elementary, primary or universal' (Bull 1995:16). Upholding international order could be seen as a primary goal because it allowed for the pursuit of the good life in context of the modern state (see Chapter 10). But changes in statehood promote a different agenda of order which must be increasingly concerned with what Bull called 'world order', meaning order among humankind as a whole. That is because the pursuit of the good life in postcolonial and postmodern states is much more dependent on and tied in with the 'international' context than was the case in the segregated modern states. Issues of international and of world order are therefore tied together to an extent that raises problems about the clearcut distinction which Bull made between them. How should the relationship between international and world order be comprehended under the new conditions? Are states less important than earlier for the creation of world order? What kinds of world order are possible in a situation where constitutional independence continues to define a society of sovereign states while substantial statehood and the regulative rules of sovereignty reflect a much higher degree of association and integration between 'domestic' and 'international'?

Finally, there are the values of wealth and welfare. The economic integration in context of uneven globalization, together with the 'domestic' economic weakness of postcolonial states has created a situation where the pursuit of wealth and welfare in postmodern and postcolonial states is intimately connected to the 'international' level. How and to what extent can states provide wealth and welfare under the new conditions? Is it possible to harness global market forces so as to preserve their beneficial effects and to avoid the drawbacks? Is development, that is, the creation of wealth and welfare always possible in all postcolonial states? If not, what are the necessary and sufficient 'domestic' and 'international' preconditions for development to take place?

Overall, one must hope that sustainable solutions can be found to the security predicament of the populations in weak, postcolonial states. One must also hope that effective and democratic solutions can be found to the governance problems in postmodern states. None of what has been said here denies that solutions can be found. But there is reason to believe that postmodern states and weak, postcolonial states will be with us for some considerable time. They set the conditions for the daily lives of a very large number of people. That is why an examination of their distinctive features, of their peculiar security dilemmas, and of their unique sovereignty games remains so very important.

# Notes

## 1 An Analytical Framework

1  In a seminal article, Peter Gourevitch (1978) urged scholars to examine domestic and international politics 'as a whole'. Kenneth Waltz notes that 'any theory of international politics requires also a theory of domestic politics, since states affect the system's structure even as it affects them' (1986:331). Justin Rosenberg speaks of the need for an 'integrating frame of reference' and for the necessity to 'perceive reality in terms of a social totality' (1994:96,100). Robert Walker laments 'the account of politics reified in the spatial categories of theories of international relations' (1995:313). Finally, Robert Cox emphasizes the interrelationship between 'forms of state', 'social forces' and 'world orders'; 'each [is] containing, as well as bearing the impact of, the others' (1996:101).

2  Ethan Kapstein notes that the treatment of domestic and international as a whole 'continues to be a major, if elusive, goal' (1995:755). Gabriel Almond writes that the interaction between domestic and international is 'a complex dynamic process which offers no simple answers or solutions' (1989:257).

3  For excellent overviews, see Müller and Risse-Kappen (1990) and Evangelista (1997).

4  According to neorealism these forces lead toward the creation of 'like units'; this view is further explored later, in Chapter 2.

5  See the fine discussion in Doyle (1997).

6  The debate between 'defensive' and 'offensive' realism is continued in the review article of Fareed Zakaria's book by Sean M. Lynn-Jones (1998).

7  It is not clear how much democracy that is needed in order to achieve the democratic peace. Fragile democracies, in the early stages of a democratization process, often exhibit more instead of less violent conflict (Sørensen 1997a). Therefore, some consolidation of democracy is needed before a peaceful domestic political culture can form the basis of peaceful international relations. Such consolidation has clearly not been achieved in the case of many of the frail democratizations in the South and in the East; and setbacks towards authoritarianism are to be expected. Republican liberal theory therefore often appears overly optimistic and it has not been able precisely to identify when the domestic conditions for the democratic peace are in place.

8  There are, however, a few recent attempts by liberal analysis to further explore change in context of a domestic–international interplay (Keohane 1995; Deudney and Ikenberry 1999; Moravcsik 1997). They will be taken up later, where some of the results will be incorporated in the present analysis.

9  'The literature on domestic structures has served as a way of bridging the debate between internal and external explanations for foreign policy in issue-areas ranging from international political economy to international security policy. . . . In both fields scholars have identified cases in which countries with divergent domestic structures faced common international pressures. They tested propositions derived from the competing internal and external theories and found that the relative power of each theory's predictions depended on the domestic structure' (Evangelista 1997:204).

10  See also Müller and Risse-Kappen (1990:384).

11  Which includes: (a) the nature of political institutions; (b) the structure of society; and (c) the nature of the coalition-building processes in the policy-networks linking state and society (Risse-Kappen 1991).

12  The effects of international forces on domestic structures was addressed in another study by Peter Katzenstein. 'Small States in World Markets' (Katzenstein 1985) traces the development of corporatism in a selection of small, West-European states. Corporatist structures developed in response to the need for rapid and flexible adaptation to constantly changing circumstances in the world market. At the same time, the specific corporatist models in the countries under study vary in their make-up according to their domestic structures, especially their historical patterns of industrialization. A project led by Robert Keohane and Helen Milner (1996) examines the effects of economic internationalization on domestic politics and stresses that 'the clearest effect of internationalization has been to undermine governments' autonomy in the domain of macroeconomic policy...' (Milner and Keohane 1996:256).

13  Roger Scully notes that the research following Putnam's argument 'has been empirically restricted because it focuses on individual, onetime instances of cooperative agreements to the exclusion of ongoing and institutionalized cooperative relationships. This research has also been conceptually restricted, because it maintains a strict division between the "domestic" and the "international"' (Scully 1998:373).

14  This view of structure is quite similar to Waltz's notion of structure as a set of constraining conditions. But note also that Cox is explicit about the substance of historical structures; they consist of material capabilities, ideas and institutions.

15  For various attempts to remedy this state of affairs, see Cox (1996), Buzan (1991), Halliday (1994), and most recently, Wendt (1999).

16  In addition to the 'IR-view', there are thus at least three major theoretical traditions to draw on in discussing the state: the liberal-pluralist; the Marxist; and the Weberian tradition (cf. Greenberg 1990; Wendt 1999).

17  Waltz's neorealist theory is keen to demonstrate that states possess (and control) clearly identifiable national economies, because if that were not the case, 'the structure of international politics would have to be redefined' (Waltz 1979:94). My argument in later chapters is that Waltz is right the sense that the structure of international politics should be redefined (or at least seriously modified), precisely because the assumption does indeed not hold: many states do not have clearly identifiable national economies.

18  Robert Cox and Alexander Wendt have both emphasized this view. Cox notes that historical structures consist of 'material capabilities, ideas, and institutions' (Cox 1996:98). Wendt says that '[s]ocial structures have three elements: shared knowledge, material resources and practices' (Wendt 1995:73).

19  As emphasized by Wendt, this is not merely a matter of adding an 'ideas factor' to a 'material' factor. Existing structures are never purely material on purely non-material. Political–military power, for example, is thus not purely material power; it is also constituted by ideas, that is, 'the discursive conditions' (Wendt 1999:135) that makes it work.

20  Or even supply quantitative evidence in support of a theory: 'Nor is there any objection to the counting of phenomena that do not differ from one another in any relevant respect, and presenting this as evidence in support of a theory' (1969:33).

21  Consequently, Bull's own work in the classical tradition is full of examples of such reasoning.

22  The existence of such a space does not mean that various positions have reached agreement, not to mention consensus. It merely means that there is common room for a meaningful, pluralistic pursuit of interrogating international relations.

## 2   Theories on the Effect of 'International' on 'Domestic'

1  For example, liberals expect liberal democracy to prevail universally (homogeneity) but they also make a distinction between a liberal democratic, modern part of the world, and a non-democratic, non-modern part of the world for present purposes (heterogeneity).
2  One recent discussion of the issue is by Hendrik Spruyt; he identifies two types of processes that lead to institutional isomorphism; one is competition, the other is learning. He concludes that 'the emergence of isomorphism in terms of sovereign territoriality has thus elements of competition and evolution as well as learning. In a rough sense, competition indicates which units perform better than others. But this does not work in the sense of an agent-less and non-intentional manner. Individuals consciously choose to imitate such forms and only tolerate types of organization which can similarly commit themselves to agreements and which have specified territorial boundaries to limit their claims to jurisdiction. Through this mechanism of mutual empowerment the state system has become a social construction' (Spruyt 1994a:18). In other words, the convergence on sovereign statehood as dominant institutional form involves both competition and learning. We can by no means take for granted that the sovereign state system will persist in its present form. New institutions may emerge, as demonstrated by the European Union.

## 3   Political–Military Power Shaping Domestic Structures: Homogeneity or Heterogeneity?

1  For arguments along these lines, see Halliday (1994:121); see also Waltz (1979:127–8).
2  The basic problem was the so-called 'scissors crisis': when sufficient industrial consumer goods were not emerging in the market at attractive prices, the peasants would withhold their produce from the market and consume it themselves instead. And so there was an insufficient agricultural surplus available to support a faster rate of industrial accumulation. Solving the problem by making more goods available for the peasants would merely mean that more of the available surplus remained in agriculture.
3  Therefore, liberalism has not been completely defeated in Russia. One indication of this is that Boris Yeltsin did not order a *coup* in 1996, as his memoirs seem to report he almost did (*New York Times*, 8 October 2000). I owe this point to Robert Keohane.

## 4   International Norms Shaping Domestic Structures: Homogeneity or Heterogeneity?

1  That peace undermined the power of the church and strengthened secular power. The choice between Catholicism and Protestantism became the privilege of local rulers; that is the principle of *cujus regio ejus religio*. The corresponding secular principle gives the King authority over his own realm: *Rex in regno suo est Imperator regni sui*. Dispersed medieval authority was replaced by centralized modern authority, the

King and his government. The world did not change overnight at one specific point in time; elements of the old system remained in place for a long period. Still, it is justified to look at 1648 as a crucial point in the transition from feudal to modern authority. The old system was decaying; a new system, with sovereign statehood as its basic principle of political organization, was growing ever stronger.

2  Three aspects of those conditions should be emphasized. First, the psychological atmosphere; Japanese travellers to the West could report of a level of industrial progress that Japan could not begin to match. Together with the treaties, this pushed a feeling of racial inferiority in 'a proud people for whom a certain self-imputed racial superiority was an important aspect of identity' (Gong 1984:172). Second, the old order in Japan was already crumbling under the weight of its inbuilt weaknesses; the Tokugawa regime would most probably have been brought down in any case, even in the absence of external pressure (Storry 1968:94; Scalapino 1977). Finally, given the maturity of its pre-industrial economy and the level of literacy, Japan had optimum preconditions for a process of modernization (cf. Kemp 1983:21).

3  In the case of the Soviet Union, its power position was without question overrated, as indicated in Chapter 3. In terms of economic and cultural power, the Soviet Union was surely no match for the West (cf. Gaddis 1997:284). But the combination of Soviet efforts in the war including Stalin's prominent role in setting up the postwar order in Yalta and Potsdam; its rapid acquisition of a large stock of nuclear weapons; and perhaps also its ideological appeal to many Westerners as a strong, crisis-free, egalitarian system; all these elements pushed the Soviet Union to a postwar position on par with the United States.

4  As emphasized by Robert Jackson, this practice of respecting existing borders 'is a fundamental normative change from the basis of state jurisdiction historically, which could be determined by military force, by Machiavellian diplomacy, by commercial transaction, by dynastic marriage, and by other such means' (Jackson 1995b:66).

5  But in France and Italy in the 1950s, the reform settlements amounted to a 'marginalization of the working class' (Cronin 1996:58). The strong communist parties in those countries were squeezed out of the coalition governments in 1947 and it would be several decades before systems of representation emerged that better reflected wage labour interests.

6  The Basic Law aimed at creating the political stability that had been absent in the Weimar Republic; at the same time it sought to avoid the creation of a too strong political centre. West Germany became a parliamentary republic with a strong chancellor and a weak president, and with substantial authority vested in the states (the *Länder*). This federal construction is based on a set of overlapping competencies (Katzenstein 1987). One aspect of this is the administrative and legislative powers of the *Länder*. Another concerns the institutional division of powers at the central level; the Bundesrat in Karlsruhe; the central administration in Bonn (now Berlin); and the monetary authorities in Frankfurt. Finally, this is combined with a party and an election system which promotes consensual policies. In sum, the system contains a far-reaching division of powers combined with a centre containing an in-built preference for consensus.

# 5  Economic Power Shaping Domestic Structures: Homogeneity or Heterogeneity?

1  For good analyses see for example Held, McGrew *et al.* (1999), Pieterse (1997), Keohane and Milner (eds) (1996), Clark (1998), and Scholte (2000).

2  In that sense the labels of 'internationalization' (cf. Goldman 1999) or 'de-nationalization' (cf. Zürn 1998) are more precise. But they then downplay some of the new aspects that are unique to present processes of globalization.

3  There are two aspects of economic globalization; one is 'more of the same', that is, the increase in well-known economic ties, such as trade, investment and other elements of economic interdependence. The other aspect is the emergence of a new 'global economy' where design, production, finance, and distribution take place on a world scale. That is, the primary framework for economic activity is the world, not the national economy. In earlier days, companies were most often national before they became transnational. In a global economy, even small companies immediately function on a global scale; design and production may take place in several different and often very distant locations; and the marketplace is global.

4  For reasons having to do with the Cold War they were granted privileged access to the American market in the 1960s. Their export strategy was so successful that they faced import limitation measures from the West together with increased pressure for opening up their own economies.

5  For a brief discussion of the economic situation in Russia, see Chapter 3.

6  There is consensus that state intervention along neoliberal lines is not enough and state intervention along orthodox socialist lines is too much. In the space between these positions, there are two broad areas for the state to deal with: the creation of a sound social and economic infrastructure for production in order to further economic growth, and issues which have to do with redistribution and welfare. It is clear that the actual (and proper) state/market mix must vary across societies and within societies over time (World Bank 1997).

# 6  Types of State in the Present International System

1  Charles Tilly (1990) has summarized the main approaches to state formation in an instructive way, making a distinction between world systems analysis (for example, Wallerstein 1974); mode of production analysis (for example, Anderson 1974); geopolitical analysis (for example, Rosenau 1970); and statist analysis (for example, Gilpin 1988; Waltz 1988). While the authors of the different approaches should not be seen as determinists arguing solely the view of their analytical corner, they do work with very dissimilar arguments.

2  One dangerous factor in such an undertaking should be mentioned immediately: it might appear that history is predetermined in that the feudal state 'had to' grow out of the Roman empire; medieval, more centralized statehood 'must' follow feudalism in some combination with the existence of city-states; these in turn were 'bound to' be superseded by absolutist states and further down the road the modern state was the inescapable consequence of absolutism. No such predetermination is argued here, of course. The proper analytical stance must be one of structured contingency: at a certain point in time a number of different paths of development are possible but some are always more likely than others. Humans can change the world but they are enabled and constrained by the social structures in which they live.

3  This brief overview is indebted to the excellent synthesis in Opello and Rosow (1999).

4  This definition draws on Giddens (1992:121); Mann (1993:55); and Skocpol (1979:29).

5  Further distinctions are possible on the latter aspect, because ethnicity and culture can be separated analytically; for example, the ethnic community does not necessarily

overlap with the cultural community, that is, within a state different types of *Gemeinschaft* are possible.

6   But that legitimacy is also the basis for state power; without it, the state would have to rely on coercion; with it, the state has infrastructural power, meaning 'collective power, "power through" society, coordinating social life through state infrastructures' (Mann 1993:59).

7   To the extent that states are not characterized by cohesion in this sense, the notion of national security becomes problematic because that concept rests on the idea that the state is indeed a cohesive unit (Buzan 1991:96–107). Therefore, a stringent concept of national security cannot be projected backward in history, because the nationhood of modern states is a recent creation; it will be argued later that it cannot be applied to a large number of states in the present system either.

8   A number of weak, postcolonial countries have not been able to construct unified national economies. And a number of advanced liberal market economies have developed beyond the traditional notion of a national economy, as indicated in Chapter 5. That is, there are other types of state in the present international system than the modern state with the national economy. These other types are introduced in what follows.

9   Focusing on the Soviet Union however, it is clear that it deviates from modern statehood especially in the sense that nationhood was not developed the same way as in the liberal states. The state was always less legitimate, with less cohesion between state and nation, and instead of infrastructural power based on the rule of law, the Soviet state had to rely much more on coercion. The consequences of this for security and for international relations will be explored later.

10  I have struggled at length with the appropriate terminology for this type of state. It is clear that not all postcolonial states are as weak as implied by the ideal type. It is therefore relevant to reemphasize that my focus here is on *weak* postcolonial states. Robert Keohane has suggested an alternative label to me, namely 'Retro-Modern' states; that might be a more precise terminology, but I have chosen to stay with the 'weak, postcolonial' or merely 'postcolonial' label on the ground that this terminology is already well established in the literature, in spite of its possible inaccuracy. In addition, Robert Keohane also suggests that there are some states which are 'fractured modern': they exhibit a mixture of modern and weak, postcolonial characteristics in that they possess effective government and self-sustained economies (as do modern states), but this is combined with incohesive nationhood (as in postcolonial states). Relevant examples are Israel, (former) Yugoslavia, and (former) South Africa. Furthermore, some states seem threatened by this situation, including Belgium, India, and even Canada. This might be an interesting category of states to explore further, but in the present analysis I retain focus on modern, postmodern, and weak, postcolonial states. I do hope, however, that my reflections will help initiate further debate about the most appropriate typology of states.

11  A recent comprehensive analysis has made the claim that much of international law develops from below the state level, pushed by a host of societal actors (Snyder 1999).

12  There is much debate about what the European Union really is. See for example. Keohane and Hoffmann (eds) 1991; and Nørgaard (1994).

13  Yet even the treaty-bargains made by state elites are subject to scrutiny at lower levels because treaties have to be ratified.

14  Some observers see the emergence of a global civil society from these processes, supported by transnational grass-roots movements and the development of notions

of universal values such as human rights (Held 1995); while the case for such a global civil society remains fairly weak, there can be little doubt about the movement away from purely nation-based identities.

15 In the case of the European Union, for example, over the last three decades (up to 1997), intra-EU exports as percentage of total exports has increased from an average of 50 to 63 per cent (figures from Caporaso 2000:16–17).

16 The argument is not that this has happened to all modern states in equal measure and that there are no elements whatsoever left of a 'national' economy. If one looks at export ratios, for example, it is clear that most West European economies are highly globalized and that Japan and the United States are less so; the notion of 'uneven globalization' pertains to this group of countries as well.

## 7   The Domestic Dimension of Security Dilemmas

1 The state does not provide complete security in the sense of absence of any possible threat, such as natural disasters, incurable disease, or self-inflicted pain; the social contract underlying the state is meant to protect people from each other. That includes threats from other individuals and groups, including other states.

2 It is true, of course, that the pursuit of self-interest can have some positive spin-offs in terms of security and order, because state rulers need some modicum of order and legitimacy to stay in power. My premise here is that self-interest alone is not sufficient to overcome the Hobbesian dilemma. That this is confirmed by practice has already been indicated and further examples follow below.

3 The claim is not that the security of the individual and the security of the state are one and the same. As emphasized by Buzan (1991:51), there must be a contradiction between the security of the single individual and the state because the state can be a source of protection as well as of threat. The argument still stands: without some positive relationship between the protection of the state and the protection of the individuals in the state, there could not be a security dilemma in the Herz–Hobbesian sense. For a general discussion of the concept of security, see Baldwin (1997).

4 John Herz did actually point to the problem in 1951 when he identified an important weakness 'of Political Realism: It overlooks the fact that 'units' of power such as states or nations are usually not coherent groups, but units based on internal power relationships, which one or the other 'inside group' may try to overthrow, even at the risk of endangering or destroying the unit as such' (Herz 1951:28).

5 Yet eighteenth-century France, was plagued by 'violence, rowdyism, petty thieving and the like' (Le Goff and Sutherland quoted from Giddens 1992:189), so there remained significant differences between countries.

6 Furthermore, Michael Mann has demonstrated how military power continued to also turn inward, being used to dispel riots requiring 'a show of force – principally food riots, smuggling disturbances, labor disputes, and riots against military impressment' (Mann 1993:406).

7 With Stalin's consolidation of his power, the Soviet Union was in every respect a totalitarian society, displaying the characteristics laid out by Carl Friedrich: '(1) a totalist ideology; (2) a single party committed to this ideology and usually led by one man, the dictator; (3) a fully developed secret police; and three kinds of monopoly or, more precisely, monopolistic control: namely that of (a) mass communications; (b) operational weapons; (c) all organizations, including economic ones' (Friedrich, quoted from Giddens 1992:296).

8   In context of answering that question, a puzzle from Chapter 3 can also be taken up: given that the Soviet leadership was for many years very well aware of the domestic economic and other weaknesses of the Soviet system, why didn't anybody before Gorbachev try to do something effective about it, for example by way of emulating the capitalist West? The answer in Chapter 3 stressed the importance of nuclear weapons; in what follows it is argued that the special situation of the Soviet elite must also be taken into account.

9   Classical realists, in contrast to neorealists, have emphasized this point in their analyses; see for example Hoffmann (1965) and Aron (1966). Yet they also see sharp limits in the difference that domestic factors can make; Hobbesian anarchy can at most be mitigated, not abandoned, cf. Chapter 1. In that sense their argument combines the essentialist continuity of anarchy criticized above with the historical specificity of different domestic structures. See the helpful discussion in Doyle (1997:136–60).

10  The argument should not be mistaken for a 'Primat der Innenpolitik' view. As noted in Chapter 1, the realist tradition in IR continues a long analytical practice arguing for the primacy of foreign foreign policy – Primat der Aussenpolitik – going back to Leopold von Ranke who coined the term. It stands against another tradition, arguing the primacy of domestic affairs – Primat der Innenpolitik. This distinction indicates that a choice should be made between the two; that is, international relations can be explained from either one or the other view. The position taken here is that both views are always necessary and that 'international' conditions 'domestic' and vice versa. Therefore, one view should not be given analytical privilege over the other.

## 8   The Security Dilemma in Postcolonial States

1   The document is reprinted in Braillard and Dalili (eds) (1986). My remarks on this are heavily indebted to the penetrating analysis in Jackson (1993a).

2   These are extreme options, of course, and there are many possible combinations in between. For clarity, however, it is helpful to discuss the extreme options.

3   'Up to half of Ghana's cocoa crop was smuggled into Côte D'Ivoire and Togo in the early 1980s, and Zaire lost at least US$300 million in revenues through the smuggling of coffee in 1976 alone' (Sandbrook 1985:42).

4   This should not be taken to mean that there cannot be a 'primordial' element in ethnic identity; but that element requires a connection to a socio-political and/or economic context which serves to recruit it as a component in open conflict between groups.

5   Gurr's list includes 'all ethnopolitical conflicts in which *substantial levels of life-threatening coercion* have recently been used (in 1993–94) by one or all contenders. Mass repression, genocidal massacres, and forcible resettlement of communal groups by public officials are symptomatic of serious conflict; so are rebellion, guerilla warfare, recurrent rioting, and terrorist campaigns by communally based political movements' (Gurr 1994:352).

6   ' "winning", from the African state's point of view, consisted in getting as much adjustment aid as possible … while delivering as little policy reform as possible in exchange … African governments, indeed, rapidly became as adept at evading the demands of international financial institutions as their people were at evading those of their own governments' (Clapham 1996a:177).

7   '.. Western states also retained interests in the continent [Africa], and sought to ensure that these would be served and not undermined by political conditionalities' (Clapham 1996a:199).

8  1,800 candidates of twenty-six political parties ran for election in Benin, a country of four million inhabitants. Fourteen candidates were on the ballot for the presidential election. Ninety-six parties requested registration in Zaire (now Congo) when liberalization made that possible.

9  An armed conflict is 'a contested incompatibility which concerns government and/or territory where the use of armed force between two parties, of which at least one is the government of a state, results in at least 25 battle-related deaths'. Minor armed conflict: more than 25, less than 1,000 battle-related deaths in the course of the conflict. Intermediate armed conflict: an accumulated total of at least 1,000 battle deaths, but fewer than 1,000 per year. War: 1,000 or more battle-deaths per year. Quote and definition from Wallensteen and Sollenberg (1999:605).

10  With state failure as a process of state decay, it is clear that there can be different stages on the way; Gros (1996) has used that as a starting point for identifying different types of failed state. Such further distinctions are not necessary for the present analysis.

11  Defined as 'dictatorial or coercive interference in the sphere of jurisdiction of a sovereign state to protect or relieve individuals facing persecution, mass oppression, genocide or humanitarian disaster' (Bull 1984:1).

12  For an emphasis on early response rather than early warning, see George and Holl (2000).

13  A few possible exceptions are discussed in Jackson (1994).

14  Boutros Ghali emphasized the point in 1992: 'If every ethnic, religious or linguistic group claimed statehood, there would be no limit to fragmentation, and peace, security and economic well-being would become ever more difficult to achieve . . . the sovereignty, territorial integrity and independence of States within the established international system and the principle of self-determination of people's . . . must not be permitted to work against each other . . . Solutions to these problems should enhance the situation of minorities as well as the stability of states' UN (1992).

15  For a comprehensive treatment of secession, see Bartkus (1999); for the proposals set forth here, see also Jackson (1992); Clapham (1998); and especially Joseph and Herbst (1997).

16  The present security situation on Taiwan remains complex, not least because some groups on the island support reunification with mainland China and some oppose it. It is the early turn-around of the Jiang Kaishek regime which is interesting in the present context.

17  William Reno has recently demonstrated how this lack of interest, combined with a perceived absence of viable alternatives, has led to increased willingness of developed countries to use private security companies (such as Executive Outcomes of South Africa) in dealing with the problems of very weak or collapsed states (see Reno 2000).

# 9  Postmodern States: from Security Dilemma towards Challenges to Effective Governance

1  There is variation between countries in this respect and the process is probably most pronounced in the case of EU. For an elaboration of the general argument, see Wendt (1994; 1999).

2  This is not a sweeping claim that traditional national interests have disappeared; the claim is that substantial structural changes in statehood also have consequences for

perceptions of interest. That interests are constructed and not given is the major point made in constructivist analysis; see for example Wendt (1994, 1999), Jepperson, Wendt and Katzenstein (1996), and Adler (1997).

3  The relationship between economic change and peace in emphasized in Rosecrance (1995).

4  'Opting out of the world market is no longer an option' (Strange 1994:215). The claim is not that radical protectionism is impossible, but that it has become extremely costly.

5  'Today, it is rather states which are embedded within (transnational, GS) markets than national economies which are embedded within the boundaries of states' (Habermas 1999:48). If the state is 'just about through as an economic unit' as Charles Kindleberger declared the case already in 1969, then according to Waltz, 'the structure of international politics would have to be redefined' (Waltz 1979:94). The state is not 'through'; but the change from modern to postmodern statehood significantly redefines the context for economic activity.

6  Adler and Barnett (1998) prefer to distinguish between 'loosely coupled' and 'tightly coupled' pluralistic security communities, where the latter 'possess a political regime that lies somewhere between the sovereign state and centralized regional government' (Adler 1998:176). I prefer the other term in order to emphasize that with a measure of common government such a community is no longer a subcategory of pluralistic security communities.

7  Deudney and Ikenberry (1999:186) correctly emphasize that the tendency of some liberal scholars to see a displacement of the state in the development of transnational relations may be wrong. Yet on both sides of this issue there is agreement that transnational relations help promote the formation of a security community.

8  Recent reflections on the issue can be found in Adler (1998) and Adler and Barnett (1998).

9  A recent RAND report for the US Secretary of Defense defined economic security as follows: 'Economic security is the ability to protect or to advance US economic interests in the face of events, developments or actions that may threaten or block these interests. . . . The objective of economic security is to reduce uncertainty about continued economic well-being' (Neu and Wolf 1992:xi).

10  Robert Reich used the example of a Japanese firm producing typewriters in the United States; the firm pressed antidumping charges against the US International Trade Commission because an American firm imported typewriters to the United States from its off-shore factories in Indonesia and Singapore (Reich 1991a). In broader terms, the forging of business alliances and globalized production raises the awkward question of 'Who is US' (Reich 1991b); see also Ruggie (1997); Moran (1990).

11  'When markets evolve to the point of becoming international in scope, the effectiveness of traditional instruments of economic policy is often greatly reduced or even nullified', Richard Cooper (1986:96); see also Zürn (1999); Milner (1988).

12  As reflected in Robert Reich's remark about a changed context for economic security: 'Rather than increase the profitability of corporations flying its flag, or enlarge the worldwide holdings of its citizens, a nation's economic role is to improve its citizens' standard of living by enhancing the value of what they contribute to the world economy' (Reich 1991b:301).

13  The RAND report mentioned earlier formulates the issue as follows: 'True national security – of either the military or the economic variety – requires a unified populace with a common understanding of national interests and capable of standing together in the face of foreign challenges. This kind of unity will be promoted by a domestic

distribution of income and economic well-being that is perceived to be broadly fair. Although the continuing integration of the US economy into the broader international economy has unquestionably benefited most of the US population, lower-skilled US workers increasingly find themselves in competition with an enormous pool of low-skilled and low-paid labor in the rest of the world. If these workers are left out of the general prosperity, US economic security will be undermined' (Neu and Wolf 1992:xviii); see also Kapstein (1996).

14  Economic globalization is not the only factor involved in the determination of patterns of inequality, of course. The most important element is probably the modes of public policy in different countries which in turn derive from different state-society complexes (cf. Cox 1996; Ruggie 1997).

15  Moran (1990:69). Moran believes that it remains possible for the United States to 'develop strategies to reduce the potential for foreign manipulation to a minimum, while maintaining maximum access to the growing global pool of technological and management skills', but he also emphasized that 'there will always be, in an era of globalization, an irreducible minimum threat of foreign control and foreign manipulation' (*ibid.*, p.98).

16  Consider, for example, that quintessentially all-American product, the Barbie doll. Its label says 'Made in China', but behind this is a complex global product: 'China provides the factory space, labour, and electricity, as well as cotton cloth for the dress...Japan supplies the nylon hair, Saudia Arabia provides oil, Taiwan refines oil into ethylene for plastic pellets for the body, Japan, the US, and Europe supply almost all the machinery tools, most of the molds...come from the US, Japan, or Hong Kong...the United States supplies cardboard packaging and paint pigments, and Hong Kong supplies the banking and insurance and carries out the delivery of the raw materials to factories in South China together with the collection of the finished products and shipping. Two Barbie dolls are marketed every second in 140 countries around the world by Mattel Inc. of El Segundo, California' (Snyder 1999:8–9). Moran's considerations on the US defence industry demonstrate how the issue of complex networks not merely pertains to dolls, cf. Moran (1990).

17  This is also recognized in the RAND report mentioned earlier: '...there is a growing recognition that exchange-rate stability, and international financial stability more generally, will be achieved only through increased cooperation among policymakers in the world's industrialized countries. Such cooperation will necessarily involve some loss of national freedom of action in economic matters. Ironically, though, giving up some national sovereignty in this regard will probably be essential to the pursuit of international financial stability and thus to the pursuit of national economic security' (Neu and Wolf 1992:xvii).

18  Former NATO Secretary-General Javier Solana was appointed to that post in 1999.

19  Such definition is also affected by historical alliance patterns, especially the relationship to the United States, as emphasized by William Wallace (2000).

20  First, blame for current problems might as well be put at the doorstep of a variety of social actors, including TNCs; second, the premise that these three problems areas radically undermine the current system is open to debate. For an opposing view, see for example Garrett (1998).

21  An overview of global governance issues is presented in Simai (1994). See also Streeten (1992), Tita (1998), and Cox (1993).

22  'How are global economic networks – including transatlantic economic networks – governed? I suggest that they are governed by the totality of strategically determined, situationally specific, and often episodic conjunctions of a multiplicity of sites

throughout the world. These sites have institutional, normative, and processual characteristics. The totality of these sites represents a new form of legal pluralism' (Snyder 1999:1); see also Sassen (1996).

23  Defined as 'a dense web of relations' between functionally distinct parts of state institutions, that is, courts, regulatory agencies, or executives, cf. Slaughter (1997:184).

24  'Throughout the nineteenth and twentieth centuries theorists of democracy have tended to assume a "symmetrical" and "congruent" relationship between political decision-makers and the recipients of political decisions. In fact, symmetry and congruence have often been taken for granted at two crucial points: first, between citizen-voters, and the decision-makers whom they are, in principle, able to hold to account; and secondly, between the "output" (decisions, policies and so on) of decisions-makers and their constituents-ultimately, "the people" in a delimited territory' (Held 1995:16).

25  For an elaboration of this line of analysis, see Klaus Dieter Wolf (1996).

26  The proper way of looking at the interests of state elites is probably through a more balanced combination of the competing views: on the one hand, postmodern state elites are basically democratic in that they pursue a number of political goods for their populations to the best of their ability; at the same time, they may entertain their own agenda of maximizing their autonomy. For such a balanced view, see also Zürn (1999:12).

27  Habermas is confident that this process of taking 'national consciousness and social solidarity' (1999:58) beyond national borders is possible; he refers to the similar obstacles faced by the movement from local to national levels in context of the creation of modern states.

28  '... a strong idea of some sort is a necessary component of a secure state ... If the idea of the state is strong and widely held, then the state can endure periods of weak institutions ... without serious threats to its overall integrity. If the idea of the state is weakly held, or strongly contested ... then a lapse in institutional strength might well bring the whole structure crashing down ...' (Buzan 1991:82).

29  Some scholars define this issue as one of 'societal security', meaning 'the ability of a society to persist in its essential characteristics under changing conditions.' (Wæver *et al.* 1993:23).

30  'The decline in nation-state autonomy has compromised the pact between citizens and the nation-state. It has made it difficult for governments to mediate between their citizens and the rest of the world, and to manage the relationship of the individual to the global economy of which he is a part' (Horsman and Marshall 1995:172).

31  Michael Zürn argues that the lack of regionalist claims for autonomy in the United States is due to the already large measure of autonomy given to states in the federation (Zürn 1998:278).

32  As noted by Bill McSweeney, a 'strong sense of societal identity could very likely, and not just pathologically, coincide with resistance to the state' (McSweeney 1996:93).

33  In Europe, a dominant idea among these movements is that the (ethnically 'pure') nation can take care of itself (cf. Zürn 1998:264–73), by strengthening its borders against outside influences and by sending 'the strangers' back where they came from.

34  Such amalgamation might eventually take place in the regional context of the EU, but it will hardly take place in context of the larger postmodern realm.

## 10 Sovereignty and Changes in Statehood

1 Only a selection of important contributions can be mentioned here: Hinsley (1986); James (1986); Lapidoth (1992); Krasner (1988; 1999); Onuf (1991); Jackson (1993a, 1993b); Keohane (1995); Lyons and Mastanduno (eds) (1995); Bartelson (1995); Barkin and Cronin (1994); Biersteker and Weber (eds) (1996); Christiansen (1994); Jackson (ed.) (1999b).

2 The game metaphor is also employed in Jackson (1993a:34), but the game is constructed in a different way than suggested here. My reflections on sovereignty games are greatly indebted to discussions with Robert Jackson.

3 A distinction introduced by Rawls (1955); the use of it here is based on Searle (1995).

4 For a similar point see Philpott (1999).

5 Taiwan, for example, may have all the attributes of a sovereign state (territory, people and government), but it is not recognized as such and is therefore not a full member of the society of states with the rights and obligations that follow.

6 Ruggie (1998:191); Ruggie is quoting Charles Tilly.

7 Some even argue that the situation of historically diffuse principles of recognition continue right up to the present day; see Österud (1997). For the view that there is a detectable pattern in recognition practices, see Hyldelund (1997).

8 Keohane (1986). The full definition offered by Keohane runs: 'Reciprocity refers to exchanges of roughly equivalent values in which the actions of each party are contingent on the prior actions of the others in such a way that good is returned for good, and bad for bad' (1986:8).

9 'Sovereign states are free political systems in the negative meaning of freedom: freedom from. They enjoy a right of nonintervention. They are not necessarily free in the positive meaning of freedom: freedom to' (Jackson 1999b:455).

10 The Most Favoured Nation principle is the expression of classical reciprocity: equal treatment of all parties. The Generalized Scheme of Preferences is the expression of nonreciprocity: special treatment for the weak party.

11 A similar conclusion is set forth by Robert Jackson: 'The reality is not that the law of welfare – nonreciprocity – has replaced the law of liberty – reciprocity...Nor is it likely. Rather, it is that poor states today assert both negative and positive norms at one and the same time...And contemporary international society is trying to operate with both' (Jackson 1993a:135).

12 Christopher Clapham, by contrast, argues that the international norms connected with sovereignty no longer affords any special protection to postcolonial state elites and that 'the era of sovereignty as a universal organizing principle for the management of the global system has ended' (Clapham 1999:537). The position taken here is that the institution of sovereignty has been developed and modified to accommodate weak, postcolonial statehood.

13 That lack of stability is clearly demonstrated in the analysis by Clapham (1999).

14 As noted by Keohane (1995) and Zürn (1999), other countries are increasingly involved in multilevel governance as well. In Chapter 9 the coordinated security community of postmodern states was comprised of an inner circle of EU-Europe, followed by Western Europe and Western Europe/North America, and Western Europe/North America/Japan and an outer circle of the OECD members.

15 Cf. Wallace (2000).

16 'The Court itself has aggressively molded the various treaties and laws of the Union into a constitutional charter...It has not only established the supremacy of Union law but also simultaneously augmented the power of the national courts by giving

them the authority to invalidate national legislation on the basis of Union law'
(Caldeira, Gibson and Klein 1995:4).

17  While classical reciprocity has been modified, it has not disappeared. To some extent redistribution to poor regions are parts of larger compromises where this is part of a compensation to poorer countries for accepting other measures of integration; yet this remains more a cooperation game than a competition game.

18  It has been suggested that such cooperation is emerging not only in context of the EU, but also in the larger postmodern realm, see Brock and Albert (1995).

19  'States have ceased to act as gatekeepers between domestic and international politics in intra-European relations.' (Wallace 2000:205).

20  The debate is presented in Jackson (1999b).

21  For an emphasis of this point, see Jensen (1999).

22  For a similar view, see Zürn (1998;1999) and Keohane (1995). This is not to suggest, of course, that postmodern states will emerge an an 'EU-community' writ large; they most probably will not.


# 11   Types of State and International Theory

1  'Self-help is necessarily the principle of action in an anarchic order' (Waltz 1979:111).

2  Waltz (1979:91). Raymond Aron notes that 'each political unit aspires to survive. Leaders and led are interested in and eager to maintain the collectivity they constitute together by virtue of history, race, or fortune' (Aron 1966:64); Stephen Krasner says that 'all states share the same minimalist objectives of preserving territorial and political integrity' (Krasner 1985:28).

3  Some realists argue that this leads state to maximize their relative power; others find that states will 'seek the minimum level of power that is needed to attain and to maintain their security and survival' (Grieco 1997:167).

4  'States do not willingly place themselves in situations of increased dependence. In a self-help system, considerations of security subordinate economic gain to political interest' (Waltz 1979:107); see also Grieco (1997:168).

5  See Jackson (1993a:171) and Wendt (1999).

6  'So long as the major states are the major actors, the structure of international politics is defined in terms of them' (Waltz 1979:94).

7  Doyle and Ikenberry (1997:11). See also Gilpin (1986) and Waltz (1986).

8  I owe this point to Stephen Krasner: 'If there is self-help, there will be some circumstances when political leaders will decide that constraining some aspect of the domestic politics or institutions of another state, or accepting such constraints on one's own state, is the best policy option. In these cases self-help undermines autonomy. A theory that asserts that actors, in this case states, can do everything they please subject only to the reactions of other autonomous states, but at the same time cannot do some other things, is not logically coherent' (Krasner 1999:53; see also Hoffmann 1984). Note that the 'voice opportunity' theory offered by Grieco above has yet to confront this inconsistency.

9  This brief summary of liberalism draws on Zacher and Matthew (1995) and Jackson and Sørensen (1999). See also Nye (1988) and Keohane (1989).

10  This is a basic element in the neomarxist dependency critique of liberal modernization theory. See for example Kay (1989).

11  For en emphasis of this point, see Keohane (1995:185).

12  The following remarks are based on the analysis in Chapter 9.

13 Four important contributions in this regard are Moravcsik (1997); Deudney and Ikenberry (1999); Rosecrance (1996); and Keohane (1995). Keohane explicitly indicates that advanced democracies will develop international institutions that are 'inconsistent with rigid maintenance of traditional conceptions of sovereignty' (Keohane 1995:184); that points in the direction of the postmodern sovereignty game.

14 This is an assumption which rationalism shares with realism: 'the two major paradigms of classical international theory [realism and rationalism, GS]...presuppose states as valuable places where the good life, if not always realized fully, is nevertheless a definite possibility. This is the traditional justification of the state in political theory' (Jackson 1990:267).

15 For some English school theorists this has led in the direction of a Kantian, solidarist view, stating that the international society of states have a right to intervention in sovereign states in the case of grave violations of human rights. Others hold on to the pluralist view of basically respecting state sovereignty and nonintervention. An analysis of the debate is presented in Wheeler (1992).

16 The analysis of the substance of weak states by Robert Jackson and Carl Rosberg (1982) is not within the purview of the English school.

17 Bull adds the goals of peace, and of 'limitation of violence...the keeping of promises and the stabilization of possession by rules of property' (1995:17–18), but these can be seen as corollaries to the goals mentioned in the text.

18 The creation of such a qualitatively different order is recommended by several analysts. For different suggestions, see Linklater (1998), Held (1995), and Falk (1991).

19 I owe this point to Jesper Bjerregaard Langkjær (1999:103).

20 'The method of historical structures is one of representing what can be called limited totalities. The historical structure does not represent the whole world but rather a particular sphere of human activity in its historically located totality...Historical structures are contrast models; like ideal types they provide, in a logically coherent form, a simplified representation of a complex reality and an expression of tendencies...' (Cox 1996:100).

21 A further possibility raised by Cox is a nonhegemonic order, 'of conflicting power centres' (1996:114).

22 Cox notes that these elites have an orientation which is 'indeterminate. It can be either conservative or radical. It may either bargain for a better deal within the world economy of international production, or it may seek to overcome the unequal internal development generated by international capital' (Cox 1996:116); either way, the view stresses economic subordination in contrast to the autonomy derived from constitutional independence.

23 'Post-Fordism means a shift away from large plants mass-producing standardized goods, towards shorter-run production for a greater variety of more specialized markets' (Cox 1996:277; 286).

24 The issue was formulated as follows in Chapter 9: 'There is a real sense in which effective governance and democracy is for the weak; the strong can take care of themselves. The resourceful groups can seize the opportunities created by postmodern statehood; the less resourceful groups face the risk of marginalization or exclusion.'

25 '...even if there is no guarantee that cultural time in international politics will move forward, I do think one can argue that it will not move backward, unless there is a big exogenous shock...with respect to its endogenous dynamic, the argument suggests that the history of international politics will be unidirectional: if

there are any structural changes, they will be historically progressive' (Wendt 1999:312).

26  See for example John Mearsheimer (1995; 1994–95).

27  The assumptions include the ascription of objective national interests to states, interests that refer to 'the reproduction requirements or security of state-society complexes'. These interests include: physical survival, autonomy, economic well-being, and collective self-esteem (Wendt 1999:234–6). As demonstrated in Chapter 8, the idea that unified state-society complexes share such national interests does not sit well with the unusual features of weak, postcolonial statehood.

28  Wendt's core argument for this separation of unit and systemic levels is that 'in the contemporary international system political authority is organized formally in a bifurcated fashion: vertically within states ("hierarchy"), horizontally between ("anarchy")' (Wendt 1999:13); that is true, because sovereign states have constitutional independence; but changes in the regulative rules of the sovereignty game have created some new aspects of the organization of political authority which require analytical attention.

29  It would appear possible to develop constructivist analysis to include the domestic level; yet constructivists may not want to move in that direction because they are satisfied that identities and interests of states are primarily a consequence of systemic interaction rather than of domestic factors. At the same time, systemic theorizing has to be based on a set of assumptions concerning the constituent state units, as indicated above. When these assumptions are put in question, that creates an incentive to pursue the analysis of domestic realms.

30  The point was made recently by Robert Jackson: 'International political theory and domestic political theory diverge at certain points but they are branches of one overall political theory...' (Jackson 1990:261). Andrew Linklater notes how '[p]olitical thought was divided into two largely self-contained branches which reflected the sharp contrast between the domestic and international realms which appeared with the rise of the Westphalian era... One of the consequences of distinguishing political theory as the theory of the good life from international theory as the theory of survival... has been the dearth of analysis of the origins, development and actual or conceivable transformation of the bounded territorial state' (Linklater 1998:35).

31  'There is not one vocabulary for international politics and another for domestic politics' (Jackson 1990:269). For a similar view, see also Milner (1998).

32  This is the procedure chosen by Waltz (1979:116).

33  It is indeed the case today that both the language of power, the language of legality, and the language of morality is employed in the study of 'international' as well as in the study of 'domestic' affairs. 'In practice, each discourse belongs to international and domestic politics alike. And insofar as theories seek, in the Hegelian manner, to give a philosophical account of pre-existing practices, we cannot adequately theorize each sphere in only one idiom either' (Jackson 1990:270).

34  For an argument emphasizing the richness and continued relevance of the great traditions, see Doyle (1997); Linklater (1998) is a direct attempt to rethink political community in a context which rejects any sharp division between 'domestic' and 'international'.

35  Cf. Schmidt (1998). Schmidt's remark about Waltz is instructive in this regard: 'The idea advanced in Waltz's *Theory of International Politics*, that states can be considered "like-units"... would have been considered very unrealistic by many of the scholars discussed in this study' (p. 238).

## 12  Conclusion

1  See for example Waltz (1959) who discusses the liberal second image at length.
2  In the United States, income inequality has grown since the early 1970s; the income of the poor has even fallen in absolute terms since 1979. The richest one per cent of families captured 70 per cent of the total rise in family income in the United States between 1977 and 1989 (Birdsall 1998).
3  It is clear, of course, that good and honest leaders are not enough, especially if they are committed to bad policies. Julius Nyerere of Tanzania was an honest man who did much good for his country, but his policies of a state-led economy and a basically non-democratic polity also led to disastrous results.
4  The standard procedure has been to discuss those two issues in more or less total isolation from each other. Chapter 8 indicated that this is highly misleading.
5  The general interplay, or 'elective affinity', between material conditions and ideas about identity and community is emphasized in Cox (1996) and Senghaas (1998).

# Bibliography

Adams, Patricia (1992). 'The World Bank and the IMF in Sub- Saharan Africa: Undermining Development and Environmental Sustainability', *Journal of International Affairs*, 46:1, 97–117.

Adeleke, Ademola (1995). 'The Politics and Diplomacy of Peacekeeping in West Africa: The ECOWAS Operation in Liberia', *The Journal of Modern African Studies*, 33:4, 569–93.

Adler, Emmanuel (1997). 'Seizing the Middle Ground: Constructivism in World Politics', *European Journal of International Relations*, 3, 319–63.

Adler, Emmanuel (1998). 'Condition(s) of Peace', in Tim Dunne, Michael Cox, and Ken Booth (eds), *The Eighty Years' Crisis*, Cambridge: Cambridge University Press, 165–93.

Adler, Emmanuel and Michael Barnett (eds) (1998). *Security Communities*, Cambridge: Cambridge University Press.

Alavi, Hamza and Theodor Shanin (eds) (1982). *Introduction to the Sociology of 'Developing Societies'*, London: Macmillan – now Palgrave.

Albrow, Martin (1996). *The Global Age. State and Society Beyond Modernity*, Oxford and Cambridge: Polity Press.

Alderson, Kai (1997). 'Convergence Under Anarchy: Does International Competition Cause State Socialization?' Paper for International Studies Association annual meeting, Toronto, March.

Almond, Gabriel A. (1989). 'Review Article: The International–National Connection', *British Journal of Political Science*, 19, 237–59.

Alter, Peter (1992). 'Nationalism and German politics after 1945', in John Breuilly (ed.), *The State of Germany*, London: Longman, 154–76.

Amin, Samir (1976). *Unequal Development*, New York: Monthly Review Press.

Anderson, Perry (1974). *Lineages of the Absolutist State*, London: New Left Books.

Anderson, Perry (1994). 'The Invention of the Region 1945–1990', Working Paper 94/2: European University Institute, Florence.

Andreff, Wladimir (1984). 'Quelles streategies d'aptations dans les economies nationales des pays de l'est?', Paper for the VIth International Colloquium on the World Economy, Paris.

Aron, Raymond (1966). *Peace and War: A Theory of International Relations*, Garden City, NY: Doubleday.

Åslund, Anders (1995). *How Russia Became a Market Economy*, Washington, DC: Brookings Institution.

Aspaturian, Vernon V. (1984). 'The Stalinist Legacy in Soviet National Security Decision Making' in Jiri Valenta and William Potter (eds), *Soviet Decision Making for National Security*, London: Allen and Unwin, 23–73.

Ayoob, Mohammed (1995). *The Third World Security Predicament*, Boulder, Co.: Lynne Rienner.

Bahro, Rudolf (1977). *Die Alternative: Zur Kritik des real existierenden Sozialismus*, Köln: Eurpäische Verlagsanstalt.

Baldwin, David (1997). 'The Concept of Security', *Review of International Studies*, 23:1, 5–26.

Barkin, Samuel and Bruce Cronin (1994). 'The State and the Nation: Changing Norms and the Rules of Sovereignty in International Relations', *International Organization*, 48:1, 107–31.

Barner-Barry, Carol and Cynthia A. Hody (1995). *The Politics of Change. The Transformation of the Former Soviet Union*, New York: St. Martin's Press.

Bartelson, Jens (1995). *A Genealogy of Sovereignty*, Cambridge: Cambridge University Press.

Bartkus, Viva Ona (1999). *The Dynamic of Secession*, Cambridge: Cambridge University Press.

Bates, Robert H. (1981). *Markets and States in Tropical Africa: the Political Basis of Agricultural Policies*, Berkeley: California University Press.

Bayart, Jean-François (1993). *The State in Africa: the Politics of the Belly*, London: Longman.

Beck, Ulrich (1992). *Risk Society: towards a new modernity*, London: Sage.

Beck, Ulrich (1993). *Die Erfindung des Politischen. Zu einer Theorie reflexiver Modernisierung*, Frankfurt Main: Suhrkamp.

Bennett, Christopher (1995). *Yugoslavia's Bloody Collapse – Causes, Course and Consequences*, London: Hurst and Company.

Berger, Thomas U. (1996). 'Norms, Identity, and National Security in Germany and Japan', in Peter J. Katzenstein (ed.), *The Culture of National Security. Norms and Identity in World Politics*, New York: Columbia University Press, 317–56.

Berki, R. N. (1986). *Security and Society: Reflections of law, order and politics*, London: J. M. Dent.

Betts, Raymond F. (1998). *Decolonization*, London: Routledge.

Biersteker, Thomas J. and Cynthia Weber (eds) (1996). *State Sovereignty as Social Construct*, Cambridge: Cambridge University Press.

Birdsall, Nancy (1998). 'Life Is Unfair: Inequality in the World', *Foreign Policy*, 111, 76–93.

Bjerregaard Langkjær, Jesper (1999). *En analyse af realismens, liberalismens og rationalismens præskriptive anvendelighed*, MA thesis, Aarhus: Department of Political Science.

Boutros-Ghali, Boutros (1992). *An Agenda For Peace: Preventive Diplomacy, Peacemaking and Peace-Keeping*, A/47/277, New York: United Nations.

Braillard, Philippe and Mohammad-Reza Djaliili (eds) (1986). *The Third World and International Relations*, Boulder, Co.: Lynne Rienner.

Brock, Lothar and Mathias Albert (1995). 'Debordering the World of States: New Spaces in International Relations', Working Paper 2, Frankfurt Main: World Society Research Group.

Bull, Hedley (1969). 'International Theory: The Case for a Classical Approach', in Klaus Knorr and James N. Rosenau (eds), *Contending Approaches to International Politics*, Princeton: Princeton University Press, 20–38.

Bull, Hedley (1984). 'Introduction', in Hedley Bull (ed.), *Intervention in World Politics*, Oxford: Clarendon Press, 1–7.

Bull, Hedley (1995 [1977]). *The Anarchical Society. A Study of Order in World Politics*, London: Macmillan – now Palgrave.

Bull, Hedley (ed.) (1984). *Intervention in World Politics*, Oxford: Clarendon Press.

Buzan, Barry (1991). *People, States and Fear: An Agenda for International Security Studies in the Post-Cold War Era*, Hemel Hempstead: Harvester Wheatsheaf.

Buzan, Barry, Charles Jones, and Richard Little (1993). *The Logic of Anarchy: Neorealism to Structural Realism*, New York: Columbia University Press.

Buzan, Barry, Ole Wæver, and Jaap de Wilde (1997). *Security. A New Framework for Analysis*, London: Lynne Rienner.

Caldeira, Gregory A., James L. Gibson and David E. Klein (1995). 'The Visibility of the Court of Justice in the European Union', paper for the 1995 APSA Meeting, Chicago.

Callaghy, Thomas M. (1991). 'Africa and the World Economy: Caught Between a Rock and a Hard Place', in John W. Harbeson and Donald Rothchild (eds), *Africa in World Politics*, Boulder, Co.: Westview, 39–69.

Camilleri, J. A. and J. Falk (1992). *The End of Sovereignty?*, Aldershot: Edward Elgar.

Cardoso, Fernando H. and Enzo Faletto (1979). *Dependency and Development in Latin America*, Berkeley: University of California Press.

Caporaso, James (2000). *The European Union: Dilemmas of Regional Integration*, Boulder, Co.: Westview.

Cardoso, Fernando Henrique and Enzo Faletto (1979). *Dependency and Development in Latin America*, Berkeley: Univesity of California Press.

Carlo, Antonio (1976), 'Structural causes of the Soviet coexistence colicy', in Egbert Jahn (ed.), *Soviet Foreign Policy: Its Social and Economic Conditions*, London: Allison & Busby, 57–91.

Carothers, Thomas (1997). 'Democracy Without Illusions', *Foreign Affairs*, 76, 85–99.

Carr, Edward H. (1963). *The Bolshevik Revolution, vol. two*, London: Macmillan – now Palgrave.

Carroll, Barbara Wake and Terrance Carrol (1997). 'State and Ethnicity in Botswana and Mauritius: A Democratic Route to Development?', *The Journal of Development Studies*, 33:4, 464–86.

Cerny, Philip G. (1993). 'Plurilateralism: Structural Differentiation and Functional Conflict in the Post-Cold War World Order', *Millennium*, 22:1, 27–51.

Cerny, Philip (1995). 'Globalization and the changing logic of collective action', *International Organization*, 49:4, 595–625.

Chazan, Naomi, Robert Mortimer, John Ravenhill, and Donald Rotchild (1988). *Politics and Society in Contemporary Africa*, London: Macmillan – now Palgrave.

Christiansen, Thomas (1994). 'European Integration Between Political Science and International Relations Theory: The End of Sovereignty', *EUI Working Paper RSC 94/4*, Florence: European University Institute.

Clapham, Christopher (1996a). *Africa and the International System*, Cambridge: Cambridge University Press.

Clapham, Christopher (1996b). 'Rwanda: The Perils of Peace- Making', paper for African Studies Biennial Conference, University of Bristol.

Clapham, Christopher (1998). 'Degrees of statehood', *Review of International Studies*, 24, 143–57.

Clapham, Christopher (1999). 'Sovereignty and the Third World', *Political Studies*, 47:3, 522–38.

Clark, Ian (1998). 'Beyond the Great Divide: Globalization and the Theory of International Relations', *Review of International Studies*, 24:4, 479–99.

Clarke, Walter and Jeffrey Herbst (1996). 'Somalia and the Future of Humanitarian Intervention', *Foreign Affairs*, 72, 109–23.

Conquest, Robert (1986). *The Harvest of Sorrow: Soviet Collectivization and the Terror-famine*, New York: Oxford University Press.

Cooper, Richard (1986). *Economic Policy in an Interdependent World*, Cambridge: MIT Press.

Cooper, Robert (1996). *The Post-Modern State and the World Order*, London: Demos.

Cornett, Andreas P. (ed.) (1996). *Økonomiernes Internationalisering*, København: Jurist- og Økonomforbundets Forlag.

Corydon, Bjarne (2000). *Et Demokratisk Europa?*, MA Thesis, Aarhus: Department of Political Science.

Cox, Robert W. (1993). 'Towards a post-hegemonic conceptualization of world order: reflections on the relevancy of Ibn Khaldun', in James N. Rosenau and Ernst-Otto Czempiel (eds), *Governance without government: order and change in world politics*, Cambridge: Cambridge University Press, 132–60.

Cox, Robert W. (1996). 'Social Forces, States, and World Orders: Beyond International Relations Theory' in Robert W. Cox with Timothy J. Sinclair, *Approaches to World Order*, Cambridge: Cambridge University Press, 85–124.

Cronin, Bruce (1994). 'Distinguishing Between a Domestic and an International Issue: The Changing Nature of Sovereignty and Obligation in International Relations', paper for the American Political Science Association annual meeting, Washington, DC, September 1–4.

Cronin, James E. (1996). *The World the Cold War Made. Order, Chaos, and the Return of History*, New York: Routledge.

Czempiel, Ernst-Otto (1989). 'Internationalizing Politics: Some Answers to the Question of Who Does What to Whom', in Ernst-Otto Czempiel and James N. Rosenau (eds), *Global Changes and Theoretical Challenges. Approaches to World Politics for the 1990s*, Lexington, Mass.: Lexington Books, 117–35.

Dahl, Robert A. (1992). 'Democracy and Human Rights under Different Conditions of Development', in Asbjørn Eide and Bernt Hagtvet (eds), *Human Rights in Perspective*, Oxford: Blackwell, 235–52.

David, Steven R. (1991). *Choosing Sides: Alignment and Realignment in the Third World*, Baltimore, Md: Johns Hopkins.

Davies, Norman (1996). *Europe: A History*, Oxford: Oxford University Press.

Day, Richard B. (1973). *Leon Trotsky and the Politics of Economic Isolation*, Cambridge, Mass.: Harvard University Press.

De Visscher, C. (1968). *Theory and Reality in Public International Law*, Princeton: Princeton University Press.

Des Forges, Alison L. (1999). *'Leave None to Tell the Story': genocide in Rwanda*, New York: Human Rights Watch.

Deudney, Daniel and G. John Ikenberry (1999). 'The nature and sources of liberal international order', *Review of International Studies*, 25, 179–96.

Deutsch, Karl *et al.* (1957). *Political Community and the North Atlantic Area*, Princeton: Princeton University Press.

Diamond, Larry (1996). 'Is the Third Wave Over?', *Journal of Democracy*, 7, 20–37.

Dinan, Desmond (1994). *Ever Closer Union? An Introduction to the European Community*, Boulder, Co.: Lynne Rienner.

Donnelly, Jack (1993a). *International Human Rights*, Boulder, Co.: Westview Press.

Donnelly, Jack (1993b). 'Human Rights, Humanitarian Crisis, and Humanitarian Intervention', *International Journal*, XLVIII, 607–40.

Doyle, Michael W. (1983). 'Kant, Liberal Legacies and Foreign Affairs, 1–2', *Philosophy and Public Affairs*, 12:3, 205–35 (Part 1), and 12:4, 323–54 (Part 2).

Doyle, Michael W. (1986). 'Liberalism and World Politics', *American Political Science Review*, 80:4, 1151–69.

Doyle, Michael W. (1997). *Ways of Peace and War*, New York: W. W. Norton & Company.

Doyle, Michael W. and G. John Ikenberry (1997). 'Introduction: The End of the Cold War, the Classical Tradition, and International Change', in Michael W. Doyle and G. John Ikenberry (eds), *New Thinking in International Relations Theory*, Boulder, Co.: Westview Press, 1–19.

Drucker, Peter (1989). *The New Realities: In Government and Politics, in Economy and Business, in Society and in World View*, New York: Harper Row.

Druwe, Ulrich (1991). *Das Ende der Sowjetunion. Krise und Auflösung einer Weltmacht*, Weinheim: Beltz.

Elklit, Jørgen (1994). 'Is the Degree of Electoral Democracy Measurable?', in David Beetham (ed.), *Defining and Measuring Democracy*, London: Sage, 89–111.

Elster, Jon, Claus Offe, and Ulrich K. Preuss (1998). *Institutional Design in Post-Communist Societies*, New York: Cambridge University Press.

Ergas, Zaki (ed.) (1987). *The African State in Transition*, London: Macmillan – now Palgrave.

Evangelista, Matthew (1988). *Innovation and the Arms Race: How the United States and the Soviet Union Develop New Military Technologies*, Ithaca: Cornell University Press.

Evangelista, Matthew (1997). 'Domestic Structure and International Change, in Michael W. Doyle, and G. John Ikenberry (eds), *New Thinking in International Relations Theory*, Boulder, Co.: Westview Press, 202–28.

Evans, Peter (1989). 'Predatory, Developmental and Other Apparatuses: A Comparative Political Economy Perspective on the Third World State', *Sociological Forum*, 4:4, 561–87.

Evans, Peter B., Harold K. Jacobson, and Robert D. Putnam (eds) (1993). *Double-Edged Diplomacy: International Bargaining and Domestic Politics*, Berkeley: University of California Press.

Falk, Richard (1991). 'Theory, Realism, and World Security', in Michael T. Klare and Daniel C. Thomas (eds), *World Security. Trends & Challenges at Century's End*, New York: St. Martin's Press, 6–25.

Featherstone, Mike (ed.) (1990). *Global Culture: Nationalism, Globalization, and Modernity*, London: Sage.

Frank, Andre Gunder (1969). *Capitalism and Underdevelopment in Latin America. Historical Studies of Chile and Brazil*, New York: Monthly Review Press.

Fröbel, Folker, J. Heinrichs, and O. Kreye (1977). *Die Neue Internationale Arbeitsteilung*, Hamburg: Rohwolt.

Gaddis, John Lewis (1997). *We Now Know. Rethinking Cold War History*, Oxford: Clarendon Press.

Gaddy, Clifford and Barry Ickes (1998). 'Russia's Virtual Economy', *Foreign Affairs*, 77:5, 53–67.

Gaile, Gary L. and Alan Ferguson (1996). 'Success in African social development: some positive indications', *Third World Quarterly*, 17:3, 557–72.

Garrett, Geoffrey (1998). 'Global Markets and National Politics: Collision Course or Virtuous Circle?', *International Organization*, 52:4, 787–824.

George, Alexander L. and Jane E. Holl (2000). 'The Warning-Response Problem and Missed Opportunities in Preventive Diplomacy', in Bruce W. Jentleson (ed.), *Opportunities Missed, Opportunities Seized. Preventive Diplomacy in the Post-Cold War World*, Lanham, MD: Rowman & Littlefield, 21–36.

Gellner, Ernest (1983). *Nations and Nationalism*, Ithaca: Cornell University Press.

Gershenkron, Alexander (1962). *Economic Backwardness in Historical Perspective*, Cambridge, Mass.: Harvard University Press.

Giddens, Anthony (1984). *The Constitution of Society*. Cambridge: Polity Press.

Giddens, Anthony (1990). *The Consequences of Modernity*, Stanford: Stanford University Press.

Giddens, Anthony (1992). *The Nation-State and Violence*, Cambridge: Polity Press.

Gilpin, Robert (1986). 'The Richness of the Tradition of Political Realism', in Robert O. Keohane (ed.), *Neorealism and Its Critics*, New York: Columbia University Press, 301–21.

Gilpin, Robert (1987). *The Political Economy of International Relations*, Princeton: Princeton University Press.

Gilpin, Robert (1988). 'The Theory of Hegemonic War', *Journal of Interdisciplinary History*, 18, 591–614.

Godt, Christine (1998). 'Der Bericht des Appellate Body der WTO zum EG-Einfuhrverbot von Hormonfleisch. Risikoregulierung im Weltmarkt', *Europäisches Wirtschafts- und Steuerrecht*, 9:6, 202–9.

Gold, Thomas B. (1986). *State and Society in the Taiwan Miracle*, New York: East Gate Books.

Goldman, Kjell (1999). 'Politikens internationalisering: en introduktion', unpublished ms., Stockholm: University of Stockholm.

Gong, Gerrit W. (1984). *The Standard of 'Civilization' in International Society*, Oxford: Oxford University Press.

Gorbachev, Mikhail (1987). *Perestroika: New Thinking for Our Country and the World*, New York: Harper & Row.

Gourevitch, Peter (1978). 'The Second Image Reversed: The International Sources of Domestic Politics', *International Organization*, 32:4, 881–911.

Gourevitch, Peter (1986). *Politics in Hard Times: Comparative Responses to International Economic Crises*, Ithaca: Cornell University Press.

Gramsci, Antonio (1971). *Prison Notebooks*, New York: International Publishers.

Greenberg, Edward S. (1990). 'State Change: Approaches and Concepts' in Edward S. Greenberg and T. F. Meyer (eds), *Changes in the State: Causes and Consequences*, Newbury Park, Ma.: Sage, 11–41.

Grieco, Joseph M. (1997). 'Realist International Theory and the Study of World Politics', in Michael W. Doyle and G. John Ikenberry (eds), *New Thinking in International Relations Theory*, Boulder, Co.: Westview Press, 163–202.

Gros, Jean-Germain (1996). 'Towards a taxonomy of failed states in the New World Order: decaying Somalia, Liberia, Rwanda and Haiti', *Third World Quarterly* 17:3, 455–71.

Gruner, Wolf (1992). 'Germany in Europe: The German question as burden and as opportunity', in John Breuilly (ed.), *The State of Germany*, London: Longman, 201–23.

Gurr, Ted Robert (1994). 'Peoples Against States: Ethnopolitical Conflict and the Changing World System', *International Studies Quarterly*, 38, 347–77.

Gusfield, Joseph (1971). 'Tradition and Modernity. Misplaced Polarities in the Study of Social Change', in Jason L. Finkle and Richard W. Gable, *Political Development and Social Change*, New York: Wiley, 15–27.

Habermas, Jürgen (1999). 'The European Nation-State and the Pressures of Globalization', *New Left Review*, 235, 46–60.

Halliday, Fred (1994). *Rethinking International Relations*, Vancouver: UBC Press.

Hamilton, Clive (1987). 'Can the Rest of Asia Emulate the NICs?', *Third World Quarterly*, 9:4, 1227–53.

Hansen, Thomas Blom (1997). *The Saffron Wave. Democratic Revolution and the Growth of Hindu Nationalism in India* (3 vols.), Roskilde: International Development Studies.

Harbeson, John W. (1988). *The Ethiopian Transformation. The Quest for the Post-Imperial State*, Boulder, Co.: Westview Press.

Hassner, Pierre (1993). 'Beyond nationalism and Internationalism: Ethnicity and World Order', in Michael E. Brown (ed), *Ethnic Conflict and International Security*, Princeton: Princeton University Press, 125–41.

Held, David (1991). 'Democracy, the nation-state and the global system', in David Held (ed.), *Political Theory Today*, Cambridge: Polity Press, 197–235.

Held, David (1995). *Democracy and the Global Order*, Cambridge: Polity Press.

Held, David, Anthony McGrew *et al.* (1999). *Global Transformations: Politics, Economics and Culture*, Cambridge: Cambrige University Press.

Herbst, Jeffrey (1989). 'The Creation and Maintenance of National Boundaries in Africa', *International Organization*, 43:4, 673–92.

Herbst, Jeffrey (1990). 'Migration, the Politics of Protest, and State Consolidation in Africa', *African Affairs*, 89, 83–203.

Herbst, Jeffrey (1996–97). 'Responding to State Failure in Africa', *International Security*, 21:3, 120–44.

Herz, John (1950). 'Idealist Internationalism and the Security Dilemma', *World Politics*, II:2, 157–81.

Herz, John (1951). *Political Realism and Political Idealism. A Study in Theories and Realities*, Chicago: The University of Chicago Press.

Herz, John (1959). *International Politics in the Atomic Age*, New York: Columbia University Press.

Hettne, Bjorn (1990). *Development Theory and the Three Worlds*, Burnt Mill, Harlow: Longman.

Hilferding, Rudolf (1968 [1910]). *Das Finanzkapital. Eine Studie über die jüngste Entwicklung des Kapitalismus*, Frankfurt: Europäische Verlagsanstalt.

Hinsley, F. H. (1986). *Sovereignty*, 2nd edn, Cambridge: Cambridge University Press.

Hintze, Otto (1962–67 [1906]). *Gesammelte Abhandlungen*, vols. I–III, Göttingen: Vandenhoeck und Ruprecht.

Hirschman, Albert O. (1970). *Exit, Voice, and Loyalty*, Cambridge, Mass.: Harvard University Press.

Hirst, Paul and Grahame Thompson (1992). 'The Problem of 'Globalization': International Economic Relations, National Economic Management and the Formation of Trading Blocs', *Economy and Society*, 21, 341–72.

Hobbes, Thomas (1946). *Leviathan*, Oxford: Blackwell.

Hobsbawm, Eric (1993). *Nations and Nationalism Since 1780*, Cambridge: Cambridge University Press.

Hobsbawm, Eric (1994). *Age of Extremes. The Short Twentieth Century 1914–1991*, London: Michael Joseph.

Hoffer, Frank (1992). *Perestroika*, Marburg: Metropolis.

Hoffmann, Stanley (1965). *The State of War*, New York: Praeger.

Hoffmann, Stanley (1984). 'The Problem of Intervention', in Hedley Bull (ed.), *Intervention in World Politics*, Oxford: Clarendon Press, 7–28.

Holm, Hans-Henrik and Georg Sørensen (1995). 'International Relations Theory in a World of Variation', in Hans-Henrik Holm and Georg Sørensen (eds) (1995). *Whose World Order? Uneven Globalization and the End of the Cold War*, Boulder, Co.: Westview Press, 187–206.

Holsti, Kalevi J. (1996). *The State, War, and the State of War*, Cambridge: Cambridge University Press.

Hoogvelt, Ankie (1997). *Globalisation and the Postcolonial World. the New Political Economy of Development*, London: Macmillan – now Palgrave.

Horsman, Mathew and Andrew Marshall (1995). *After the Nation- State. Citizens, Tribalism and the New World Disorder*, London: HarperCollins.

Hoselitz, Bart F. *et al.* (1960). *The Sociological Aspects of Economic Growth*, New York: Free Press.

Howe, Herbert (1996/97). 'Lessons of Liberia. ECOMOG and Regional Peacekeeping', *International Security*, 21:3, 145–76.

Huntington, Samuel P. (1996). *The Clash of Civilizations and the Remaking of World Order*, New York: Simon & Schuster.

Hydén, Goran (1983). *No Shortcuts to Progress*, London: Heinemann.

Hyldelund, Karin (1997). *Anerkendelsesprincipper*, MA thesis, Aarhus: Department of Political Science.

Hymer, Stephen (1975). 'The Multinational Corporation and the Law of Uneven Development', in Hugo Radice (ed.), *International Firms and Modern Imperialism*, Harmondsworth: Penguin, 37–63.

Jackson, Robert (1990). 'Martin Wight, International Theory and the Good Life', *Millennium: Journal of International Studies*, 19:2, 261–72.

Jackson, Robert (1992). 'The Security Dilemma in Africa', in Brian L. Job (ed.), *The Insecurity Dilemma. National Security of Third World States*, Boulder, Co.: Lynne Rienner, 81–93.

Jackson, Robert (1993a). *Quasi-states: sovereignty, international relations and the Third World*, Cambridge: Cambridge University Press.

Jackson, Robert (1993b). 'Continuity and Change in the States System', in Robert Jackson and Alan James (eds), *States in a Changing World*, Oxford: Clarendon Press, 346–69.

Jackson, Robert (1993c). 'The Weight of Ideas in Decolonization: Normative Change in International Relations', in Judith Goldstein and Robert O. Keohane (eds), *Ideas & Foreign Policy. Beliefs, Institutions and Political Change*, Ithaca: Cornell University Press, 11–39.

Jackson, Robert (1994). 'International Boundaries in Theory and Practice', paper for XVIth World Congress of the International Political Science Association, Berlin, August 21–25.

Jackson, Robert (1995a). 'The Political Theory of International Society', in Ken Booth and Steve Smith (eds), *International Relations Today*, University Park: Pennsylvania State University Press, 110–28.

Jackson, Robert (1995b). 'International Community Beyond the Cold War', in Gene M. Lyons and Michael Mastanduno (eds), *Beyond Westphalia. State Sovereignty and International Intervention*, Baltimore: Johns Hopkins University Press, 59–87.

Jackson, Robert (1999a). 'Introduction: Sovereignty at the Millennium', in Jackson, Robert (ed.) (1999). 'Sovereignty at the Millennium', *Political Studies*, 47:3, 423–31.

Jackson, Robert (1999b). 'Sovereignty in World Politics: a Glance at the Conceptual and Historical Landscape, in Robert Jackson (ed.), 'Sovereignty at the Millennium', *Political Studies*, Special Issue, 47:3, 431–56.

Jackson, Robert and Carl G. Rosberg (1982). *Personal Rule in Black Africa: Prince, Autocrat, Prophet, Tyrant*, Berkeley: California University Press.

Jackson, Robert and Georg Sørensen (1999). *Introduction to International Relations*, Oxford: Oxford University Press.

Jackson-Preece, Jennifer (1999). 'Self-Determination, Minority Rights and Failed States', paper for Failed States Conference, Purdue University, April 7–11.

Jacoby, Neil H. (1966). *US Aid to Taiwan*, New York: Praeger.

Jakobsen, Peter Viggo (1996). 'National Interest, Humanitarianism or CNN: What Triggers UN Peace Enforcement After the Cold War?' *Journal of Peace Research*, 33:2, 205–15.

James, Alan (1986). *Sovereign Statehood: The Basis of International Society*, London: Allen and Unwin.

James, Alan (1999). 'The Practice of Sovereign Statehood in Contemporary International Society', *Political Studies*, 47:3, 457–74.

Jameson, Frederick (1991). *Post-Modernism or the Cultural Logic of Late Capitalism*, London: Verso.

Jensen, Anne-Sofie (1999). *Suverænitet, identitet og citizenship*, MA thesis, Aarhus: Department of Political Science.

Jepperson, Ronald L., Alexander Wendt, and Peter J. Katzenstein (1996). 'Norms, Identity, and Culture in National Security', in Peter J. Katzenstein (ed.), *The Culture of National Security. Norms and Identity in World Politics*. New York: Columbia University Press, 33–79.

Johnson, Chalmers (1982). *MITI and the Japanese Miracle*, Tokyo: Charles E. Tuttle.

Joseph, Richard (1998). 'Africa, 1990–97: From *Abertura* to Closure', *Journal of Democracy*, 9:2, 3–17.

Joseph, Richard and Jeffrey Herbst (1997). 'Correspondence', *International Security*, 22:2, 175–84.

Jost, Kenneth (1995). 'Democracy in Africa', CQ Researcher 5 (March 24), quoted in Henry Bienen and Jeffrey Herbst, 'The Relationship between Political and Economic Reform in Africa', *Comparative Politics*, 29:1, 23–42.

Jørgensen, Knud Erik and Thomas J.Christiansen (1995). 'Conceptualizing the Changing Nature of Borders in Western Europe', paper for the Second Pan-European Conference of the ECPR Standing Group on International Relations, Paris, September.

Kant, Immanuel (1992 [1795]). 'Perpetual Peace', printed in Hans Reiss (ed.), *Kant's Political Writings*, Cambridge: Cambridge University Press, 93–131.

Kapstein, Ethan B. (1995). 'Is realism dead? The domestic sources of international politics', *International Organization* 49:4 (Autumn), 751–74.

Kapstein, Ethan B. (1996). 'Workers and the World Economy', *Foreign Affairs*, 75:3, 16–37.

Katzenstein, Peter J. (1976). 'International Relations and Domestic Structures: Foreign Economic Policies of Advanced Industrial States, *International Organization*, 30:1, 1–45.

Katzenstein, Peter J. (1985). *Small States in World Markets*, Ithaca: Cornell University Press.

Katzenstein, Peter J. (1987). *Policy and Politics in West Germany: The Growth of a Semisovereign State*, Philadelphia, Pa: Temple University Press.

Kay, Cristóbal (1989). *Latin American Theories of Development and Underdevelopment*, London: Routledge.

Kehr, Eckart (1977). *Economic Interest, Militarism and Foreign Policy: Essays on German history*, Berkeley: University of California Press.

Kelly, Sean (1993). *America's Tyrant. The CIA and Mobutu of Zaire*, Washington, DC.: The American University Press.

Kemp, Tom (1967). *Theories of Imperialism*, London: Dobson.

Kemp, Tom (1983). *Industrialization in the Non-Western World*, London: Longman.

Kennan, George F. (1960). *Russia and the West under Lenin and Stalin*, Boston, Mass.: Little Brown.

Kennedy, Paul (1993). *Preparing for the Twenty-First Century*, New York: Vintage.

Kennedy-Pipe, Caroline (1995). *Stalin's Cold War. Soviet Strategies in Europe, 1943 to 1956*, Manchester: Manchester University Press.

Keohane, Robert O. (1984). *After Hegemony: Cooperation and Discord in the World Political Economy*, Princeton: Princeton University Press.

Keohane, Robert O. (1986). 'Reciprocity in International Relations', *International Organization*, 40, 1–27.

Keohane, Robert O. (1989). *International Institutions and State Power: Essays in International Relaions Theory*, Boulder, Co.: Westview Press.

Keohane, Robert O. (1990). 'Multilateralism: an agenda for research', *International Journal*, 45, 731–55.

Keohane, Robert O. (1995). 'Hobbes's Dilemma and Institutional Change in World Politics: Sovereignty in International Society', in Hans-Henrik Holm and Georg Sørensen (eds), *Whose World Order? Uneven Globalization and the End of the Cold War*, Boulder, Co.: Westview, 165–87.

Keohane, Robert O. and Stanley Hoffmann (eds) (1991). *The New European Community: Decisionmaking and Institutional Change*, Boulder, Co.: Westview.

Keohane, Robert O. and Stanley Hoffmann (eds) (1993). *After the Cold War: International Institutions and State Strategies in Europe, 1989–91*, Cambridge, Mass.: Harvard University Press.

Keohane Robert O. and Helen V. Milner (eds) (1996). *Internationalization and Domestic Politics*, Cambridge: Cambridge University Press.

Knudsen, Tonnny Brems (1999). *Humanitarian Intervention and International Society: Contemporary manifestations of an explosive doctrine*, Aarhus: Department of Political Science.

Krasner, Stephen D. (1978). *Defending the National Interest. Raw Materials, Investments, and U.S. Foreign Policy*, Princeton: Princeton University Press.

Krasner, Stephen D. (1985). *Structural Conflict: The Third World Against Global Liberalism*, Berkeley: University of California Press.

Krasner, Stephen D. (1988). 'Sovereignty. An Institutional Perspective', *Comparative Political Studies*, 21, 66–94.

Krasner, Stephen D. (1993). 'Westphalia and All That', in Judith Goldstein and Robert O. Keohane (eds), *Ideas & Foreign Policy*, Ithaca: Cornell University Press, 235–64.

Krasner, Stephen D. (1999). *Sovereignty. Organized Hypocrisy*, Princeton: Princeton University Press.

Laakso, Liisa and Adebayo O. Olukoshi (1996). 'The Crisis of the Post-Colonial Nation-State Project in Africa', in Laakso and Olukoshi (eds), *Challenges to the Nation-State in Africa*, Uppsala: Nordic Africa Institute, 7–40.

Lapidoth, Ruth (1992). 'Sovereignty in Transition', *Journal of International Affairs*, 45, 50–74.

Lash, Scott (1993). 'Reflexive modernization: the aesthetic dimension', *Theory Culture and Society*, 10:1, 1–25.

Lash, Scott and John Urry (1994). *Economies of Signs and Space*, London: Sage.

Lebow, Richard Ned (2000). 'The Rise and Fall of the Cold War in Comparative Perspective', in Michael Cox, Ken Booth and Tim Dunne (eds), *The Interregnum: Controversies in World Politics 1989–1999*, Cambridge: Cambridge University Press, 21–41.

Lenin, V. I. (1939 [1917]). *Imperialism: The Highest Stage of Capitalism*, New York: International Publishers.

Linklater, Andrew (1998). *The Transformation of Political Community*, Cambridge: Polity Press.

Lipietz, Alain (1987). *Mirages and Miracles: The Crisis of Global Fordism*, London: Verso.

List, Friedrich (1966). *The National System of Political Economy*, New York: Augustus M. Kelley.

Lundestad, Geir (1986). 'Empire by Invitation? The United States and Western Europe, 1945–1952', *Journal of Peace Research*, 23, 263–77.

Luttwak, Edward N. (1999). 'Give War a Chance', *Foreign Affairs*, 78:4, 36–44.

Lynn-Jones, Sean M. (1998). 'Realism and America's Rise', *International Security*, 23:2, 157–82.

Lyons, Gene and Michael Mastanduno (eds) (1995). *Beyond Westphalia? Sovereignty and International Intervention*, Baltimore: Johns Hopkins Press.

Mandelbaum, Michael (1991–92). 'The end of the Soviet Union', *Foreign Affairs*, 71:1, 160–83.

Mann, Michael (1993). *The Sources of Social Power, vol. II*, Cambridge: Cambridge University Press.

Marer, Paul (1974). 'Soviet Economic Politicies in Eastern Europe', in John P. Hardt (ed.), *Reorientation and Commercial Relations of the Economies of Eastern Europe*, Washington, DC.: Government Printing Office.

Marks, Gary *et al.* (1995). 'European Integration Since the 1980s. State-Centric Versus Multi-Level Governance', paper for American Political Science Association Meeting, Chicago, 31 August–3 September.

Martinussen, John (1997). *Society, State & Market. A Guide to Competing Theories of Development*, London: Zed Books.

Marx, Karl and Friedrich Engels (1973). 'Manifesto of the Communist Party', in Karl Marx, *Revolutions of 1848*, (David Fernbach, ed.), vol. 1, Harmondsworth: Penguin Books.

Mayall, James (1999). 'Sovereignty, Nationalism and Self- Determination', *Political Studies*, 47:3, 474–503.

Mazarr, Michael J. (1993). 'The Military Dilemmas of Humanitarian Intervention', *Security Dialogue*, 24:2, 151–62.

McFaul, Michael (1997). 'Russia. Transition Without Consolidation', *Freedom Review*, 28:1, 30–49.

McGowan, P. and T. Johnson (1986). 'Sixty Coups in Thirty Years: Further Evidence regarding African Coups', *Journal of Modern African Studies*, 24, 539–46.

McMichael, Philip and David Myhre (1991). 'Global Regulation vs. the Nation-State: Agro-Food Systems and the New Politics of Capital', *Capital and Class*, 43, 82–94.

McNulty, Mel (1997). 'A Double Discrediting: France, Rwanda and Military Intervention', *International Peacekeeping*, 4:3, 24–44.

McSweeney, Bill (1996). 'Identity and security: Buzan and the Copenhagen School', *Review of International Studies*, 22:1, 81–93.

Mearsheimer, John (1991). 'Back to the Future: Instability in Europe After the Cold War', in Sean M. Lynn-Jones (ed.), *The Cold War and After. Prospects for Peace*. Cambridge, Mass.: MIT Press, 141–92.

Mearsheimer, John (1994–95). 'The False Promise of International Institutions', *International Security*, 19, 5–49.

Mearsheimer, John (1995). 'A Realist Reply', *International Security*, 20:1, 82–93.

Merkl, Peter H. (1965). *Die Entstehung der Bundesrepublik Deutschland*, Stuttgart: W. Kohlhammer Verlag.

Miller, J. D. B. (1981). *The World of States. Connected Essays*, New York: St. Martin's Press.

Milner, Helen (1991). 'The assumption of anarchy in international relations theory: a critique', *Review of International Studies*, 17, 67–85.

Milner, Helen V. (1988). *Resisting Protection: Global Industries and the Politics of International Trade*, Princeton: Princeton University Press.

Milner, Helen V. (1998). 'Rationalizing Politics: The Emerging Synthesis of International, American, and Comparative Politics', *International Organization*, 52:4, 759–86.

Milner, Helen V. and Robert O. Keohane (1996). 'Internationalization and Domestic Politics: A Conclusion', in Robert O. Keohane and Helen V. Milner (eds) (1996). *Internationalization and Domestic Politics*, Cambridge: Cambridge University Press, 243–59.

Mitchell, G. Duncan (1968). *A Hundred Years of Sociology*, Chicago: Aldive.

Monga, Celestin (1997). 'Eight Problems with African Politics', *Journal of Democracy*, 8:3, 156–70.

Müller, Harald and Thomas Risse-Kappen (1990). 'Internationale Umwelt, gesellschaftliches Umfeld und aussenpolitischer Prozess in liberaldemokratischen Industrienationen', *Politisches Vierteljahresschrift*, Sonderheft 21, 375–400.

Moran, Theodore (1990). 'The Globalization of America's Defense Industries: Managing the Threat of Foreign Dependence', *International Security*, 15:1, 57–99.

Moravcsik, Andrew (1997). 'Taking preferences seriously: A liberal theory of international politics', *International Organisation*, 51, 513–53.

Moravcsik, Andrew (1998). *Choice for Europe. Social Purpose and State Power from Messina to Maastricht*, Ithaca: Cornell University Press.

Mosley, Paul, Turan Subasat and John Weeks (1995). 'Assessing Adjustment in Africa', *World Development*, 23:9, 1459–73.

Muraja, Koti (1998). 'Changes in Civil-Military Relations in the Post-Cold War Japan', paper for Third Pan-European IR Conference, Vienna, September.

Murphy, Deane (2000). 'Southern Africa has Trappings of Democracy but Substance Lacking', *Los Angeles Times*, March 11, A14–15.

Naisbitt, John (1994). *Global Paradox*, New York: Avon.

Neu, C. R. and Charles Wolf, Jr. (1992). *The Economic Dimensions of National Security*, RAND Report for the Office of the Secretary of Defense, Washington, DC.: National Defense Research Division.

Nisbet, Robert A. (1969). *Social change and history: aspects of the Western theory of development*, New York: Oxford University Press.

Nye, Joseph S. (1988). 'Neorealism and Neoliberalism', *World Politics*, 40:2, 235–51.

Nye, Joseph S. (1990). *Bound to Lead: The Changing Nature of American Power*, New York: Basic Books.

Nye, Joseph S., Jr. (1999). 'Redefining the National Interest', *Foreign Affairs*, 78:4, 22–35.

Nørgaard, Asbjørn Sonne (1994). 'Institutions and post-modernity in IR: the "new" EC', *Cooperation and Conflict*, 29, 245–87.

OECD (1993). *STI Review 13*, Special Issue on Globalization.

Ohmae, Kenichi (1993). 'The Rise of the Region State', *Foreign Affairs*, 72:2, 78–87.

Oman, Charles (1979). 'Changing International Investment Strategies: The "New Forms" of Investment in Developing Countries', Paris: OECD.

Onuf, Nicholas (1991). 'Sovereignty: Outline of a Conceptual History', *Alternatives*, 16, 425–46.

Opello, Walter C. Jr. And Stephen J. Rosow (1999). *The Nation-State and Global Order. A Historical Introduction to Contemporary Politics*, Boulder, Co.: Lynne Rienner.

Österud, Øyvind (1997). 'The Narrow Gate: Entry to the Club of Sovereign States', *Review of International Studies*, 23, 167–84.

Ottaway, Marina (1995). 'Democratization in Collapsed States', in I. William Zartman (ed.), *Collapsed States. The Disintegration and Restoration of Legitimate Authority*, Boulder, Co.: Lynne Rienner, 235–51.

Ougaard, Morten (1989). *Magt og intereresser i den globale samfundsformation*, Aarhus: Department of Political Science.

Palan, Ronen and Barry Gills (eds) (1994). *Beyond the Global-State Divide: A Neo-Structuralist Approach*, Boulder, Co.: Lynne-Rienner.

Pieterse Jan Nederveen (1997). 'Going Global: Futures of Capitalism', *Development and Change*, 28, 367–82.

Philpott, Daniel (1999). 'Westphalia, Authority, and International Society', *Political Studies*, 47:3, 566–90.

Piccioto, Sol (1991). 'The Internationalisation of the State', *Capital and Class*, 43, 32–49.

Pinder, John (1968). 'Positive and Negative Integration. Some Problems of Economic Union in the EEC', *World Today*, 24:3, 88–110.

Pisar, Samuel (1970). *Coexistence and Commerce: Guidelines for Transactions Between East and West*, New York: McGraw-Hill.

Polanyi, Karl (1957 [1944]). *The Great Transformation: The Political and Economic Origins of Our Time*, Boston: Beacon Books.

Pooley, Sam (1991). 'The State Rules, OK? The Continuing Political Economy of Nation-States', *Capital and Class*, 43, 69–81.

Porter, Bruce D. (1994). *War and Rise of the State. The Military Foundations of Modern Politics*, New York: The Free Press.

Powaski, Ronald E. (1998). *The Cold War. The United States and the Soviet Union 1917–1991*, New York: Oxford University Press.

Prunier, Gérard (1995). *The Rwanda Crisis*, New York: Columbia University Press.

Putnam, Robert D. (1988). 'Diplomacy and Domestic Politics. The Logic of Two-Level Games', *International Organization*, 42, 427–60.

Rawls, John, (1955). 'Two Concepts of Justice', *Philosophical Review*, 64, 1–33.

Reich, Robert (1991a). 'Dumpsters', *The New Republic*, 10 June, 9.

Reich, Robert (1991b). *The Work of Nations*, New York: Alfred Knopf.

Rengger, N. J. (2000). *International Relations, Political Theory and the Problem of Order*, London: Routledge.

Reno, William (2000). 'Internal Wars, Private Enterprise, and the Shift in Strong State–Weak State Relations', *International Politics*, 37, 57–74.

Risse-Kappen, Thomas (1991). 'Public Opinion, Domestic Structure, and Foreign Policy in Liberal Democracies', *World Politics*, 43:4, 479–544.

Risse-Kappen, Thomas (ed.) (1995). *Bringing Transnational Relations Back In*, Cambridge: Cambridge University Press.

Roberts, Adam (1996). 'Humanitarian Action in War' *Adelphi Paper 305*, London: The International Institute for Strategic Studies.

Robinson, William I. (1996). *Promoting Polyarchy. Globalization, US Intervention, and Hegemony*, Cambridge: Cambridge University Press.

Rosecrance, Richard (1995). 'The End of War Among Trading States', *New Perspectives Quarterly*, 21:1, 44–51.

Rosecrance, Richard (1996). 'The Rise of the Virtual State', *Foreign Affairs*, 75:4, 45–61.

Rosenau, James N. (1970). *The Adaptation of National Societies: A Theory of Political System Behavior and Transformation*, New York: McCaleb-Seiler.

Rosenau, James N. (1990). *Turbulence in World Politics: A Theory of Change and Continuity*, Princeton: Princeton University Press.

Rosenau, James N. (1993). 'Citizenship in a changing global order', in James N. Rosenau and Ernst-Otto Czempiel (eds), *Governance without government: order and change in world politics*, Cambridge: Cambridge University Press, 272–95.

Rosenau, James N. (1994). 'New Dimensions of Security: The Interaction of Globalizing and Localizing Dynamics', *Security Dialogue*, 25:3, 255–81.

Rosenau, James N. (1997). *Along the Domestic–Foreign Frontier. Exploring Governance in a Turbulent World*, Cambridge: Cambridge University Press.

Rosenberg, Justin (1994). 'The International Imagination: IR Theory and 'Classic Social Analysis'', *Millennium: Journal of International Studies*, 23:1, 85–108.

Rosenberg, Justin (1996). 'Dethroning the Balance of Power'. Paper for International Studies Association annual meeting, San Diego.

Rostow, Walt W. (1960). *The Stages of Economic Growth*, Cambridge: Cambridge University Press.

Ruggie, John G. (1982). 'International regimes, transactions, and change: embedded liberalism in the postwar economic order', *International Organization*, 36:2, 195–231.

Ruggie, John G. (1997). 'Globalization and the Embedded Liberalism Compromise: The End of an Era?', Columbia International Affairs Online Working Papers.

Ruggie, John G. (1998). *Constructing the World Polity*, London: Routledge.

Russell, Jeffrey B. (1968). *Medieaval Civilization*, New York: John Wiley and Sons.

Russett, Bruce M. (1993). *Grasping the Democratic Peace: Principles for a Post-Cold War World*, Princeton: Princeton University Press.

Rustow, Dankwart A. (1970). 'Transitions to Democracy', *Comparative Politics*, 2:3, 337–65.

Samuels, Richard J. (1994). *'Rich Nation Strong Army'. National Security and the Technological Transformation of Japan*, Ithaca: Cornell University Press.

Sandbrook, Richard (1985). *The Politics of Africa's Economic Stagnation*, Cambridge: Cambridge University Press.

Sandbrook, Richard (1993). *The Politics of Africa's Economic Recovery*, Cambridge: Cambridge University Press.

Sassen, Saskia (1996). *Loosing Control? Sovereignty in an Age of Globalization*, New York: Columbia University Press.

Scalapino, Robert A. (ed.) (1977). *The Foreign Policy of Modern Japan*, Berkeley: University of California Press.

Schaller, Michael (1997). *Altered States. The United States and Japan Since the Occupation*, New York: Oxford University Press.

Scharpf, Fritz W. (1996). 'Politische Optionen im vollendeten Binnenmarkt' in Markus Jachtenfuchs and Beate Kohler-Koch (Hrsg.), *Europäische Integration*, Opladen: Leske und Budrich, 109–40.

Schatz, Sayre P. (1994). 'Structural Adjustment in Africa: a Failing Grade So Far', *The Journal of Modern African Studies*, 32:4, 679–92.

Schatz, Sayre P. (1996). 'The World Bank's Fundamental Misconception in Africa', *The Journal of Modern African Studies*, 34:2, 239–47.

Schmidt, Brian C. (1998). *The Political Discourse of Anarchy: A Disciplinary History of International Relations*, Albany, N.Y.: State University of New York Press.

Scholte, Jan Aart (2000). *Globalization – a critical introduction*, London: Macmillan – now Palgrave.

Scully, Roger M. (1998). 'Understanding Domestic–International Linkages', *Mershon International Studies Review*, 42, 372–4.

Schulze, Hagen (1996). *States, Nations and Nationalism*, Cambridge: Blackwell.

Searle, John R. (1995). *The Construction of Social Reality*, London: Penguin.

Senghaas, Dieter (1985). *The European Experience. A Historical Critique of Development Theory*, Leamington Spa: Berg Publishers.

Senghaas, Dieter (1998). *Zivilisierung wider Willen*, Frankfurt Main: Suhrkamp.

Shanin, Theodor (1983). *Late Marx and the Russian Road*, London: Routledge.

Shaw, Martin (1994). *Global Society and International Relations*, Cambridge: Polity Press.

Simai, Mihaly (1994). *The Future of Global Governance. Managing Risk and Change in the International System*, Washington, DC.: United States Institute of Peace.

Sivard, R. L. (1987). *World Military and Social Expenditures, 1986–7*, Washington, DC: World Priorities Inc.

Skocpol, Theda (1979). *States and Social Revolutions*, Cambridge: Cambridge University Press.

Slater, William (1994). 'Russia: The Return of Authoritarian Government?' *RFE/RL Research Report*, 3:1.

Slaughter, Anne-Marie (1997). 'The Real New World Order', *Foreign Affairs*, 76:5, 183–98.

Smith, Jean Edward (1990). *Lucius D. Clay. An American Life*, New York: Henry Holt and Company.

Smith, Steve (1995). 'The Self-Images of a Discipline: A Genealogy of International Relations Theory', in Ken Booth and Steve Smith (eds), *International Relations Theory Today*, University Park: Pennsylvania State University Press, 1–37.

Smith, Steve (1997). 'New Approaches to International Theory', in John Baylis and Steve Smith (eds), *The Globalization of World Politics*, Oxford: Oxford University Press, 165–90.

Snyder, Francis (1999). 'Global Economic Networks and Global Legal Pluralism', paper for conference on 'Globalization, Statehood and World Order', Florence, Sept. 30–Oct. 1.

Snyder, Jack (1991). *Myths of Empire: Domestic Politics and International Ambition*, Ithaca, NY: Cornell University Press.

Soysal, Yasemin Nuhoglu (1994). *Limits of Citizenship*, Chicago: The University of Chicago Press.

Spero, Joan E. and Jeffrey A. Hart (1997). *The Politics of International Economic Relations*, London: Routledge.

Spruyt, Hendrik (1994a). 'The Evolution of Sovereignty and Institutional Isomorphism', Paper for American Political Science Association Meeting, New York, September 1–4.

Spruyt, Hendrik (1994b). *The Sovereign State and Its Competitors*, Princeton: Princeton University Press.

Storry, Richard (1968). *A History of Modern Japan*, Harmondsworth: Penguin Books.

Strange, Susan (1994). 'Wake up, Krasner! The world *has* changed', *Review of International Political Economy*, 1:2, 209–19.

Strange, Susan (1996). *The Retreat of the State. The Diffusion of Power in the World Economy*, Cambridge: Cambridge University Press.

Strange, Susan (1999). 'The Westfailure system', *Review of International Studies*, 25:3, 345–55.

Strayer, Joseph R. (1965). *Feudalism*, Princeton: Van Nostrand.

Streeten, Paul (1992). 'Global Governance for Human Development', UNDP: Human Development Report Office, *Occasional Papers* 4.

Sørensen, Curt (1976). *Marxismen og den sociale orden*, vols. I–II, Kongerslev: GMT Press.

Sørensen, Georg (1983). *Transnational Corporations in Peripheral Societies*, Aalborg: Aalborg University Press.

Sørensen, Georg (1991a). *Democracy, Dictatorship and Development. Economic Development in Selected Regimes of the Third World*, London: Macmillan – now Palgrave.

Sørensen, Georg (1991b). 'Strategies and Structures of Development: The New 'Consensus' and the Limits to Its Promises', *European Journal of Development Research*, 3:2, 121–46.

Sørensen, Georg (1992). 'Kant and Processes of Democratization: Consequences for Neorealist Thought, *Journal of Peace Research*, 29:4, 397–414.

Sørensen, Georg (1994). 'International Relations After the Cold War: What Has Changed? Toward a Theory of Units', San Diego: School of International Relations and Pacific Studies.

Sørensen, Georg (1996). 'Individual Security and National Security: The State Remains the Principal Problem', *Security Dialogue*, 27:4, 371–87.

Sørensen, Georg (1997a). 'Det liberale fredsperspektiv i teori og praksis', *GRUS*, 53, 7–27.

Sørensen, Georg (1997b). 'Suverænitet: Formel og faktisk', *Focus Paper*, Copenhagen: Danish Institute for International Affairs

Sørensen, Georg (1998). 'IR theory after the Cold War', *Review of International Studies*, 24, 83–100.

Sørensen, Georg (2000). 'Muddy Waters. The Debate on States, Markets, and Globalization', Aarhus: Department of Political Science.

Ticktin, Hillel (1976), 'The relation between détente and Soviet economic reforms' in Egbert Jahn (ed.), *Soviet Foreign Policy: Its Social and Economic Conditions*, London: Allison & Busby, 41–57.

Tilly, Charles (1990). *Coercion, Capital, and European States, AD 990–1990*, Cambridge: Basil Blackwell.

Tita, Alberto (1998). 'Globalization: A New Political and Economic Space Requiring Supranational Governance', *Journal of World Trade*, 32:3, 47–57.

Toennies, Ferdinand (1955). *Community and Association*, London: Routledge and Kegan Paul.

Touval, Saadia (1967). 'The Organization of African Unity and African Borders', *International Organization*, 21:1, 102–27.

Toye, John (1987). *Dilemmas of Development*, Oxford: Blackwell.

Trotsky, Leon (1930). *My Life*, New York: Schribner.

Trotsky, Leon (1980). *The History of the Russian Revolution*, New York: Pathfinder Press.

UNCTAD (United Nations Conference on Trade and Development) (1997). *1997 World Investment Report*, Geneva: UNCTAD.

UNDP (United Nations Development Programme) (1999). *Human Development Report 1999*, New York: Oxford University Press.

United Nations (1992). *An Agenda for Peace: Preventative Diplomacy, Peacemaking and Peace-Keeping*, A/47/277.

United Nations (1994). *Report of the Secretary-General on the Situation in Rwanda*, S/1994/640, New York: The United Nations.

United Nations (1997). *World Economic and Social Survey 1997*, New York: UN.

Vernon, Raymond (1966). 'International Investment and International Trade in the Product Cycle', *The Quarterly Journal of Economics*, LXXX, 190–207.

Victor, David G. (1999). 'Risk Management and the World Trading System: Regulating International Trade Distortions of National Sanitary and Phytosanitary Policies', unpublished paper, New York.

Vincent, R. J. (1983). 'Change and international relations', *Review of International Studies*, 9, 63–71.

Walker, R. B. J. (1995). 'International Relations and the Concept of the Political', in Ken Booth and Steve Smith (eds), *International Relations Theory Today*, University Park, Pa: Pennsylvania State University Press, 306–27.

Wallace, William (2000). 'Europe after the Cold War: Interstate Order or post-Sovereign Regional System?', in Michael Cox, Ken Booth, and Tim Dunne (eds), *The Interregnum: Controversies in World Politics 1989–1999*, Cambridge: Cambridge University Press, 201–25.

Wallensteen, Peter and Margareta Sollenberg (1999). 'Armed Conflict, 1989–98', *Journal of Peace Research*, 36:5, 593–606.

Wallerstein, Immanuel (1974). *The Modern World System*, New York: Academic Press.

Wallerstein, Immanuel (1979). *The Capitalist World Economy. Essays*, Cambridge: Cambridge University Press.

Wallerstein, Immanuel (1984). 'World Networks and the Politics of the World-Economy', in Immanuel Wallerstein, *The Politics of the World Economy. The States, the Movements and the Civilizations. Essays*, Cambridge: Cambridge University Press, 1–12.

Waltz, Kenneth N. (1959). *Man, the State, and War*, New York: Columbia University Press.

Waltz, Kenneth N. (1979). *Theory of International Politics*, Reading, Mass.: Addison-Wesley.

Waltz, Kenneth N. (1986). 'Reflections on *Theory of International Politics*: A Response to My Critics', in Robert O. Keohane (ed.), *Neorealism and Its Critics*, New York: Columbia University Press, 322–47.

Waltz, Kenneth N. (1988). 'The Origins of War in Neorealist Theory', *Journal of Interdisciplinary History*, 18, 615–28.

Waltz, Kenneth N. (1993). 'The Emerging Structure of International Politics', *International Security*, 18:2, 44–79.

Waltz, Kenneth N. (1994). 'The Validation of International–Political Theory', paper for 1994 Meeting of the American Political Science Association, New York, September 1–4.

Weber, Cynthia (1995). *Simulating Sovereignty: Intervention, the State and Symbolic Exchange*, Cambridge: Cambridge University Press.

Weber, Max (1949). *The Methodology of the Social Sciences*, translated by Edward A. Shils and Henry A. Finch, New York: The Free Press of Glencoe.

Weber, Max (1964). *The Theory of Social and Economic Organization*, New York: Free Press.

Wendt, Alexander (1992). 'Anarchy is what states make of it', *International Organization*, 46, 394–419.

Wendt, Alexander (1994). 'Collective Identity Formation and the International State', *American Political Science Review*, 88, 384–96.

Wendt, Alexander (1995). 'Constructing International Politics', *International Security*, 20:1, 71–81.

Wendt, Alexander (1999). *Social Theory of International Politics*, Cambridge: Cambridge University Press.

Wheeler, Nicholas (1992). 'Pluralist or Solidarist Conceptions of International Society: Bull and Vincent on Humanitarian Intervention', *Millennium*, 21:3, 463–87.

Wight, Martin (1977). *Systems of States*, Leicester: Leicester University Press.

Wight, Martin (1991). *International Theory. The Three Traditions* (ed. by Gabriele Wight and Brian Porter), London: Leicester University Press.

Wolf, Klaus Dieter (1996). 'Defending State Autonomy. Intergovernmental Governance in the European Union', Working Paper 5, World Society Research Group, Darmstadt: Technische Hochschule.

Wolfers, Arnold (1962). *Discord and Collaboration. Essays on International Politics*, Baltimore: Johns Hopkins.

World Bank (1994). *Adjustment in Africa: Reforms, Results, and the Road Ahead*, New York: Oxford University Press.

World Bank (1997). *World Development Report. The State in a Changing World*, New York: Oxford University Press.

World Bank (1999). *World Development Report. Entering the 21st Century*, New York: Oxford University Press.

Wæver, Ole, Barry Buzan, and Jaap de Wilde (1993). *Identity, Migration and the New Security Agenda in Europe*, London: Pinter.

Yeltsin, Boris (1990). *Against the grain: an autobiography*, translated by Michael Glenny, New York: Summit Books.

Young, Crawford (1991). 'The Heritage of Colonialism', in John W. Harbeson and Donald Rothchild (eds), *Africa in World Politics*, Boulder, Co.: Westview, 19–39.

Zacher, Mark V. (1992). 'The decaying pillars of the Westphalian temple: implications for international order and governance', in James N. Rosenau and Ernst-Otto Czempiel (eds), *Governance without government: order and change in world politics*, Cambridge: Cambridge University Press, 58–102.

Zacher, Mark V. and R. A. Matthew (1995). 'Liberal International theory: Common Threads, Divergent Strands', in C. W. Kegley, Jr. (ed.), *Controversies in International Relations: Realism and the Neoliberal Challenge*, New York: St. Martin's Press, 107–50.

Zakaria, Fareed (1995). 'Realism and Domestic Politics: A Review Essay', in Michael E. Brown, Sean M. Lynn-Jones, and Steven E. Miller (eds), *The Perils of Anarchy. Contemporary Realism and International Security*, Cambridge, Mass.: MIT Press, 462–84.

Zartman, William I. (1995). 'Introduction', in William I. Zartman, (ed.), *Collapsed States. The Disintegration and Restoration of Legitimate Authority*, London: Lynne Rienner, 1–11.

Zartman, William I. (1995a). 'Putting Things Back Together', in William I. Zartman, (ed.), *Collapsed States. The Disintegration and Restoration of Legitimate Authority*, London: Lynne Rienner, 267–73.

Zürn, Michael (1995b). 'The Challenge of Globalization and Individualization: A View from Europe', in Hans-Henrik Holm and Georg Sorensen (eds), *Whose World Order? Uneven Globalization and the End of the Cold War*, Boulder, Co.: Westview, 137–65.

Zürn, Michael (1998). *Regieren jenseits des Nationaalstaates. Globalisierung und Denationalisierung als Chance*, Frankfurt Main: Suhrkamp.

Zürn, Michael (1999). 'The State in the Post-National Constellation – Societal Denationalization and Multi-level Governance', unpublished paper, Bremen: University of Bremen.

# Index

Africa, Sub-Saharan
  economic development in, 67–8
  security dilemma in, 109–11
Amin, Samir, 31–2
anarchy
  constructivist view of, 9, 176
  neorealist view of, 6, 15–16, 25
  and postmodern states, 127–8

Bull, Hedley, 22–3, 170–1, 187–8

capitalism
  leading to homogeneity, 27–8
  uneven development of, 31–3
Cerny, Phil, 131
China, 52
  development of, 182
  economic development in, 64–5
classical approach, the, 22
classical economic liberalism, 81–2
constructivism, 16, 175–6
  connection between 'international' and
    'domestic', 9
Cox, Robert, 18, 19–20, 172–5

decolonization, 57–60, 83
  changes leading to, 57–9
  leading to homogeneity and
    heterogeneity, 60
democracy
  liberalist view of, 7
  and postcolonial states, 85, 114–16
  and postmodern states, 136–7, 181
dependency theory, 184
Deutsch, Karl, 128
'domestic'
  connection with 'international', 10–12,
    14–15, 21, 145–6, 177, 180, 184
  definition of, 19–21

Eastern Europe
  economic development in, 65
economy, 20, 91
  in modern states, 80–2
  in postcolonial states, 66–8, 85–6,
    109–10

in postmodern states, 68–70, 89–90, 126,
    129–2
embedded liberalism, 53–4, 130–1, 134–5,
    162
emulation, 25, 46–7, 161–2
English school, the, 16, 170–2
  connection between 'international' and
    'domestic', 8
epistemology, 22–3
Ethiopia, 51
European Union
  and democracy, 136–7, 181–2
  multilevel governance in, 87–8, 132–3
  and nationhood, 88–9
  and the postmodern sovereignty game,
    158–61
  realist explanation of, 165–6
Evangelista, Matthew, 9

*Gemeinschaft*, 78
Germany
  development into a postmodern state,
    54–7
  postwar allied policies in, 54–5
  postwar domestic political forces in, 56–7
*Gesellschaft*, 78
*glasnost*, 43
globalization, economic, 62–71
  definition of, 62
  and heterogeneity, 66–8
  and homogenization, 63–6
  liberal view of, 62–3, 66–7
  Marxist view of, 62–3, 66–7
  and postmodern states, 68–70, 129–2
  uneven, 62, 70, 139–40, 162, 183
Gorbachev, Mikhail, 42–4, 101
Gourevitch, Peter, 9–10
government, 91
  in modern states, 75–7
  in postcolonial states, 83–5, 109
  in postmodern states, 87–8, 126–7,
    132–7
Gramsci, Antonio, 21

Habermas, Jürgen, 137
Herz, John, 93, 94